THE ANATOMY OF ARCADIA

LAKKA

VASSILATIKA

PAXOS

MYRTIA

GAIOS
PANAGIA
AG. NIKOLAOS

BOUGAZI

MOGGONISI
KALCHIONISSI

GREMOS

AGRILIDA

KALOURI

ANTIPAXOS

THE ANATOMY
of ARCADIA

David Solway

Véhicule Press

MONTRÉAL

Published with the assistance of The Canada Council.

Cover art and design: J.W. Stewart.
Design & imaging: ECW Type & Art
Printing: Imprimerie d'Édition Marquis Ltée

CANADIAN CATALOGUING IN PUBLICATION DATA

Solway, David, 1941–
   The anatomy of Arcadia

ISBN 1-55065-026-2

   1. Travelers' writings — Criticism and interpretation.
2. Greece in literature.   3. Arcadia in literature.
1. Title.

PN56.3.G73S55 1991   809'.9359104   C92-090269-3

Published by Véhicule Press, P.O.B. 125, Place du Parc Station,
Montreal, Quebec, Canada H2W 2M9.

Distributed in Canada by University of Toronto Press, and in the
United States by Bookslinger Inc. (St. Paul, MN) and Inland Book
Company (East Haven, CT).

Printed in Canada on acid-free paper.

for Karin

χωρις αυτην τιποτε

N O T E

The Anatomy of Arcadia was written in the mid-1980s. In the process of revision, I have tended to leave certain details that pertain to the time of writing intact in order to remain true to the spirit in which the book was composed.

Despite efforts in the direction of scrupulousness, however, I have permitted myself a certain onomastic nonchalance for reasons of simplification and familiarity. In some of the names that appear in the following pages, for example, the Greek *chi* (X) is generally rendered as English 'H,' and the terminal 's' is sometimes omitted. It is safe to say that, in general, I tend to rely on phonetics rather than accuracy.

The use of travelling is to regulate imagination by reality, and instead of *thinking* how things may be, to *see* them as they are.
— Samuel Johnson

No; I cannot stop a moment to give you the character of the people their genius their manners their customs their laws their religion their government their manufactures their commerce their finances, with all the resources and hidden springs which sustain them: qualified as I may be, by spending three days and two nights amongst them, and during all that time, making these things the entire subject of my enquiries and reflections.
— Laurence Sterne, *Tristam Shandy*

Don't get me wrong. I love the Greeks. But, sometimes, they can break your heart.
— Helen MacInnes, *Decision at Delphi*

PREFACE

What do we mean by travel? An even more pertinent question: what is meant by modern travel? Modern travel is vitiated, as Daniel Boorstin saw in his brilliant book, *The Image*, by the reciprocal needs to make the exotic commonplace and the commonplace exotic. We accomplish the former by planning our journeys in advance, usually with the help of a 'travel agent,' so that the spontaneous eruption of experience is controlled and expurgated. Discomfort is banished. Significant encounters are reduced to a minimum. We are carefully insulated from people, landscape, atmosphere, violence, boredom, the unpleasant, the unpredictable; tours are packaged, amenities provided, the "natives" properly groomed, selected and dressed up to conform to our illusion of "the authentic." This is not travel but tourism.

Boorstin notes that the word 'travel' is related to 'travail' ('work' in French and 'torment' in English) and derives from the Latin 'trepalium,' a three-staked instrument of torture. Thus the traveller is active, he takes risks, endures discomfort, is ready to improvise, anticipates shock and disappointment but is also capable of genuine exaltation. The word 'tourism' comes from the Latin 'tornus,' which itself derives from a Greek word for a tool describing a circle. Accordingly the tourist is passive, he expects interesting things to happen to him without risk or effort, and remains comfortably ensconced in his privileged circle of prefabricated, Bowdlerized event.

So the exotic is rendered commonplace, but the commonplace in turn becomes meretriciously exotic through the illusions, the panderings, of our vast entertainment industry. We sit before our television screens and watch Michael Wood voyage up the Congo River fighting off mosquitoes, bartering for monkey flesh, and spending the night in a whorehouse he mistook for a hotel. Adventures! We have not stirred a muscle or scratched a single bite. We have not paid for anything in the currency of exposure. But we have been magically transported into the realm of the fabulous, the exotic, the safely menacing.

In both cases we have willingly and gratefully succumbed to the Arcadian dream, where we experience *nothing* but our own illusions and pre-existent expectations. We have refused to *endure* reality in our quest for the strange and the new, with the inevitable result that we have enjoyed nothing more than a trivial fantasy. Being neither tempted nor tested, we learn little and change less. This is the nature of our modern Arcadia.

Thus, we meet nothing and no one but ourselves in our unreconstructed state. Roland Barthes writes: "Open a travel guide: usually you will find a brief lexicon which strangely enough concerns only certain boring and useless things: customs, mail, the hotel, the barber, the doctor, prices. Yet what is travelling? Meetings. The only lexicon that counts is the one which refers to the rendezvous."

The Anatomy

OF ARCADIA

September, 1983. Glyfada. Arrival.

First day in Greece after an absence of fifteen months. Seems I've learnt nothing from the years I've put in here. Like Simplicius Simplicissimus, I let myself be taken for a ride, both literally and figuratively, by the taxi driver I hired to take us to Athens. First I neglected to look at the meter. I found out later from my son Alki that there were already 286 drachmas on it from the previous fare. (The poor kid is as naive as I am, he thought it was the standard procedure.) Secondly, I let him take us the long way round by the coast road instead of cutting through Vougliameni Avenue. Thirdly I permitted him to drive 'privately,' like Sterne's impetuous postilion, hitting speeds of up to 160 kilometres per hour. Granted the traffic was thin, and I assumed this was Greece after all where the highways are considered as extensions of Formula One racetracks; still, out of mere diffidence I placed my family in some jeopardy. The driver was one of those classic urchin types: coarse-featured, bored, laconic, chewing gum and smoking at the same time, the modern Atlas-figure one finds everywhere in this country carrying a planetary grievance on his shoulders. And I let him get away with it, which I see as a moral failure or a weakness of character on my part. I may have been somewhat intimidated by the massive indifference mixed with muscular resentment that made up the nature of my antagonist. Not a very flattering portrait of myself. I will have to work on this in the coming year.

❖

In what other country can you enter a restaurant and find yourself after a few minutes deep in conversation with the owner on the subject of the relation between madness and genius? The food was all but forgotten. Karin and the kids fretted outside at the table while Angelos, the proprietor of the Chestnut Cafe in Glyfada, and I debated the issue. Genius cannot be measured by the same standard of insanity that is applied to commonplace folk, said Angelos, and as if to prove the point reached into the till over which he presided and extracted a black, hard-bound, impressive-looking volume, a Greek translation of *Thus Spake Zarathustra*. Thumping the book like a preacher at his exhortations, Angelos developed his theme: that madness, benign madness founded in frustration, had to be expected where the brain was too big to fit the skull. "You mean," I said, "like too much wine in too small a glass." "Exactly," he replied, and sent a bottle of retsina to the table. "This bottle you empty by drinking," he explained, "but in the vessel of Nietzsche's brain, the wine was too potent. One day it re-fermented and exploded." "That's a good analogy," I replied, "like Kabbalah." "*Acrivos*, exactly." "You know about all these things?" I queried, astonished. "Of course, I teach theology on the side," he confided.

❖

Morning in Syntagma Square over coffee and lemonade, before setting off to the Plaka. The waiter, whose name was Thomas, a seedy, disreputable-looking, corpulent man in his late forties, guessed that I was Canadian. I was so impressed by this feat of clairvoyance, I asked him the source of his extraordinary powers. "I read minds," he replied. "How did you develop that talent?" "I am more than I appear," he said, and after a short intense silence in which he stared hard into my eyes, "I am a policeman."

"A policeman?"

"Yes. My cover is being a waiter. I am searching for drugs."

"How can you tell who is carrying drugs?"

"One can tell by the gestures and by the eyes."

I asked him to guess my profession, and here he made his first mistake, assuming that I was "a mechanic," by which he meant "engineer." I had to disappoint him. "Well then," he replied, "you are the direct opposite."

"Pretty good for a policeman."

He smiled disarmingly. "I am not really a policeman. I was just having a little joke." And then he inquired, for the first time, "What is your profession, exactly?"

"Drug carrier," I said, deadpan.

He laughed good-naturedly. From there, in some obscure way, we began discussing the anthropomorphic religion of the pagan Greeks. The connection in Thomas' mind seemed to have something to do with the non-hallucinogenic lucidity of his early forbears.

"Do you know what the Greeks made?" he asked rhetorically. "They made twelve gods. And they made them imperfect to cover their own infidelities." He was very fond, I noticed, of the word 'cover.' "And then they made a thirteenth god, in case they forgot anything."

"You mean the unknown god that St. Paul preached about?"

"Exactly. St. Paul was very clever. He used the thirteenth god as a cover for Jesus. And you see the result . . ." he pointed in the direction of Lycabettus "a rich church and a poor people."

It was time to leave. The morning was getting on and the kids restless. Tom and I shook hands just as Hannah dropped her glass of lemonade on the pavement, which we chose to consider as a libation to the thirteenth god.

Paxos

Martin Young in his book on the Ionian islands remarks how the Paxiots used to *fish* for birds from the high cliffs, using nets and lime. The custom has been superseded by the ubiquitous shotgun. Everyone shoots, even the women. And even though they swear there is no danger, we have been cautioned not to let the child wander about during the bird season, which some of our neighbours on the hill above Lakka, in Moungelatika and Apergatika, describe as a *polemos*, a war. The hunters say there is no danger because they are shooting *up*. It seems to have escaped their attention that shooting *up* from a vantage point lower down the slope of the hill does involve certain hazards for those who live on the crest. Two evenings ago a spray of pellets sang right past my ear and peppered the whitewash on the front wall.

We have been settled in for only a month and are already looking for alternatives. The island is so small, six miles long by less than two wide, that it affords no place to hide from the madness that rages about us. The bird-shooting season is on and the island has gone crazy with the sport. The roads and footpaths radiating out from the top of the hill past our house in Moungelatika are festooned with gaily-coloured, spent buckshot cartridges — red, green, yellow — like bits of scissored bunting and confetti. At six in the morning the air ripples, whistles and booms with maniacal detonations, making sleep one of the casualties along with the coveted turtledoves, *trigonia*, that adorned the sky when we first moved in here. Instead we have the spectacle of rifle-toting people marching out of the forest like the hunters in *Peter and the Wolf*, 'shooting as they came.'

Yesterday morning I had my first political confrontation with the community over the orgy of shooting in which we are immersed. It was still dark when the reverberation of gunfire jolted us out of bed. There was no telling if the shot had been fired right beside the bedroom window or if it was merely the echo that rattled the panes. The result was the same anyway. We were furious not only at being so rudely awakened ourselves but because Hannah, who is only three and having a hard time adjusting to life in what she calls "a very strange place," does not need to be further traumatized. We sat outside at the garden table sipping our coffees and listening to the gunshots exploding somewhere at the back of the house. Suddenly there was a rattling sound in the leaves of the olive tree above our heads and a shower of sizzling pellets plunked straight down into my coffee cup. I'd had enough. I walked through the gate, up the road past the Villa Eftithia, and into a field of scrub and bush where the hunter stood, his cartridge belt slung across his breast like a Mexican bandit in a third-rate film, and his rifle held upright the way orthodox priests clutch the crucifix in processions.

Very politely I informed him that we had a sleeping child in the house and that his bullets had just landed in my coffee, and could he therefore move further back into the bush so we might get on with ordinary life.

"I have permission to shoot," he replied.

"At six in the morning?"

"At any hour."

"In that case, please do us a favour."

He stood very straight, as if offended in his deepest manhood, glared over the barrel of his rifle, and said in a curt and solemn tone, making it clear the conversation was over: "*Ime sti patrida mou.*" I am in my country.

I returned to the house determined to leave his country. *His* country! There are five million Greeks in Germany, Australia, the United States, and Canada, almost as many, in fact, as remain in the *patridas*, the homeland. The world has been hospitable to them. I recalled waiting in line at a bank in Aghios Constantinos behind an elderly Greek Canadian who had retired to the *patridas* and was happily cashing his Canadian pension cheques so he could live worry-free, at favourable rates of exchange, in the homeland. And of course the year we intend to remain here will cost us, everything considered, between three and four million drachmas, money that will come to roost in local pockets. And oddly enough, none of the hoteliers, car rental agents, ticket agents, restaurateurs, shop-keepers and landlords appears to be refusing this tainted currency from the pride of *patridas*. But the hunter was in his homeland and I, as a *xenos*, a foreigner, had infringed upon his rights, as if courtesy were equivalent to exile.

I don't remember ever having been so angry in this country, not even that time a few years back when out neighbours on the island of Alonissos, with whom we shared a wall in common, planted dynamite in their kitchen to break up the floor-stones and nearly brought the house down. I cursed myself for having opened an account in the local bank and deposited a substantial amount of money in non-convertible drachmas. And I began ranting to the neighbours until all of Lakka down the hill was buzzing with the scandal. By evening the entire episode including the hunter's response was common knowledge. And this led to the denouement at supper in Myro Mourtis' restaurant, where we were joined by the somewhat crestfallen hunter (with the pastoral name of Theophrastus) who had obviously been coached by his friends to deliver a rather trembly apology. We agreed to put the affair down to an unfortunate misunderstanding. He thought I had ordered him off the land, that I had barked "Fige!" beat it! and so he had reacted out of dignity. This was obviously not the case, but I let it pass and apologized in turn for my faulty Greek. All was forgiven, and Alki and I received an invitation to participate in the hunt, which I reciprocated by inviting the *trigoni*-shooters to the house for morning coffee, provided there were no bullets in it.

The cats in this part of the island are a breed apart. Greece is notorious for its legions of mangy, disease-ridden, underfed, wild marauding cats. They are everywhere, in the mountains where the screams can be heard eerily in the night and under every restaurant table where they claw and grapple for fishbones. Occasionally they allow themselves to be tamed, but even then they remain private. Here in Lakka town and on the hill above, where we live, a new genetic strain has appeared on the scene. The eyes are a sort of intense, electric green and in their behaviour they are almost all friendly and inquisitive, even the 'wild' variety. A cat will often pop out of a bush and accompany you on a stroll, pausing for a bit of stroking, and then return to hunting lizards. More startling is the prevalence of the couple. Cats tend to pair off here and establish long-standing marriages. Gata and Gatos, perpetual visitors, are rarely to be found apart. They sleep together in the olive nets folded at the bottom of the trees, take walks together in the garden behind the house, and arrive punctually at the food dish three times a day where they display the most exemplary table manners, Gatos waiting patiently while Gata has her fill and only then advancing to the dish himself. A more affectionate couple I have never known on any phylogenetic level. They are constantly rubbing up against one another, stroking one another's flanks and heads, and when Gatos strays a few inches distance, Gata curls her tail into a makeshift lasso and gently tugs him back against her side. Other such cat couples, perhaps not so loving but apparently as uxorious, are to be found throughout the streets of Lakka, lying together on verandas, under restaurant awnings, in rubble-strewn corners.

Our biggest surprise was our third housecat, whom we christened 'Misery' owing to his scurfy, bedraggled appearance, one eye glaucous, ears and neck depilated by what we took to be hunger or sickness. After a short while we discovered that he actually belonged to Anglaia further up the hill, was called 'Tzonny' (the Greeks do not pronounce the 'J'), and was eighteen years old, the venerable progenitor of uncountable generations of the Lakka feline population. It is odd to think of him as being three years older than my son. His other crowning achievements, apart from longevity, are his hankering for beer and his resigned willingness to give his paw when solicited. He has decided to move in permanently with us and gets along amicably with Gatos and Gata (who are probably his offspring) — in fact he gets along with everybody in his quiet, dignified way.

Despite the clamour I raised two weeks ago, the bird-shooting has been going on unabatedly, beginning every morning without fail at around six and continuing sporadically till nine in the evening. Last week I went into Gaios, the 'capital' six miles to the south of Lakka, to consult the police on the strict interpretation of the hunting statute. This consists of two articles: a) shooting is permitted only between 7:00 a.m. and 10:00 a.m.; b) shooting is prohibited within a perimeter of 100 meters from the *last* house in the vicinity. Both these prohibitions are regularly broken. I find cartridges in abundance, so incongruously colourful, a few feet from our bedroom window or scattered by the front gate. Last week I was assured by the townspeople that the hunting season would be over in six days, but I afterwards learned that the shooting goes on indiscriminately all year, especially during the two great seasonal *trigoni* migrations, tapering off only for the tourist season which begins in May and ends in September. As someone said in Myro's restaurant the other night, "After the tourists leave, there are 2,500 people on the island with nothing to do. So they shoot." So it appears there are basically two seasons in Paxos, the hunting season and the tourist season (the latter just another form of hunting).

The gunfire started this morning a little earlier than usual, around five, and blew another good night's sleep to smithereens. As we stumbled round the corner to the kitchen, which is a separate structure like the bathroom, the first sight that met the eye was a speckled rorschach of fresh arterial bird's blood across the raked gravel path and reddening the milk in the cat's bowl. There is a real sense of menace in the air, what with the continual shooting, the rattle of grapeshot in the trees, the blood gouts, the spent cartridges crackling underfoot, and the weird stormlight thickening the atmosphere. It has rained three of the last four days.

The debacle has its cartoonish side as well. Peering over the stone wall at the neighbour's house to find out why Rocky is barking so furiously, we see the long double-barrelled proboscis of a shotgun slowly and inexorably extruding itself from the front door, followed eventually by sixty-year old Areti, Yanni the butcher's wife, out for an early morning shoot. A minute later a deafening roar, amplified by the hollow water urn beside our door. Karin's comment: amputees on this island have dispensed with wooden legs, they merely fasten a rifle stock to the stump.

On the way back from Gaios, Panayotis, our English-speaking taxi-driver, stops briefly by a small, whitewashed house set back from the road to deliver a parcel, and launches into an animated conversation with an elderly woman, somber-faced and dressed in the obligatory black. It is not so much a conversation as a classical paradigm of a scolding, the old woman bristling with gestures and Panayotis standing before her, meek, abashed, scratching his bald pate. When we drive away he tells us the story. A few months ago her son, who was doing his military service, was granted leave to write a set of examinations that would determine his future. He failed. Shortly afterwards, he committed suicide. As if this were not enough, her husband abandoned her for an eighty-four year old woman (who, Panayotis assures us, "looks like seventy") with whom he is now living in a tiny cottage some fifty metres up the road. The abandoned wife is destitute and helpless and has already tried to commit suicide three times, on one occasion throwing herself into the sea from the Corfu pier when she arrived to meet her son's funeral cortege. Panayotis has now become her link with the larger world of Gaios and Lakka, bringing her groceries and medicines several times a week. The scolding he received was for not appearing the day before.

Two years ago when I was here, Paxos was entirely free of jellyfish, unlike Alonissos where scooping the jellyfish out in buckets to clear a swimming hole in the sea was part of the daily Lobster Quadrille. Now the jellyfish have begun to infest the Ionian. Received my first sting in three years last week, swimming off the breakwater in Lakka harbour. The collective migratory undulations of this species of sea-junk has become part of the mythological resonance of contemporary Greece, a country in which there are no ultimate explanations for anything, in which the concept of truth has entered the dimension of Quantum duplicity.

The geodesic impulse is anathema to the Greek soul. I spent an entire summer on Alonissos trying to discover the reason the *koinotita* was pumping scarcely any water to the village on the summit of the mountain, the ancient capital of the island. I consulted the local people, and made two or three visits to the mayor down in Patatiri, the present capital, and even telephoned the authorities in Volos on the mainland. The first reason I was given for the water shortage was the general drought all Europe was presently enduring which, as a reason, seemed legitimate enough. Who was I to complain of having no water in the house when half of Europe's farmers were falling into bankruptcy? But then I learned that the Galaxy and Marpounta hotels were literally swimming in the stuff. So it turned out the reason we had no water in the village was that the available supply was being diverted to the hotels while the villagers and the resident foreigners who had bought and renovated houses, and who contributed more to the local economy in the long run than the transient tourists putting up at the hotels, were left to go without. A few days later I discovered that a fleet of pick-up trucks plied regularly all night between the wells at the other, uninhabited end of the island and the two major hotels, which meant that the hotels were indeed in the same dry straits as the village and were not siphoning off the reservoir as I had originally been given to understand. Another visit to the mayor. This time I was informed that there was in fact no water shortage at all, there was plenty of water gushing from the springs which abounded on the island; only, the pump on the side of the mountain which fed the reservoir on the summit was broken, and spare parts were daily expected to arrive from Volos. After another week without water in the taps and one of my children sick from the infected muck I drew up in buckets from an exhausted sterno in the lower part of the village, (since not all the water could be boiled and we were often without propane) I inquired further into the matter. The pump was indeed working, but a conspiracy of unscrupulous villagers was depleting the reservoir during the night to satisfy its own needs. This interpretation of events was vigorously denied by the suspected individuals. The problem *really* was that the houses in the 'lower' village' (the clutch of houses further down the slope) were receiving all the water as it laboured uphill toward the reservoir. These houses somehow tapped into the major conduit and therefore did not have to wait for the water to trickle back down each morning from the reservoir that had filled during the night, with the inevitable result that the houses in the larger 'upper village,' when the time came to open the faucets, received not water but air. This was perhaps the most plausible explanation of the *tremendum mysterium* from which the village suffered except that the lower village had recently sent a deputation to the mayor complaining about the water shortage. The only dearth we did not suffer was a dearth of explanations, and to this day I am as much in the dark as ever, and I am also convinced that *nobody* on the island, not the villagers, the hotel-keepers, the water commission, not even the mayor himself, had peeled all the integuments of that Greek onion, Truth. Detunication is an eternal process.

In the same way, everyone has his own general explanation for the plague of jellyfish that has spread across the Aegean and Ionian. It is the fault of the oil tankers threading the Suez Canal and shipping ballast in Greek waters. It is a general migration from the South Pacific. It is a kind of spontaneous coagulation of global pollution. And every-one has become an expert in predicting the location of the shoals on any given day — which beaches will be hit, which will be free — so that there has been a scholastic proliferation of specific theories to match the peristaltic invasions of the medusas. They follow in the wake of the yachts and catamarans, feeding off the refuse. But I have spent many afternoons snorkling down in the harbour without running into a single jellyfish. Another theory, which probably boasts the largest number of adherents, states that the jellyfish are really current-propelled, so that determining the prevalent wind direction will infallibly tell you which coast of the island and which beaches will be accessible. Not only have I seen the jellyfish swim effortlessly against the most strenuous currents, but the statistics I compiled over a summer clearly showed that this analysis scored no better than fifty percent and was therefore invalid. Another theory claims that jellyfish are attracted to shady waters. I have been stung absolutely irradiated by underwater sunlight.

My theory is that there was no water in the village because there was no water in the village. None of the reasons adduced to account for the phenomenon was final, or a different combination of factors may have operated on every other day in random sequence. As for the jellyfish, they drift and undulate where they will, in shade and sunlight, in refuse like flies or in pure translucencies like sea-bream, with the current and against, in blasts of wind and in dead Sargassos. Which leads me to suspect, having lived in Greece off and on for over twenty years, that *there is no ultimate reason for anything*. There are no final explanations. What we call truth is only the most recent interpretation of events, an asymptotic approximation to nothing. And this is the only and paradoxical truth, of which Greece is the eternal and mythic incarnation. You turn on the tap and hope there is water. You dive off a rock and pray the jellyfish are grazing on the other side of the island. You drink your morning coffee and wonder whether grapeshot will spatter into your cup or bird's blood freckle the cream bowl.

Paxos is a rarity among the small Greek islands for its lavish and startling opulence. The soil is miserly and brittle, yet the island is a rich canopy of green owing to the prolific olive mixed with cypress and pine. (Only Naxos, its close namesake, with its abundant streams and forests, can compare for verdure.) When the Venetians were here several hundred years ago they encouraged the Paxiots to plant olive groves by offering one ducat per tree. The result is evident today. The entire length of the island is a succession of olive groves and floating terraces, one blending insensibly into the next, and Paxos is famous in Greece as a provider of olive oil which is accounted, for flavour and consistency, as the finest to be had in the country. (Though the olives themselves, tiny, black, wrinkled ovals, are inferior to the Kalamata variety which are exported world-wide.) The Venetian ducats and later the groves themselves were the source of whatever prosperity the island enjoyed. Today Paxos has become a suburb of tourist-filled Corfu, its population during the summers increasing tenfold to 25,000, and the olive has accordingly fallen in status to that of a subsidiary industry. Now many of these magnificent trees, some thrusting up to heights of forty and fifty feet (unlike the stunted Aegean breed), are being cut down to provide the tourist villas with open spaces and clear, expansive views of the sea, as if the Department of Tourism, aware that history runs in cycles, were offering the people one ducat per felled tree to add to the island's prosperity.

In Greece, it seems everything is prohibited and nothing is forbidden. For example, on Paxos as on many other islands a foreigner is not permitted to buy a house without bringing in a Greek partner in whose name it is registered. But a loophole in the law permits the foreigner to incorporate himself as a tourist agency or become a shareholder in an already-existing agency and buy the house under its protective auspices. In either case someone else is enriched, a Greek national or a resident English tourist-baron, and always the government. But you get your house. Or again, hunting is prohibited within a hundred metre range from the last house 'in the vicinity,' but as the houses are distributed in such a random, higgledy-piggledy way that no one can be sure which is in fact the 'last house,' the law cannot be enforced. There is a way around everything in Greece, originally a nation of mariners accustomed to circumventing reefs. In the West, only a designated number of things is prohibited but these are strictly and inescapably forbidden. You can get away with parking on a sidewalk in Greece because there is nowhere else to park. In Montreal I averaged one ticket a month for parking on the wrong side of the street even though every spot on the legitimate side was taken up and there was nowhere else to put the car.

One of the most interesting characters in Lakka is a portly, dominating, and exceedingly wealthy bachelor named Haralambos. He has lived in many places around the world ("I live international," he says), including a twenty-year stint in the Sudan where he acquired his conspicuous wealth in some obscure and perhaps unmentionable way. Afterwards, he returned to Lakka in Paxos, the home of his parents, where he designed and built a monstrous, luxurious eyesore of a mansion on the raised flank of the bay, dominating the town by its bulging and garish magnificence as does the six-foot-plus Haralambos over the suddenly diminished townsfolk with whom he plays cards every morning and evening in Spiro Petrou's cafeneion. He is the object of much gossip and considerable envy. A dalmatian pup which he imported from England was mysteriously poisoned. Two of his nine cats were thrown into the sea. The Mercedes which controlled the island roads was found one morning scratched from stem to stern. He is sometimes referred to in Gaios, where I first heard of him, as "the black one" (he was notorious for his parties and the foreign women who danced all night on his marble floors), which reminds me of the traditional kenning for Dionysus, 'Melainaigis,' the dark-skinned one. In other ways he brings to mind the powerful and inscrutable hero of John Fowles' *The Magus*, Mr. Conchis.

Despite everything, Haralambos clearly enjoys his *réclame*. Though he plays cards daily and amicably with half the male population of Lakka, he professes to have no respect for the Paxiots, whom he bluntly calls "stupid," a people "no educated," and who "know naatheeing." For eight months of the year he entertains on a regal scale. One entire floor of his house, which he calls 'The Villa Blotto,' is devoted to the bar stocked with every kind of liquor imaginable, and once boasted a grand piano. His friends stream in from all over Europe, arriving in Land-Rovers, yachts and even helicopters, signalling him from the town square with megaphones. During the winter months he applies himself to rummy and tavlis (backgammon), waiting for the arrival of spring and his horde of guests, whom he can now entertain more lavishly as he just had a yacht built for himself to complement his two motorboats.

We have enjoyed several suppers together at Myro Mourtis' restaurant, the first two at his invitation — freshly caught swordfish and gallons of raw Corfu wine from his cellars. I reciprocated with a lobster dinner, which he found second-rate since the lobsters had been frozen. Last night I bought a fresh, three-kilo dentex in

Gaios and had it cooked and garnished by Myro Mourtis and his wife Marina. Haralambos proclaimed himself satisfied.

There is no doubt that he is a show-off (witness the gold lira on his keychain) and that he loves his notoriety, needing the Paxiots to set him off as they need him to enliven their otherwise television-filled nights — a perfect symbiosis. On the other hand he is a gracious and magnanimous host, sees to everyone's satisfaction at table, offers the best that can be had, and will go out of his way to provide whatever accords with the taste or requirements of his guests: a certain cognac, for example, or a musical instrument. What I like about him is the unabashed way in which he revels in his opulence. He has it, therefore why shouldn't he enjoy it in the splendid, oligarchical manner he finds congenial?

Thirty years ago he married a beautiful Turkish dancer who performed with a celebrated touring company, bringing her to live with him in Lakka. She turned out to be uncommonly possessive, jealous of every moment of Haralambos' life spent outside her presence, and was infuriated even by his manifest lack of jealousy. They divorced after one month and Haralambos left Lakka to seek his fortune in Africa. Since his return he has lived with women from time to time, but having been fried to a crisp in that early, blazing passion, he had become permanently suspicious of permanence. One affair with a young English girl lasted eight months. When Haralambos rejected her offer of marriage, the relationship sputtered out. Another time he lived with a German woman who also belonged to the sorority of possessive earth goddesses, chiding him constantly like an erring child. If he indulged his Sardinapalian appetite for food, she condemned him for growing fat. He went on a diet. She conceived an intense dislike for thin men. Keeping his new house spotless, he found himself accused of over-fastidiousness. Letting things lie about, he was excoriated for being messy and careless. One morning he brought her coffee in bed and found himself, for no reason he could discern, the object of a contemptuous rebuke. "Haralambos no like when womans speak strong for Haralambos. Why she speak strong for me? No, is not good when womans speak strong for man." And so that relationship also ended.

He is sixty-five, but looks fifty, healthy and well-fed. He is now, like Frost's Abigail, providing for an old age without family, having made arrangements with a Swiss establishment outside Geneva for his eventual retirement from the Lakka amphitheatre which he still continues to dominate.

The shooting is at its most vehement and extensive this morning. A gunshot blast at about ten metres catapulted me from bed at the usual hour. The hills are swarming with hunters — they no longer bother to conceal themselves. They are at the Villa Eftithia next door and at the Red House just across the road, stalking beneath the olives, throwing stones into the branches to dislodge the birds, and blasting away from every conceivable angle. The *lofos* on which we live is a veritable shooting arcade and when

I sit down to write in the mornings I feel mostly like a war correspondent in the midst of a revolution. Guns keep going off in our ears and our hair is full of grapeshot. There is no stopping this people, who are breaking the law twice over, not only shooting inside the legally prohibited radius but shooting without legal right. The law in Greece is generally so complicated and redundant that it invites evasion or mere disregarding. You need to buy a licence in order to own a gun and then another licence in order to use it. The people acquire the first licence but dispense with the second, so that the entire population of the island would have to be fined or arrested if the law were to be enforced. It is as if we are living in an arsenal, an island of less than twelve square miles bristling, according to the most reliable estimate, with more than seven thousand guns. The other day, walking through Apergatika in the next valley, we met a young boy (he can't have been more than six or seven) unslinging his shotgun in a copse of trees. We turned a bend in the road. The familiar explosion and a hail of pellets.

We discovered yesterday what the greatest danger is: grapeshot in the eyes, especially in the case of children who are prone to forget and look impulsively upward as the rain of hot pellets smokes downward. Blindness is a distinct possibility, and though the local people are tight-lipped about the underside of their passion, they have had their share of casualties over the years. We keep Hannah indoors until around nine and almost never take walks in the mornings.

But what fascinates me in particular is the concrete,

vivid, and unforgettable lesson the island teaches in the paradoxical duality — duplicity might be a better word — of life. Paxos is one of the most beautiful islands in the entire Greek archipelago: green, testered with olive groves, puckered with valleys and webbed with pathways leading from the hills to the beach-indented coastline. Everywhere there are flowers, hibiscus, bougainvillaea, dog rose, oleander, jasmine; the air is thick with the scent of heather, oregano, basil and sage. The sunsets rival their Caribbean competitors, the whole sky turning a smoky pink alternating with patches of pewter grey and dusty blue as the sun, swollen and fulvid, seems with its almost tactile weight, like a huge blood-pomegranate, to heave the sea upward as it sinks. The sensation of displacement is palpable. And on halcyon afternoons the topmost olive-leaves are tipped silver-green with a kind of glancing scintillation (I think of Pound's 'glaucous') so the sky seems almost sequinned or scaled with light.

Yet one goes for a walk through these light-checkered groves and the skeletons of innumerable birds crunch underfoot. For hours every morning, in the gaps between the distant incendiary crackle of gunshots and the close-range detonations, the air has the eerie stillness of a sarcophagus and reeks of cordite. Nothing moves. Nothing sings. It is almost like a bodying forth of Sophocles' half-mythical Lemnos where the birds never sang and the air was always acrid. One sits at the garden table and suddenly a singed feather drifts past one's face, from out of nowhere. Blood speckles the cream bowl. It is all pure Poussin, *Et in Arcadia Ego.*[1] For this island with its fragrance and colour is about as close to Arcadia as you can get today, and yet everywhere the perpetual reminder of gunshots; of birds trussed up in the market place, swarming with wasps that plunge their insect snouts into the eyeholes and guzzle; of little heaps of charred feathers and thin, fluted bones at the corners of the paths; and everywhere the cartridge shells, millions of them, on the road, littering every mound and tussock, in rich chromatic circles beneath the trees as if they were some tropical species of leaf, more colourful even than the burgeoning and various flora of the island, gradually replacing the island's powdery topsoil.

It is no longer possible to let oneself go in an orgy of aesthetic admiration, in exhalations of tourist rapture. Beauty comes at a price, as one tends to forget back home where life seems less concentrated, less naked, and comes to you disembowelled, as it were, like a supermarket chicken. The garden now, as I write, is full of melody, the hunt having moved further west toward Ipapantis: the curious ticking of the small finches, the plainsong of the redthroats, the thrum of the hummingbirds, and the high three-note trill of some unidentified warbler. One can still feel grateful and delighted but the mortuary under-current, the bassnote, is unavoidable. Rhapsody is cheap and sentimental, the privilege of the lunatic, the lover and the tourist. If death is the mother of beauty, as Wallace Stevens writes, it is also the sister of recollection and the wife of a belated realism.

❖

It is well known in Greece that every island and region has its own peculiar dialect, each like a small epicycle imposed on and figuring the linguistic chart of the Greek language itself. I recall in the south of Crete an old shepherd giving us directions and using words from the 'formal' language; for instance, in pointing the way to the sea he used the word 'pelagos' instead of 'thalassa.' Or in Alonissos the people have the habit of lopping off suffixes so their speech is really an idiom of contraction. 'Let us go down to Patatiri and then up to the house' in standard Greek would read or sound: 'Paome kato sti Patatiri kai meta apano sto speeti.' The Alonissiots say: 'Paom kat sti Patir k'met apan sto speet.' In Paxos the dialect is polyglottal, a dollop of Italian (e.g., the familiar 'Aghios' for 'saint' is often replaced by 'Santa,' as in Santa Demetrios, which sounds distinctly odd) and a dash of English (e.g., the proper name 'Haralambos' is almost always 'Bobby'). The most frequently repeated phrase in island speech is 'no problem' (with an uvular 'r'). Everything is 'no problem.' You ask the grocer for a half kilo of feta cheese and he replies, "Nai, endaxi, no problem." You order a coffee at the cafeneion and hear, "A mesos, Kyrie, no problem." The phrase is beginning to infiltrate my own speech habits. Alki asks me if he can turn on the 'thermosymphono' for a hot shower and I say, "Sure, son, no problem."

The main dilemma (I almost said 'problem') most of the islands face apart from the flight of youth to Athens or overseas is the chronic water shortage. Only a few are spared: parts of Crete, Naxos, Thassos to the north. The fortunate islands are blessed with a scattering of wells and springs. But Paxos relies entirely on the winter rains, which are usually abundant enough to see the people through the dry season. The few wells around Lakka are salt and the prospect of importing water in huge inflated sea-dirigibles, as is the case in Hydra, is sufficiently daunting to cause shudders of apprehension. But so far the rains have held, as regular in their winter schedules as the flocks of turtle-doves in October and April. Everyone here takes a great pride in his sterno or reservoir, which is usually the chief item of display when you make your first visit to someone's house. The other day in Vlachoplatika, we were invited for coffee at the Gaios baker's house, a place that reeks of new money. (The summer influx of tourists to Gaios have made him a wealthy man.) He engaged in mechanical, desultory conversation over thick cups of 'metreo' and then, obviously impatient to get on with the real reason for the invitation, led us on an inspection tour. The house boasted two kitchens, a washing machine, an over-decorated living-room, marble floors, a gigantic colour television set, but the *pièce de resistance* was the new sterno in the back yard, which was about the size of a large swimming pool or a small gymnasium. The baker stood with his thumbs in his belt and gloated. "It is the biggest in Paxos," he sighed, rapturously. And even Haralambos, after he had demonstrated the magnificent view from his arcaded balcony, the bathroom with its enormous green-tiled tub and sparkling bidet, and the infamous 'Villa

Blotto' bar on the lower level, paused to dilate on the architectural wonder of his reservoir, measuring it out and assuring us that he had a supply of water sufficient for three years. It is the size of these island sternos which are the gauge of a person's wealth and status here, more so than the car he drives, the olive trees he possesses, or the number of boats he has in drydock.

Met an elderly Englishwoman this morning who has been living in Ozias for the last year. She and her husband retired to Paxos a little over a year ago, after which he succumbed to a heart attack. She has decided to stay on and is about to move into a house in Makratika, which she has had restored.

Peter Bull, the English actor (best known for his role as Mr. Thwackum in the film *Tom Jones*), who owned a small house high over the bay of Lakka in a tangled brake of shrubbery, also died here of a heart attack not too long ago. He was particularly beloved of the islanders who considered him *their* resident Englishman. One day Panayotis, the bilingual taxi-driver, proudly informed me that he possessed an autographed copy of Peter Bull's book on Paxos. I told him in that case I would not give him a complimentary sample of one of my books. "Why not?" he asked. "Because I can't afford to take the chance," I replied. Panayotis promised to lend the book to me, though when I will see it is another question entirely. I have been trying to hunt down a copy of Bull's volume for some time now. George (Tzortzy), the English gardener who resides here most of the year, and is sure to have the sought-after item, is presently vacationing in England.

✣

Drove yesterday to Boikatika, a gaggle of houses perched on the cliffs above Erimitis. The views are truly 'enormous.' To the northwest the sheer drop of several hundred metres to the grotto-hollowed beach of Erimitis, and to the southwest the limestone scarps and dramatic outcrops of stark granite plummeting into the small bight of Achai. We went as far as the Subaru would take us, parked it near the chapel of Aghios Apostolis, and walked through the olive terraces into the heather and thistle fields but could not find the *monopati* down to Erimitis. On the way back we stopped by a house we had admired earlier: two stories, green shutters, whitewashed walls, set in a flagged garden flowering with basil shrubs and clusters of gardenia. A bent and sickly woman, who must have been approaching eighty, watched us from the gate. Soon we were deep in conversation. Kyria Maria had just returned from a two month convalescence in the Corfu Hospital, where she had undergone a knee operation. I raised my trouser cuffs and showed her the scar from my old menisectomy and she reciprocated by lifting the hem of her brocaded skirt and displaying the marks of recent butchery. When I told her how much I liked her house she immediately offered to sell it to me. We were invited in for coffee and sweets and then given a tour: a beautiful ancient dwelling, over three hundred years old, the original crossbeam still in place, the walls almost two feet thick — all somewhat pokey and clammy and rundown now, the shutters bolted hard against the cold evening light, but I could imagine it cleaned up, aired out and renovated. Boikatika is one of the loveliest hamlets on the island: the terrace walls built in the 'old style' with jagged crenellations of unhewn stone and the views dramatic, vertiginous, exhilarating. All this almost converted me to island life and made me wish to acquire Maria's property, despite the obstacles that stand peremptorily in the way (not the least of which, as I later discovered, being a clan of litigious relatives each claiming a morsel of the house and garden). Every day the distance between Paxos and home seems to increase, between this flawed, compelling Arcadia and the parcelled, secure existence I can never quite grow accustomed to.

This morning a small redthroat flew into the kitchen. Nothing we could do was of any avail. He fluttered round and round for several minutes, excreted on the window pane, and then settled on the roofbeam, looking about with renewed philosophical interest. Breadcrumbs did not appeal to him and the imbecilic whistling and chirping sounds we made in our efforts at communication seemed only to incite a quiet amazement in him. Finally he flew down, walloped himself against the window, found the open mullion, and was gone. "Another emblem there!"

We were astonished today at the absence of gunfire. The silence was, as they say, deafening. Soon the reason for this unexpected cease-fire became evident. A troop of children from Lakka primary school marched past on a nature expedition, spending an hour or so in the scrub around the ruined tower and filing back singing (apart from the counterpoint of the reprieved birds, the only sound in the vicinity). This inspires some bitter reflections. We also have a cheerful and quite melodious child in the house, but she is, after all, only a foreigner, and her father does not wear a cassock like the priest-teacher at the head of the procession of schoolchildren. Soon the truce will be over and the hunt will begin again around our beleaguered and encircled property. (A gunshot this very moment.)

Invited Haralambos for supper last night — Hungarian goulash and a marvelous *anakatomeni* salad Karin spent half the day preparing. A moderate success. Haralambos did not touch the salad and left over most of the sauce, going exclusively for the chunks of meat. "I don't like an unappreciative eater," was Karin's final judgment. But

Haralambos does things in grand style. He 'materialized' out of the darkness at the door (there is no other way to describe his *parousia*), arriving not by the road but through the clump of trees at the side of the hill, carrying a large box of fresh macaroons in one hand and a *galloni* of new Corfu wine in the other, installed himself on the bench behind the kitchen table (none of our chairs could hold him), and remained ensconced there until nearly midnight.

After a slow start the conversation gathered momentum. The Paxiots came in for much abuse: a greedy people unable to transcend the narrow horizons of self-interest, riven by political dissension, as stony-hearted as their soil. There is an old folk-story that when God made the Seven Islands, he scooped a handful of good earth in a great sieve, shook it several times, and dropped the rich loam into the sea. This became the island of Corfu. The stones and pebbles remaining in the sieve he threw some distance away. This became Paxos.

Recent history has been kinder on the whole to Paxos than to the other islands in the archipelago. During the Second War, the island was garrisoned by a contingent of twenty-five lazy and inefficient Italians. Nobody was executed (I recall the marble cenotaph in the dusty parking lot in the mountain village of Alonissos, commemorating the eleven islanders shot by the Germans for subversion.) Afterwards, during the civil war that cleft the country, the Paxiots took sides like everyone else in Greece but never got around to liquidating one another — not profitable, I suppose. (In this connection I think of my friend Grigory

Limnios in Lesbos. His entire family divided down the middle. During the day he and his brother fired at one another in the hills around Eftalou, a partisan encampment; during the night, the truce-period, they would shout family news back and forth across the lines. Grigory himself survived the world war unscathed; the civil war shattered his arm.)

Haralambos praised the people of the island of Zacynthos to the south. "In Zacyntho, everybody dance. In Paxos, nobody dance. In Zacyntho, everybody drink, sing. In Paxos, only drink." I asked him why in that case he did not move to Zacynthos, once known as 'the flower of the Levant.' He only laughed and answered, evasively: "Paxos people no good. Ees stupid. Only money, money, money, But ees island beeyooteefool." Karin compared Haralambos to the Old Testament God, presiding on a mountain over the commercial harbour, observing the antlike, idolatrous activities of the people, thundering and condemning relentlessly, but never abandoning them, never removing to favored Zacynthos.

We learned a little more about Haralambos' past. In his early twenties during the Second War, he was "beeg saboteur." Caught by the Germans, he was sent to the prison camp on Chios where he spent a year under daily sentence of death. "But commander ees Austrian man. Very good. Very intelligent. No shoot Haralambos." After the hostilities, he moved on to Khartoum where he acquired a fortune in business (still unspecified), getting out just in time, before the political climate changed and foreign properties were sequestered. Then he retired to Lakka where he could indulge his lordly fulminations and manifold passions without let or hindrance and be Haralambos, the black one.

Though he speaks a fluent, ornate and melodious *katharevousa* (he ostentatiously prefers the pure language to the demotic), I enjoy listening to his multiply-fractured English. He has the curious linguistic tic of placing most of his semantic eggs in the basket of the second-person singular. The pronoun 'you' not only tends to serve for all the others but often does double duty for the definite article as well. He will say, "you coming to Lakka ten years before," when he means "I came to Lakka ten years ago." Or, "you is no good people in Lakka" for "they are not . . ." "You Athens tourist group coming to make control for Paxos restaurants" means "The Athenian tourist organization is coming to inspect the Paxos restaurants." There was a disaster on Zacynthos yesterday: a sudden, violent hailstorm devastated all the crops. Haralambos reported the news as follows: "You beeg catastrof in Zacyntho. You beeg stone fall. You catastrof everytheeng."

At the end of the evening Haralambos went to the bathroom and then departed, thanking Karin for supper in his idiolectical way: "Ees okay, lady. Ees good eat."

Paxos must be one of the stoniest islands in all of Greece, though it is covered with a nap of rough green scrub. But the earth consists mainly of stones which have been dug out in inconceivable numbers and assembled into the walls that separate groves and terraces. There are walls everywhere, in Ozias, in Yfthika, in Makratika, in Magazia, in Ipapanti, on every slope, in every valley, each constructed from innumerable stones that lock into a mortised checkerboard and still, wherever one walks, one stumbles over mounds of stony rubble as if a volcano had erupted under the cobbled streets of a large city. Karin deduces the character of the islanders from these profusions of stone. All this digging, this perpetual fitting of one stone upon another, generation after generation, must explain "the tight-fisted, counting mentality" of the people. It is the same with the olives. A basket of large Kalamata olives can be emptied and toted up in a short while. But a basket of the tiny, elliptical calculi of Paxos olives appears to contain infinities, and although weighing simplifies the operation, the olives were occasionally counted. Centuries of calculating these minuscule, abounding fruit, like enumerating the Aleph-plus of stones to build into walls, have left their imprint on the character of the people, she believes, and have finally come to produce Myro Mourtis down in Lakka who never buys himself a coffee or encourages his wife Marina to take a morning off (it is twenty years since Marina has visited Gaios) or procures medicines for her phlebitis, yet he has already invested ten million drachmas in the construction of a great house on the cliffs of Vassilatika.

In Gaios and Lakka nobody ever invites anybody to his house or to a restaurant for supper, with the exception of the inimitable Haralambos (a double exception: he is rumored to be the only Paxiot who does not own a gun.) For hospitality you have to go into the outback, to Boikatika, Vlachoplatika or Ipapanti where the people still brew coffee for the stranger. The 'outback' on Paxos is a kilometre away from the larger towns. Lakka must number at least two hundred souls, a humming metropolis.

The Garden (1)

The cyclamen shoots lie coiled like bedsprings. The little red cravats are scooting among the leaves, wings thrumming, chirping mechanically. The cats are stalking under the plumbago bush, and the kitten has caught a half-fledged finch, batting it about like a bolo ball, then sinking its slender needles of teeth into the feathers around the neck. We can see the sun through a fine reticulation of olive leaves as it sinks past the unillumined lighthouse. Depending on one's frame of mind, the sun is either beautiful or grotesque, either an enormous vermilion fruit weighing down the tree of heaven or something clumsy and tumescent and absurd, a mumpish titan collapsing under his own torpid mass. A frail, translucent gecko is picking its way along the sandpaper leaves of the prickly pear.

The Garden (2)

The political slogans are sprouting on the walls of Arcadia like the tough, leathery bushes that force their way through every chink and tiny crevice. The red KKE legends are everywhere, of course, painted luridly on the white house walls on the *paralea* and along the road to Gaios. But there has been a fresh and unexpected growth of black swastikas which, by a kind of allelopathy, are beginning to strangle the dribbling red roots of the KKE patches. You see them pushing their way up the taverna walls and cracking the tarmac with their thick, black strokes. Even the Eclogues of Virgil were not free of political intent, but such malignant flora seem disproportionate and startling.

It is astonishing how diverse such a microdot island can be. It is broadly unified by the olive groves which extend everywhere and by the long, mosaic stone walls that mark the properties and truss up the earthen terraces to prevent landslides. But apart from these, the views and villages differ remarkably from one another. The sheer limestone cliffs of the west coast oppose the gradual, sloping shingle beaches of the east. The north is a rocky headland on which stands the lighthouse (only one hundred years old; the previous lighthouse tumbled from its abutment into the sea when the rock collapsed); the southern part of the island consists of a verdant peninsula which shelters the popular Mongonisi beach and a small outriding islet with its tiny chapel and straggle of goats. The Gaians are shrewd and busy; in Lakka the people are somewhat warmer though equally pawky and disingenuous. In Boikatika and Ipapanti one still finds authentic hospitality, but in Vlachoplatika behind the soccer field the newly rich are beginning to entrench themselves and the hospitality is tainted by pride and a sense of important things to attend to. From the high road one looks eastward toward the thrusting mountains of the Epirot coast and the bare southern cliffs of Corfu; westward, an expanse of open sea, Italy an imaginary boundary at the curvature of the horizon. Bogdanatika with its neat, painted houses and ancient church of Aghios Haralambos is pleasant to stroll or drive through, but Magazia half a mile up the road seems untidy and faintly disreputable (it is around Magazia that the swastika has begun to flourish). Within ten minutes from wherever one starts, one is in a different part of the world, with different perspectives and different responses on the part of the inhabitants. It is as if the contracting pressures of a sixteen mile coastline have squeezed a rich diversity from the stony subsoil to compensate for a Lilliputian patrimony.

It adds a certain pungency to my daily life here to note that the tiny community in which we rented our house on the hill above Lakka is called Moungelatika, which means roughly 'the property of one who is mute' or variously 'the community of the dumb.' (from 'moungos' = mute). I came here to work with speech, to plunge into the resources of language, to write English and speak Greek, to be voluble. I came here because of a favourable metaphorical soil in which to replant the seeds of a desiccated eloquence, and I choose to live in Moungelatika, among the stones and deserted houses.

Winter has launched its first tentative probes. The wind has driven the cats into the laundry baskets and sent cold jets of air whistling through the cracked doors and porous shutters of our barricade. Rain has penetrated the outer, tiled roof and sounds just like the pack of fruit rats that scurries and clatters over the wooden slats of the inner ceiling. Whenever we move from the central house to the kitchen or the bathroom, all separate structures, we must don boots, rainjackets and caps, so that merely going from one room to another becomes a major expedition. To complicate matters, none of the doors is provided with knobs — a doorknob in these parts is about as rare as a chess computer or a comfortable chair — which means that we must carry the one set of housekeys about with us at all times, standing in the rain while fumbling with the locks, just to brush one's teeth or fetch a spoon. (The frequent act of passing the keys back and forth reminds me of the three Gray Sisters in Greek mythology with only one eye between them.) I have to thaw out my fingers several times a day around a cup of steaming tea before I can grasp a pen or plunk the typewriter keys. The weather today is a classic example of pathetic fallacy, a clammy and tempestuous rhetoric that translates the discomfort and even the terror of our own interior climate.

There are basically two masculine names on the island: Spiro and Bobby. The first derives from Saint Spiridon, the patron saint of Corfu, and the second from Saint Haralambos, who presides over Paxos itself. Other derivatives of the latter are Harry and Lambi, though there are few Harries on the island and only one Lambi (Anglaia's husband, our neighbor up the road.) By contrast there are in the order of four hundred Bobbies and a somewhat greater number of Spiros. The remaining hundred or so masculine names are partitioned out among the obligatory Yannis, Costas, etc. The problem of reference is one of the peculiarities of life on Paxos.

I have let the rumour spread that I am interested in buying a house on Paxos. It began innocently enough — I merely told Myro Mourtis in conversation that Kyria Maria in Boikatika had offered to sell me her house. Immediately Myro grew visibly disturbed and tendered his own bid: a house "me kati elies" (with some olive trees) on the road to Vassilatika. A few days later he buttonholed me in the square and renewed his offer, looking more worried than ever. Afterward, we received our first luncheon invitation since arriving here, from our neighbor Yanni, the local butcher who also runs a tourist shop, and who owns considerable property. He offered to show me a piece of land with a 'wonderful view' toward the sea, on which I could build a house to my own specifications, and not from stone but wood. I said I would wait and see. Yesterday evening I drove to Gaios to meet Karin at the Corfu boat, and while strolling on the dock was suddenly accosted by Bobby, one of the wealthy marine entrepreneurs, who without preamble suggested I inspect several old houses in the mountains behind Gaios. It took me a moment to recover my equanimity. How could he know I was presumably in the market for a house. He is six miles away, he is constantly busy with his marine rentals, I have never seen him once in Lakka (and for many people in Lakka, Gaios is almost at the other end of the world), and certainly none of the Lakkans would have divulged the information to a competitor. I said I was only thinking about it at present.

Soon the offers will come pouring in from all over the island. I am fair game now, a 'prospect,' a 'xenos' with heaps of money that by the immutable laws of the cosmos rightfully and inevitably belongs in the pockets of a *Paxiotis*. Meanwhile, as I am treated with courtesy and respect and am becoming the recipient of numerous invitations, I allow the rumour to gather momentum and make no effort to disabuse this affable, lycanthropic society of Arcadians.

✤

People are busy preparing for the winter rains and high, choppy seas that come sloshing over the quay and down the narrow lanes and streets, sometimes to the level of a metre. What they do is extend the height of their doorstoops, either by affixing a metal gate to the jambs or simply walling up the lower half of the doorway from outside with bricks and mortar or thick slabs of concrete. Entering a house becomes a strenuous and sometimes hazardous procedure. One has to raise one's legs high and straddle the dike, and children have to be lifted into the vestibules. These incongruous demi-portals lend the town a curiously fortified look, as if an attack from the Algerian pirates or the mountain people were imminent. Especially on a day like today when the streets are empty and the square is echoing thunderously with wind.

When we first moved into this house, Maria, our young landlady, hung a *dichti*, a fishing net, in the closet for good luck, the way people place a little pot of basil on the windowsill for the same reason. I didn't realize then how appropriate a symbol the *dichti* would turn out to be. When the wind threw itself at the hilltop two days ago, the house stood like a sieve or net against it. None of the windows shut properly. The kitchen door, webbed with cracks and sliding off its hinges, may as well not have been there. The holes in the ceiling acted like little wind funnels. In bed that night, we had to cower under the pillows from the puffs of cold wind skating round nose and ears. In the morning I went down and complained to Maria's mother-in-law, Marina Mourtis, who telephoned Maria's mother Eleni. Eleni duly appeared later in the day and when I explained the matter, she replied, in the typically insouciant local manner, that I should merely shut the hall door to keep the parlour winds out of the bedroom or the bedroom winds out of the parlour. Amusement triumphed over incredulity: I patiently went over the entire house and managed to persuade her that we did indeed have 'a problem.' To her credit, she returned later in the afternoon with her husband, Bobby, who took off his cartridge belt — the Paxiot baldric — leaned his rifle against the fig tree, opened his sack of tools and fell to work. A handier, more cheerful and robust man I have rarely met: he planed every window frame, filled the cracks with shims of wood, repaired the light fixtures in the bathroom, partially rebuilt the kitchen door from whatever material he could find lying about the yard, drank a glass of brandy, smoked a pack of cigarettes, and elaborated a theory of viticulture (praising young wines and derogating aged dignity). Meanwhile Eleni dug in the garden with the *tsapa*, and when this proved inadequate, went to her knees and used her hands as scoops. (I looked at these hands: they resembled nothing so much as calloused trowels.)

These two people represent the best of a doomed generation: hardworking, good-natured, uncomplaining, and very much *there*, alert, perceptive. I was touched by Eleni, who paused when going over our bedroom, at the books under the window-ledge. She regretted that in "the old days" there was only a primary school on the island.

No one could afford to go to Corfu to complete his or her education and besides everyone was needed to work the olive groves or herd the goats in the stony pastures. She had always wanted to study. Later on, when Karin, who was digging in the garden with Eleni, called to me to help with a translation, I heard Eleni whisper loudly, "Oxi, graphi" "No, he is writing." I didn't have the heart to tell her I was merely calculating the week's expenses.

Bobby tells me there are people in Gaios who have never been to Lakka. Some of these are professional sailors and engineers who have sailed many times round the world and have visited Australia, Canada and Russia, but Lakka six miles away is another universe entirely. Driving back from Gaios last night, I realized with astonishment that the island seems to be expanding, increasing in length. The short trip seemed to take forever. I noticed all sorts of roads and paths branching off the main highway, dwellings I had never registered before, chapels, coombs, mountain peaks, views that were utterly new to me. Paradoxically, as I become more familiar with the place, it assumes a stranger and more mysterious aspect; and the longer I stay here, the less confined I feel — so far. The island slowly takes on the dimensions of a world with all its diversity and unexpectedness, and though I may be wrong I can't help but speculate that it is *people*, the underlying or superimposed stratum of *personality*, that inflates the tiny volume of the region. Just as the other day I discovered two houses in an olive grove only a hundred metres or so away from here, whose existence I had never suspected, so that the pocket community of Moungelatika seemed suddenly amplified, almost vast in the same way every person I meet (like Aristides in the cafeneion yesterday morning, who owns six hundred olive trees and five houses, has retired from active work, and spends his latter years composing poetry about cafe life and having fantasies about dolphins swimming in the sky), every person seems to add his private *locus*, his quality of feeling, perception and vision, to this sea-hemmed rock on which we live. It is as if the *human* complicates, deepens and magnifies the *natural*. Paxos is not only walls, olives and stones, it is also Big Harry's Turkish wife, Bobby's theories about wine, and Aristides' winged dolphins.

We are overrun with cats. Gata and Gatos come by daily dispensing affection for nourishment. The abandoned kitten who followed us up from the village and whom we have dubbed the traditional 'Gatoula' has settled in comfortably. Adonis, who is the largest cat I have ever seen, a spaniel-and-a-half tall, also the mildest and most retarded, has now become (as Karin says) pussy non gata after soiling the kitchen with an involuntary discharge and then using the laundry basket as a private jakes. Tzonny is a fixture and will not be budged from the supper plate. He has gained about two kilos since coming here from Anglaia's farm. As Karin said in disbelief, after he got himself stuck in the new hole in the kitchen door like Winnie the Pooh, "some cats will go to any width for food."

What astonishes me about these animals is their distinct, coherent and recognizable personalities, or their defining eccentricities. Tzonny eats tomatoes, is partial to bread soaked in beer, answers to his name, gives his paw, and demands respect for his venerableness. Adonis is a cretin and despite his canine dimensions will cringe beneath the circling flight of a moth. Gatoula will follow us down the hill to Lakka whenever we go shopping or to a restaurant, wait several hours at the corner where the steep road meets the *limani*, and pick us up again on our return. Gata is an oriental houri, prancing sideways, lifting her fat, furry bum, begging to be caressed. We have now begun to refer to them as friends and neighbours, 'gonifs' and nuisances and always by name, as if a cat were more than merely a *cat*.

Jacques Ellul, in his book *The Technological Society*, distinguishes medieval from modern technique in part according to the plenary conception of time. Modern technique is omnivorous and ubiquitous, it touches every aspect of life, its influence is pervasive, and it can never be suspended or abrogated. Medieval technique is intermittent, is subordinated to artisanal skill, and is often put away in a corner, as it were, to be taken up later when it is needed. "The time given to the use of techniques," he writes, "was short, compared with the leisure time devoted to sleep, conversation, games, or best of all, meditation."

In the Ellulian sense, Lakka must be seen as a focus of medieval attitudes and assumptions. The tourists are gone and the techniques which catered to their satisfaction (or manipulated their exploitation) have been temporarily put aside. The boats are in drydock and the restaurants are closed. Now people tend to sleep abundantly. The shops open at ten and close again at one. The cafeneion is filled with men playing cards, tavlis, occasionally chess, and conversing chiefly about the surprises and challenges of bird hunting. (They do apply a certain technique here, catapulting huge rocks into the trees to dislodge the birds. These jagged rocks are strewn all over the roads, making driving quite hazardous.) The missing element, which does not invalidate Ellul's definition but reduces its range of application somewhat, seems to be meditation. Hara-lambos claims that he "philosophizes life" and Aristides says that he "fantasizes" it. Still, with these two exceptions, Lakka is not a contemplative society. We are fond of punning on its name: something is lacking, it is very lackadaisical. Nobody yet has been able to tell me what it means in Greek.

Anglaia keeps the door of her farmhouse wide open while we secure the shutters, weatherstrip the doors with Afrolex, and sit hunched and shivering before the electric heater (which is compromised both by the expense and the frequent blackouts). She is proud of the fact that she has never found it necessary to heat her house even in the dead of winter. Her theory is that the older generation was made of sterner stuff from its effeminate successors. Eleni embraces the same hypothesis: we tend to complain about the cold because we are comparatively soft and *chalasmeni* or spoiled.

The other day when it became too bone cold to remain in the house, we donned our bunting jackets and Gore-tex shells and set out for a walk. We passed Anglaia's house with its derisory wide-open door and decided to pay a visit. The shame of the younger generation was instantly put to flight. Anglaia's house was *pumperl*-warm. Door open, shutters flung back to admit the sodden light, the house was nevertheless a natural furnace. It was built with its backside wedged firmly against a small hill, effectively calling the wind's bluff, and snuggling into the earth for warmth. Nothing entered the front door but neighbors and temperate zephyrs. The same *mutatis mutandis* is true of Yanni's and Areti's house just down the slope from ours: windowframes tight, floor raised, walls plastered, so that while we shake and chatter, Areti and Yanni are enjoying their sauna-like bucolics. The older generation, having first choice, built its houses in the right places; spending a lifetime here, it built its houses in the right way. That is really all the difference. Yet, for all my neoteric etiolations, I think I would suffocate in Anglaia's miracle of thermal efficiency, open door notwithstanding.

❖

Stroll with Karin in the eternal rain to the 'Pende Spetia' (the Five Houses) on the promontory facing the Corfu channel. (These are really five houses, but stuck one to the other like a condominium. They were constructed that way by five Italian families to circumvent the Greek law, which permits only one structure per cadastral property.) This was not a good day. Karin was in one of her contralto moods and the tension between us was so thick you *couldn't* cut it with a knife. A chainsaw, maybe. She said she was feeling unwell, debilitated. So nervous myself my knees turned to water. We pottered about the five houses, empty at this time of year, surrounded by juniper buds, blown heather, shrubs of melissa and ivy creepers, and the bizarre geranium leaves with their central red imprints like lipstick marks in napkins. None of this, as they say, spoke to me. I recall with equal vividness the blue plastic garbage bags glinting strangely in a clump of cedars by the road, and the coke tins discarded by the school-children on their 'nature excursion' a few weeks ago. Karin is now curled up in the sleeping bag and staring glumly at the ceiling as I write, counting raindrops, no doubt.

I think of the Cheshire cat grinning down mischievously at Alice and stating matter-of-factly: "We're all mad here." So it is in our Paxiot wonderland. Karin has begun preparing beds for the cats. Adonis has his own plastic-and-terry-cloth digs in the bathroom, where he repairs every evening after receiving a brisk lecture on hygiene. Alki has begun hearing mosquitoes. Every evening before bed, he sits bolt upright at the parlour table, concentrates mightily, and proclaims: "I can hear a mosquito, ever so faintly," like Orestes hounded by the invisible Furies. Of course no one else in the house can hear anything but the shutter-banging wind. Apart from that it is mid-November and the weather has turned inhospitably cold. Any surviving mosquito would need to be some kind of interstellar mutant. But Alki goes to bed cursing and muttering, sprays his room with Raid, plugs in his electric mosquito-killer, and bundles into his sleeping bag. In the morning he awakens with three mosquito bites on his neck. Last night, as he lay fussing and swearing in bed, I gave his room a thorough inspection — a small mosquito would be glaringly conspicuous on the whitewashed walls. There is absolutely nothing in the way of mosquitoes to be found on November 17 in our sub-arctic quarters, but Alki will stumble to the bathroom this morning scratching a fresh crop of bites. Yesterday when we were discussing poetry, he asked me what Gray's Allergy was. Alki is certainly allergic to something — maybe it's the loneliness — and his body has become a delicate psychographic recording instrument, faithfully producing mosquito bites overnight to corroborate his delusions.

Reflections on 'Arcadia'

To expose the Arcadian dream that inspires the modern traveller, that is, the tourist. The *modern* specification of the fictions of Theocritus and Virgil.

The technique is not 'critical' and subversive, not disintegrative. It is anatomical and descriptive. The point is to show what Arcadia is really like, its residual glories and triumphs, but also its palpable defects, its cruelties, hardships, contradictions and banalities.

Arcadia is a function of the imagination in its resistant or commutative aspect. It is useful in that it is not only an insipid reflex but also the analytic sponsor of discontent. But it can also become the sentimental revery of personal indolence and an implicit, abiding hallucination. It spoils our relationships with people. It pollyanizes love. It leads to the systematic misunderstanding of other social groups and countries, reducing them to the level of caricature. It falsifies experience by constraining us to impose a fiction, palimpsest-like, on its actual, refractory content. It leads to triviality and bad conscience.

Wonderland is a terrifying place full of absurdities and unpredictable transformations, and it offers no guarantee of return. It is a plunge into the tertiary realm of schizophrenia which can result in either terminal stagnation and withdrawal or in the renewal and reintegration of the self. Wonderland is also Looking-Glass Land in which common expectations are infallibly reversed. Both are what I mean by Arcadia and are to be found in Paxos.

Perhaps the best way to banish delusion is to experience

it, to submit to it *thoroughly*. Genuine, rigorous experience is the proper antidote to the figment and rhapsody of self-aggrandizement and its corresponding diminishment of the rest of the world. Arcadia is both a threat to sanity and the amperage of imagination. But in order for the power to flow, the threat must be controlled. A year in Paxos restores the morality of the imagination by clarifying and authenticating its natural ardour.

Technique: the journal entry in its three complementary functions.

1) To establish the authenticity of the experience *scriptively*, by avoiding the artifice of chapter breaks, the illusion of narrative. The mind recording its experience, not re-arranging it. (Artifice, since it is necessary, must remain subliminal.)

2) As parody. That is, to mimic the Arcadian procedure of discrete snapshots and slides featuring the presumed uniqueness of the event and the dominating fiction of the heroic, highlighted self.

3) Each entry should be considered as a kind of textual shard, to be fitted into an intuitive pattern that will never and should never quite cohere. Ostraca.

Down to Lakka beach with Karin and Hannah this morning on a nostalgic shell-hunting expedition. Nothing but the usual limpets, oyster drills, periwinkles and thimble-size whelks. One of these latter still contained the fragments of a hermit crab that didn't make it. The sea had tossed it too far up the beach and the constant surf had prevented it from scuttling back. Food for the gulls. Food for thought, too.

It is astonishing how densely imbricated the physical locale is here in Moungelatika, as is the case everywhere else on the island. We turned up a sideroad that we had passed a hundred times without noticing and walked through a vast olive grove, terrace succeeding terrace, along the border of which stood four houses in their small obligatory dells. One has been renovated and is rented out two months in the year; the other three are in various stages of collapse. Each retains its vestige of garden, weedy and rank, though along their perimeters dill, marjoram and savory continue to flourish.

One of the customs on the island is the discarding of houses with each passing generation to accommodate the next. The older houses are allowed to decay and crumble stone by stone, yet they rarely collapse entirely. They loom up behind their walls like shadowy tombs or heavy, sloping mastabas, secured by a scaffolding of vines and cobwebs. The newer houses are usually found in the adjacent grove, facing in the opposite direction, so that the people who live in them literally have their past directly behind them.

They are buttressed in or up, so to speak, by their collective history of which, paradoxically, they are often sublimely unconscious.

They speak about Peter Bull's death as if it were just one more of the pranks and adventures for which he was famous on the island. His death also has a calendrical function. 'Prin O Peter Bool pethane' ('Before Peter Bull died'), they will repeat, frequently dating events by one or another of the dubious or legendary incidents he seemed to accumulate about his personage, as if to say, 'Before Peter Bull bought his house' or 'Before Peter Bull made *Tom Jones*.' He seems to have been universally liked. Arete was telling me the other day about Peter Bull and his crazy friend Nikos, their pratfalls and escapades, and regretting Bull's death tearfully. The two cronies must have emptied paintpots of exuberance whenever they descended on Lakka.

Of course, Peter Bull first came to Lakka some twenty years ago when life was inconceivably different. Even ten years back scarcely anybody owned a car and travel was by foot or donkey. Gaios had not yet been overconstructed and the water in the channel was still clear enough to see in (now the Gaios channel is a seething murk of refuse, jellyfish and sewage). In the last ten years, Alki was saying last night, Paxos has probably experienced greater changes than in the previous two thousand. (Patrick Leigh Fermor in *Roumeli*, regarding the Sarakatsans: "The last quarter of a century has probably done more than the last three thousand years to change the traditional life.") He could be right. Everyone owns a car and a couple of boats. Though the island suffers the threat of chronic water shortage, the washing-machine is epidemic. The power supply is irregular, which has not prevented the influx of colour television sets. The signs of affluence are every-where to be met with, crude, blatant, inescapable. (I sometimes think the two or three donkeys one encounters from time to time are imported from Yugoslavia to appease the tourists.) The Paxiots do possess a good deal of prac-tical intelligence: as we have seen, they build enormous reservoirs to hoard the winter rains. This solution is not so obvious as it may appear. On Alonissos, for example, my old friend Tassos the local shepherd grew exceedingly wealthy from the tourist boom, selling everything from cheese to property, and built himself a magnificent villa, the capstone of which was a large, gleaming, state-of-the-art bathroom decorated with expensive majolica and faience, jade tiles, slabs of Parian marble, shower, bath and a bidet imported from France. There was only one prob-lem. Tasso had no water and the miraculous bathroom, celebrated all over the island, retains as of my last visit its glittering and untarnished, parthenogenetic chastity.

The illustrations in Peter Bull's book on Paxos, *It Isn't All Greek to Me*, by his friend, the painter Roger Furse, strike me as sentimental and dissembling. I am convinced they do not render the Paxos of twenty years ago, for all their donkeys, fishing boats and frolicking Breughel-like peasants. (The women are sketched in folkloric costume, but Haralambos assures me that these sartorial 'authenticities' never existed on Paxos, not even as props.) Furse is obviously presenting his version of the Arcadian dream, which resembles the general stereotypical eulogy of passionate, irresponsible, flamboyant Greece, the women all embroidered, the men tippling, singing, dancing with gargantuan excess. This is the European revery of modern Greece[2], just as Europe has to some extent invented classical Greece with its cool, lucid, democratic Athenians and fierce, low-browed, resentful Spartans. What one should remember about the modern Greeks is that they are, like most people, a mixed stock: some Turkish and Levantine influence, a thin genetic thread of Aryan physical traits, some Albanian, a bit of Bulgar, Vlach and Slav, and what every foreigner should keep in mind, an aquiline infusion of 'Algerian' corsair.[3]

Met Aristides the poet on the Lakka waterfront, prior to his departure for Athens where he intends to winter over, returning to Paxos in April for the spring effusions. The conversation this time was not about airborne dolphins but earthbound houses, of which he has two for sale. He tactfully suggested I might be interested in having a look at them. The rumour is carrying on the Paxos winds like burlers, which is what I intended. What nobody knows is that I am fast running out of money.

Rained again last night, indoors as well as out. The raster tilt must have been different from usual. It rained on Hannah's bed; luckily her sleeping bag is water resistant. It rained on us as well. When I tugged at the iron behemoth we sleep on to move it away from the leak in the ceiling, the warped metal crossbar came away in my hands and the bed crashed to the floor. The two of us stood there lugubriously by the ruins at two in the morning, the rain drizzling steadily in, a fragment of bedstead in my hands, like mourners round a catafalque. This morning we discovered our luggage soaked through and largely spoiled and the expensive electric heater I bought in Corfu drenched and on the blink. We are coming more and more to feel like Al Capp's Joe Btfsplk. We run about the house ranting and cursing, then fall on the wooden settle helpless with laughter.

Rosanne seems to have carried out her threat and left the island. I have rarely met a more systematically depressed person than this poor Irish lady, pregnant, married to a Greek police officer, her life in this country a concatenation of disasters. She and her husband, Manolis, recently bought a second-hand Mercedes. The papers were apparently forged and the car repossessed, but the couple was left with an enormous debt which is being met by regular, official deductions from an inadequate salary while the case is pending. And in Greece a case can pend indefinitely. Their move from Corfu, Manolis' previous assignment, to Paxos last month was another catastrophe. All their belongings were loaded on a truck to be carried down to the harbour. Fifty metres from the house, the driver, who must have had one ouzo too many, unaccountably swerved into an olive tree, damaging their furniture beyond reclamation. Here on Paxos their luck failed to turn. Rosanne found the people coarse and grasping, demanding rents three and four times as high as they had paid in Corfu. They finally agreed on a house in one of the narrow alleyways of Gaios, which was somewhat less unaffordable than the others. They soon discovered the reason for the discount: the plumbing facilities were deficient. Sewage tended to back up and vomit out the kitchen drain. Dishwashing became hazardous and the stench of ordure was everywhere. A professional nurse trained in English hospitals, Rosanne found her situation rather more intolerable than her Greek neighbours did. She decided against having her baby in a Greek hospital. "In Corfu," she told me, "they throw the afterbirth into the streets for the dogs to eat." Being stigmatized by Manolis' mother as a "foreign whore" who had schemed and inveigled her son's affections away from their maternal resting place was probably the *coup de grâce*. Whenever I meet Manolis, he looks sallow and down in the mouth, but proud and inflexible. He stands there barricaded behind his taciturn masculinity while Rosanne pours out a fresh spate of complaints and denunciations, the skin around her jowls turning rancid-colored. I haven't seen her now in over a month, so I presume she has left to have her baby in England or Ireland. She could never get my name right and persisted in calling me Brian, why I can't say. It sounded like 'brine,' which is approximately how I imagine her, salted away, her eyes like two pickled foetuses, still and weeping at the same time.

Rained yesterday, and the day before, and the day before that as well. It is raining again today. Bobby has come to repair the ceramic tiles on the roof but the storm has driven him over to Arete's for coffee. The house is becoming more and more colander-like: the roof has sprung a number of fresh leaks and the floorboards are drenched and creaking. The air inside is so damp that the long matches we use for lighting the petrolgaz stove in the kitchen fail to catch. In order to boil water for morning coffee, we must first ignite the match with a cigarette lighter and then thrust the burning splinter under the metal wick of the gas jet: two small explosions and finally a thin drizzle of flame.

I am growing very worried about Hannah, what with the constant rains that keep us indoors, the relative seclusion forced upon her by the language, and the lack of reliable companionship. Two months ago the pictures she drew were saturated with rich, vibrant colours, sunsets, gardens, abstract splotches of yellow and blue. Now she paints in unrelieved hues of black and grey, picture after picture. She has also regressed demonstrably. She has become cranky and querulous, refuses to play by herself, turns the simple act of putting on her socks in the morning into a traumatic production, and at night insists on having a cradle constructed over her bed from pillows and a blanket. She is not yet four and this may just be what parents call 'a phase' (a consoling fiction), but we remember her only a few months before as a precocious, highly articulate, astonishingly good-natured child. Now it is as if she is vaudevilling herself. If we cut short our stay here, it will be for her sake. Half her waking hours are spent in reminiscence of her friends and activities back home. The phrase she repeats over and over, like a verbal talisman, is: "When we go back to Canada. . . ."

For myself, I am exactly where I want to be. As Karin said approvingly this morning, cleaning out the potty we bought for Hannah but which the whole family has pre-empted, "All this takes the romance out of Greece." I recall mocking us tourists in Alonissos, in a poem of several years ago, as a tribe of masochists who "quaintly undertake to pay/for want of all amenities." This assessment has never been truer than it is for us now. With a year's leave and a generous grant providing enough money (at first) to travel anywhere in the world, I chose to come here, when I could have magic-carpeted the family to the Grenadines for twelve months of sea and sunshine. But that would have been too easy, too pampering, too cosmetic. Here I feel I am actually learning something and have no regrets over the steep tuition fees.

What is it I am learning? How to light wet matches, how to make do without electricity and water (when the pump knocks off), how to stay dry when the rain prizes through the roof tiles, how to huddle in front of a small, box-like,

73

inadequate heater, how to deal with the wily, cunning and likeable inhabitants of this historical backwater whose only claim to mythological notoriety is that the death of Pan was announced off its shores (as recorded by Plutarch), and how to navigate the treacherous currents of this complicated and bewildering langauge. (Appropriately, the word for the Greek language in Greek is pluralized: *ta Hellenica*, as if it consisted of many languages, as it in fact does: *katharevousa* (pure), *demotiki* (common), *archaio* (archaic), and of course the plethora of dialects. Though, more plausibly, the plural obviously refers to *grammata: ta hellenika grammata* comprising the entire phrase and translating as 'Greek letters.')

Karin is learning how to tend artichokes and boil *chorta* (dandelion stems), how to plug leaks, refasten shutters, glue Afrolex strips, cook in a half-squatting posture, and identify the myriad herbs and flowers that spring out of every rock and clump of earth, like an affirmation of Pan's continued survival. What we are really learning, I think, is how to live without the romantic delusion of a golden age, a golden clime, the chryso-alternate, that sustains us in our common, everyday existence.

It seems we all need to believe in the utopian fantasy of an innocent world we are convinced must exist somewhere, whether on the littoral of the Mediterranean or in the obscure recesses of History. There is of course no such world and there never was. The golden age was always made of iron pyrites. But it is difficult to live without rhapsody, without that interior, sustaining fiction incarnated objectively for many of us, both historically and elementally, in the tensile illusion of 'Greece.' It is a kind of psychic therapy which enables us to avoid despair and partially recoup the bankruptcy of quotidian life. There *is* a society, we assume, in which men are sane or joyful or both: Roger Furse's sketches are an attempt to replevin this sense of the lupercalian community we have partially surrendered to the reality principle. There *is* a world in which the sun bronzes and reinvigorates the tired flesh and the sea massages the industrial waste of the human body with salt and iodine. The sun, however, also peels off the skin like a housewife detunicating an onion and leaves a raw, pink tumescence in its place; and the sea stings the innocence out of us with its jellyfish and watersnakes — but such matters are conveniently forgotten, edited out of mind by sentimentality and nostalgia. The tourist manages to protect himself from such unwelcome revelations. Just as he rubs his flesh with turtle-extract, travels in air-conditioned buses and sleeps in state-inspected hotels, he is also defended by an inevitable *limitation in time*: two weeks on the Costa del Sol, three weeks in Mykonos or Rhodes. The tourist often complains about the brevity of his visit, but the longer sojourn for which he ostensibly craves would render him helpless, confused and unhappy. He is insulated by the pre-paid abbreviation of his exposure to whatever 'Greece' it is he fancies and hankers after. One more week might be enough to puncture the utopian trance. Meanwhile, he returns home furnished with cassettes, snapshots and slides which record a world that, in a very real sense (to put it paradoxically), *never happened and does not exist*. But the Kodak elysium prospers at the

75

expense of that grainy, dense, abrasive and laminated world without which we are deprived of specific weight, of emotional and intellectual substance. This is a condition, the *deficiency of the sense of reality*, which is becoming habitual.

Our protracted stay in Paxos is demythologizing us a little — not entirely, for my own sense of 'reality' compels me to admit that I will never completely exorcise the Arcadian possession. Nostalgia and hope are powerful adversaries. But Karin is right: the romance has gone out of Greece, and I for one am satisfied that it is so.

To return to the immediate problem: what to do about the child. Are we sacrificing her happiness in the name of a belated liberation from Cloudland? We have come to Greece to banish 'Greece' and we are partially succeeding in this act of romantic detoxification. But Hannah, even at three and a half, is already fully equipped with her own private Arcadia, her own nostalgic reminiscences of daycare, Amos and Fern and Nicholas, the little playground on Drolet street, all subsumed under the rubric 'Canada.' Should we return home for her sake or stick it out here equally for her sake?

Bobby has just left, having replaced the broken ceramics and repaired the kitchen door. My estimation of him has changed somewhat. He is a Jack-of-all-trades, immensely versatile and handy, yet he does nothing really well, nothing thoroughly and everything approximately. Casting around for a shim of wood to patch the hole in the lower part of the door, he seized upon our breadboard, instantly chopped it into three segments with two decisive strokes of his axe, and hammered one of the scraps into place. The wind still bullies through. He affixed several thin slats of wood over the longitudinal cracks. Now I have to flatten out the nails that poke alarmingly out the front of the door before someone inadvertently crucifies himself. The window-jambs have been planed and refitted. The only problem is that we must struggle to open them, threatening to shatter the broken panes that will apparently not be replaced.

Bobby is one of those unfortunate Greeks condemned to lifelong servitude by the mixed blessing of having sired three daughters, each of whom must be provided with a *prika* (dowry) if she is to be successfully married off. As the prikas must be reasonably substantial here — a diesel fishing boat, a house, a pick-up truck — a man in this position must devote a good part of his life to arranging for his daughters' futures. My old landlord on Hydra was crushed under the weight of six daughters. When I first met him, he had just finished building his fifth house. And Mitso on Alonissos, who must have thanked God every night for afflicting him with only one daughter, nevertheless wore the same red shirt and faded overalls for three years, but he provided his daughter with a magnificent villa — balconies, arched promenades, the works — on the hill above Patatiri. I heard some years later that the girl had made a most impressive marriage. Katina, my landlady in Kamini in Hydra back in 1968–9, showed uncharacteristic spunk. When the man she married turned out to be an incorrigible loafer who regularly fell asleep on his fishing nets when he should have been trawling, she threw him out and repossessed her *prika*, the fishing boat he had used as a sea-hammock.

The men are always on the lookout for a desirable *prika*. Venizelos used to run a borderline grocery store on the port in Hydra, and always seemed a touch distracted, apprehensive. When I returned for a visit one year, I found him transformed into a gentleman of leisure, with an ample three-storey house, a cellarful of wine, a small boat, and a wonderfully unruffled countenance. When I asked him if he loved his wife, he stared at me in disbelief. "Of course not," he said, "what has *that* got to do with it?"

The classic instance must be Aristo in Alonissos. Suave, charming, not handsome but with a flair for sociability and conversation (in three languages apart from Greek), he was nevertheless reduced to the status of glorified desk-clerk in one of the bigger hotels. I used to stop by occasionally for a chat (we had both lived on Hydra in 'the old days') and found him amiable and naturally cultivated. Then he met Violet, the ex-wife of an American millionaire, whom he quickly married. When I next saw Aristo, he was reclining voluptuously in a deck-chair on the patio of the largest and most luxurious house on the island, set in one of the remoter bays. He was entertaining several members of local 'society' and, after exchanging greetings with me, pointedly neglected an invitation. I had a short swim and departed, with a last backward glimpse of our hero accepting a long, slender drink from the hands of an adoring wife. This, for the modern Greek, is pure Horatio Alger, the sum and substance of *his* utopian fantasy.

Costas has done reasonably well with Bobby's daughter, Maria. He is at least furnished with a house in Moungelatika, ours for a brief period, which, ironically enough, was not the sweat of Bobby's labour, since Maria got it from her grandmother who in turn had it deeded to her as a gift from Haralambos' father, who was actually born within its perforated walls. But Bobby has no doubt provided for Dina, married and living in America near fabled Tsikago, and is amassing a trousseau for twenty-two year old Pepitsa who is as yet unspoken for.

Apropos the popular, incantatory formula, 'then echi provlima', no pr-r-roblem, which one hears everywhere on this problematical island. I had a brief talk with Captain Spiro in Gaios about the schedule of the *Kamelia*. Captain Spiro, having lived for many years in Belgium, insisted on maintaining his end of the conversation in a kind of blurry French which hinted at a former, unattained impeccability. His vocabulary managed to survive his pronunciation, as I thought at the moment, like those little white tufts of his beard in an undulating sea of yellow tobacco stains, and I was finally quite impressed by the continental manner of exaggeration and sceptical incredulity implicit in his manipulation of the French. When he had expounded the mystery of the schedule, he tipped his black felt sailor-cap and said, with a mixture of Gallic insouciance and Paxiot optimism, "Ah bon! Il n'y existe pas de problème."

Rained and thundered all night and again this morning. The cats had attacked the garbage bags and spread ordure all over the front walk. My first task of the day was to clean up the mess. Finally, a tepid, unaccustomed squib of sunlight through the rumpled overcast. The sun, which several weeks ago I compared to a huge blood-pomegranate, now strikes me as a brownish love-patch in stale, week-old bed linen.

A long talk with Cafeneion Spiro (Spiro Petrou) this morning about the 'old days.' In Spiro's opinion, the Rubicon which Paxos crossed irreversibly into the modern world was electricity. When electricity began to flow, life changed dramatically, and in many respects for the worse. Its effect was paradoxical and unexpected. Before electricity, says Spiro, the food was always fresh and wholesome: boats plied every day between Lakka and Corfu, in the most inclement weather (the old-fashioned caiques were made for the crossing), bringing in fresh meat and other comestibles. Now there are refrigerators and the quality of the food, frozen for days and weeks, has noticeably declined. Everyone kept twenty or thirty chickens and Spiro himself had three sheep and two goats: milk, cheese, mutton, eggs and fowl were in plentiful supply. Today the milk is imported from Italy, the cheese from Germany, the eggs from Corfu (pre-laid, as it were), there is little chicken meat and mutton is rarely available.

Moreover, there is a warm, cozy quality to lamplight which electric lighting with its hard and searing immediacy cannot approximate. As Peter Bull correctly remarks in his book, the Greeks have taken enthusiastically to the garish horripilations of neon light. Everywhere you go now in this country you are bathed in a lurid fluorescence, a cold radioactivity. The kerosene lamps, which I remember from Hydra and Lesbos and Alonissos, made reading a strain, but shed a gentle, sociable glow over the men playing cards and the women gossiping. In comparison, electric light is ruthless, tyrannical; it permits no secrets and exiles the feeling of mystery. Shadows are harsher, every discoloration and blemish is flagrantly obvious to the eye. I have noticed that in lamplight the voice tends to be subdued; in electric light noise levels rise and the voice tends to grow raucous. This is not a mere nostalgic fancy.

Since the arrival of electricity, life has become easier, allowing for the enjoyment of all kinds of amenities not available before but, as Spiro says, *mia piotita* (a certain quality) is missing. 'Brightness falls from the air' and is replaced by scintillation. George Steiner observes in his essay, 'The Distribution of Discourse,' that "the history of artificial lighting cannot be separated from that of consciousness itself" and runs together with "the turn towards and into the private room (and) the emphasis on individuation." I think his 'elucidation' is substantially correct. With abundant lighting comes reading, privacy, reflection; the energies of individual inquiry and analysis are accordingly liberated. I for one would not wish to sacrifice my eyesight and privacy to a romantic delusion. On the other hand, Spiro is incontestably right as well. With lamplight comes conviviality, warmth and intimacy. Why, after all, do expensive restaurants furnish their tables with decorative candles? And why do lovers in tender or erotic moments display such a marked antipathy to the scald of electric bulbs, choosing instead darkness, candlelight, kerosene lamps or as on Paxos the small, weak-beamed flashlight turned discretely to the wall?

Alki has just returned from a rain-protracted stay on Corfu. He went in for the day to buy a few books, enjoy a decent breakfast at the Black Cat Cafe, and wander about on his adolescent own. The weather turned stormy and the boat service was suspended, as happens regularly. Three days later and several pounds lighter, he staggered off the *Kamelia*, looking dazed and bedraggled and steeped like a teabag. His jeans are now hanging on the line in the faint prospect of drying by springtime. We are beginning to feel like the denizens of *A Hundred Years of Solitude*. To adapt the clown's song in *Twelfth Night*:

And then we came to Paxos' state,
     With a hey ho, the wind and the rain.
The wind and storm will not abate
     For the rain it raineth every day.

Paxos is certainly not the bosky sabbatical retreat I once envisioned after reading Irving Layton's poem in which he wanders indolently with his lady love through splendid and dignified summery olive groves. It had, in fact, already been contaminated by the visitations of the famous. Peter Bull introduced Albert Finney to the island, and Spiro Petrou tells the story of Finney and his girlfriend terrified in the middle of the night by curious mountain goats peering through their window. This legendary event has become part of the chronicles of Paxos. Laurence Olivier spent two nights in Spiro's rambling summer dacha, the Villa Penelo (which reminds me of Mary Stewart's well-written thriller, *This Rough Magic*, set on Corfu and involving the fortunes of a prominent Shakespearean actor, Sir Julian Gale, obviously a stand-in for Sir Laurence, who has rented a luxurious villa in which to solace his retirement). Susannah York afterwards took over the place for several months. These events were prominent renting-points when Spiro offered the Villa to me for the year at an exorbitant price. At times I feel abashed for being an obscure Canadian poet and college professor with an income substantially less than that of three-quarters of the island's population. However, as I drive about in a rented car, pay a handsome sum for my house, am obviously enjoying extensive leisure, and am ostensibly a prospective client in the real estate market, it follows that I must be rich and at least trans-Atlantically famous. I am consequently treated with an amalgam of deference and suspicion. Nobody quite knows what to make of me. I am obviously rich, but I own no property yet. I am a conspicuous gringo, a mere foreigner, but I can sail this stormy language without sinking (though capsizing frequently). And moreover I am sticking out the winter when even O Peter Bool entertained serious doubts about the clemencies of April. I complain about everything, which is accounted strictly a Greek prerogative. When I bought an umbrella in Eleni's tiny *magazi*, someone remarked that I had made a good investment, considering the perpetual rains. I replied that I was acquiring an umbrella not against the rain but the storm of grapeshot. A hush of embarrassment fell on the shop and everyone began shuffling nervously.

At the same time, I fail to maintain that sacred distance between foreigner and Greek, that thin red line no Greek is permitted to cross despite the orgiastic friendships that flare and erupt with instinctual abandon. But let some unwary Greek cross that invisible barrier, let him actually appear in London or Hamburg in honour of some friendly invitation, and the uneasiness and condescension that greet him will turn him into a dedicated xenophobe for the rest of his life. The Greeks are no fools and have unconsciously come to expect and even demand the existence of that insulating medium, that strip of no-man's land mined with cultural presuppositions. But I perversely manage to offend their sense of inverse delicacy by refusing to garrison the citadel of foreign supremacy. The Greeks, who are no fools, are also sublimely irrational. They have great difficulty respecting those who insist on respecting them back, an attitude which reminds me of Groucho's old chestnut about being unwilling to join a club that would have someone like him as a member. My relations with the Greeks have always been strained and ambiguous as a result of these conflicting elements. The difference is that now, after so many years, I am aware of these involutions and even take a perverse delight in them.

It adds a certain piquance, a sharp mythological flavour to the 'chronicles of Paxos,' when I recall that Pan, whose death was announced off these shores, was the principal god of Arcadia. Arcadia, of course, is a real geographical site, located in the heart of the Peloponnese, wild, mountainous goat-country. But through a creative transmutation in the pages of the bucolic poets, it gradually came to be identified with the idyllic region of playfulness, innocence and love located in the heart of the human imagination. As such it has become the fabulous locale, the geomythic *arrondissement* of the free, improvisatory spirit in man. And Pan is its tutelary presence. As Michael Stapelton asserts in the Hamlyn Dictionary, "His name, 'the pasturer' or 'feeder' of flocks, identifies him as a spirit as ancient as man himself."

As long as men continue to feel nostalgia over their vanished youth and to languish for a simpler and more jubilant destiny than the real world supplies, Arcadia will survive the militant incursions of the reality principle. It is necessary that this should be so, otherwise we could expect the total surrender of the buoyant, imaginative self to the aggressions of cynicism, despair and abulia. How often is the profession of 'realism' merely a cover (to quote the Athenian waiter Thomas) for *tedium vitae* or a cold, atrabilious response to the world?

This said, and conceded, I must revert to my original warning and the intention behind these pages. Arcadia, born of the human longing for peace, simplicity and joy, is at the same time the gravest threat to the human need for balance, clarity and self-awareness. If the desire for the pastoral resolution of the manifold complexity of life is not checked and monitored, it will begin to colour our perception of the world and tempt us to hasty, ill-considered actions in every sphere of our conduct. Even the most sophisticated and educated people start behaving like simpletons, whether on the domestic level of material acquisition or in the political realm of massive and sibylline mobilizations. Arcadia corrupts. As any student of mythology knows, there is an intimate and reciprocal connection between the Garden of Eden and the Thousand Year Reich, between the Isles of the Blessed and the Dictatorship of the Proletariat: in other words, between the intuition of mythic banishment and the enfranchisements of political utopia. On a humbler plane, Arcadia is the source of much personal dissatisfaction and unhappiness in the dogged

86

unwillingness to accept imperfection. We lose a considerable portion of our lives in useless and indulgent revery or in the frenetic quest for imaginary treasure: love, youth, immortality, and even, paradoxically, wealth itself (for in a certain sense all treasure is imaginary) which the dragon of reality will under no circumstance relinquish from its custody.

Paxos is my subject, my hypostasis of the Arcadian dream, and it is providentially fitting as well as ironic that the death of Pan, the god of Arcadia, should have been proclaimed off its very coast.

Unless, of course, as some mythologists affirm, the oracle was ambiguous and an extra comma should be inserted to construct an apposition. Instead of the mythic bulletin, presumably addressed to the Egyptian pilot Thamus, reading:

Thamus, Great Pan is dead . . .

it might equally be construed as addressed to Pan:

Thamus, Great Pan, is dead . . .

That is, the Sumerian deity, Tammuz, one of the two Gatekeepers in the pantheon, whose worship arrived in Greece in the seventh century B.C. from Cyprus and was incorporated into the Dionysian ritual of the dying and reviving god, had now been repudiated and superseded by the reign of Pan himself.[4]

If that is the case, then it is just possible that Pan has

survived the vicissitudes of time and infidelity, and is up to his old mischief, concealed behind clumps of heather and gorse bushes, waiting to terrify the unsuspecting passer-by, to cause 'panic.' Perhaps the cicadas which rarely cease their stridulations even on the coldest nights are merely refracting the shrill melodies of his syrinx. Arcadia is infinitely resilient.

Long walk to Vassilatika, a largely deserted village located inland and roosting on the mountain chain that overlooks the high, western plateau of the island, somewhat like Poe's Bessop's Castle. It consists of about two dozen *kalivia*, hovels in various stages of decrepitude, dominated by two great manorial houses that must once have served as summer residences for the rich, landowning Corfiot families in the olive trade. The whole set-up wears that impregnable medieval look: walls, cisterns, the huts bowed serf-like round the huge baronial enclosures. The vegetation is unrelievedly desolate: nettle, scrub, inextricable tangles of Christ-thorn, and those immense olive groves casting an unbroken gloom, a kind of eerie water-light, over the countryside. Here and there an astonishing dendrological freak caught our attention, such as the natural trinity formed by an ancient olive, a fig and an unidentifiable nut-bearing tree, that seemed to have pooled their roots and branches and grown together, twined and inseparable. Another fig tree had been grafted onto the trunk of an olive and sprouted higher up the bole, so that it resembled a gigantic spider or kraken quietly digesting its prey.

On the western side of the slope we came upon what is reputed to be the oldest dwelling on the island, an 'Algerian' pirate stronghold (the infamous Aegean and Ionian corsairs are referred to by the people as 'Algerians'), complete with armorial bearings (lion's head over the arched gateway, six-petalled flower on the lintel of the inner door), narrow vertical gunslits at various levels beneath the staggered merlons, and a series of squat, quasi-Doric pillars supporting the sagging ashlars of the portico. Karin fell in love with the whole complex and on the way back was seriously considering the logistics of purchase and restoration. We enquired about the history of "the fort" from an elderly woman replacing candles at a roadside shrine. All she could say was that the place was very old, older than herself, and she was seventy-five!

Saw Haralambos this morning in Gaios basking in the revenant sun. We pointedly ignored one another. An inexplicable estrangement has arisen between us since the night he came over for supper. I have run across him often at Spiro's cafeneion or the Lakka mini-market with nothing but a perfunctory nod from that massive, leonine head ('Algerian' heraldry?). I have trouble putting his laconic presence together with that voluble, expansive and endearingly preposterous character with whom we shared so many 'banquets' at Myro Mourtis' restaurant. I must have offended him in some inexplicable way. Karin thinks he simply objected to the menu we offered. I suspect we are simply not rich or flamboyant enough. But discretion forbids reconnaissance. Perhaps we have merely joined what he regards as the Paxiot canaille.

One day of sunshine to ten days of rain: this seems to me a reasonable approximation to the calculus of daily experience and contentment. It is, put plainly, the reality quotient.

There are three kinds of literary 'failures,' considered from the point of view of audience-potential as well as intrinsic merit. There is the book whose imaginative trajectory takes it far beyond the level of its readership, deep into oblivion or, as sometimes happens, into an appreciative but indiscernible future. Its mental propulsion outstrips the fiscal gravitation of its publisher's intention. Then there are the twin miscarriages of diminished range, books which undershoot their audience but for opposite reasons. One is like a Cyclopean boulder, heavy and unwieldy, lumbering a short distance from the creaking trebuchet of its author's imagination and lying somewhere mossy and forgotten. The other ballistic mishap is the result of either too little kinetic energy or too little mass or both, like a pellet of goat dung shot from an elastic band stretched between index and middle finger.

Peter Bull's account of Paxos, *It Isn't All Greek to Me*, falls squarely into this third category, displaying little propulsive force and even less critical mass. It suffers from almost every conceivable flaw of intention and execution that can mar the pages of a single book. This is the only form of ecumenism it exhibits, as if it were the author's unstated purpose to ransack the annals of travel writing for every possible embarrassment, opacity, maladroitness and stylistic dereliction he could find and marshal them all encyclopedically into his own personal compendium.

For example, the irritating habit of capitalization to achieve a spurious importance, as in "I don't even know What I Like" or "Being a mine of absolutely Useless Information" or "When I go to Greece I go there principally to Write." Of course, it is not supposed to be taken literally, but the self-mockery is by no means parodic and carries with it precisely that element of self-importance it is ostensibly deflating. In other words, the author takes himself seriously enough to caricature his motives and ambitions with a diligence that argues the prior conviction of his pre-eminence.

The same can be said of his compulsion to sprinkle contractions about like breadcrumbs in Trafalgar Square: the ubiquitous 'v' for 'very,' as in "And v. nice they looked" or, another of his favourite verbal loppings, "In that partic year." What I find most exasperating is the patronizing benediction of the word "inhabs," the lighter version of the colonial "natives." And always the popping phrasal chestnuts he simply can't take out of the fire: "I thought I'd better get to Athens and the dear old Akropolis and all that Over"; "Que sera sera (what will be will be) as dear old Dame Doris Day used to sing"; and he refers to Antigone as "Dear old Oedipus' daughter." (As the dust jacket assures us, the reader "need have no fear that he (Bull) has delved deep into the mythology or history of Greece. He has just transferred to another country his talent for being unable to take anything very seriously.")

His tendency to pepper that bland, anonymous style with jargon and patois only points up its lack of taste and substance. Everything is dodgy and conkers. "The sight that met our eyes was about the prettiest I remember in all my puff." Somebody causes "a sensationette." With premonitory acumen the author discloses that he "knew there was going to be troubola." From time to time he gets on the boat "as quickly as poss" and is either "clocking in" or "clocking out."

Even the Greek is frequently garbled, a lapse for which there is no excuse given his long residence on the island. The definite article is windily aspirated, (almost never the case any longer), as in "Ho Phillow Mou" and "Ho Pappas," as if Santa Claus had decided to learn the language and could not keep his merriment out of his pronunciation. He makes simple acoustic mistakes like writing 'martho' for 'matho' (to learn) and substituting plosives for velars ('Kerete' for 'Chyerete'). Speaking Greek is a bit like stumbling barefoot through the nettles and creepers that abound in this landscape, but writing it out in English should not be that phonetically intimidating.

His reading of character and custom is also on a level with his mishandling of either language. A certain restaurateur, for example, whom Peter Bull memorializes, is lovingly characterized as "a dear little man." He does have his endearing side, I presume, but that does not prevent him from being a tightfisted little miser who will not lift a finger to procure essential medicines and treatment for his wife's phlebitis and other ailments, but exerts himself mightily to water down his cognac. On a larger scale, Bull's interpretations of family relations might embellish the pages of a travel brochure: "It seems to me that in Greece everyone is enchanting to their old relations and there is never any question of them being neglected or abandoned." Certainly not. They are far too valuable as cheap labour, especially the grandmothers who function as nannies, cooks, chars and chimney sweeps till they sink, bent and haggard, into the stony Greek soil. Their reward comes in the form of sepia encadrements, stuffy and conventionalized, hanging crookedly in rented-out bedrooms.

Perhaps what annoys me most about the book and the mind that percolates through its stylistic grounds is the manifest *attitude*, blatantly evident in the profusion of hokey, arch and ostentatious references to himself, the reader and the book.

"See page one. You must have got that far."

"Or whatever firm of messrs may be pirating this load of rubbish."

"The already near-nauseating flavour of these recollections." ". . . character I have already discussed at length in an earlier and probably less boring chapter."

Always that pride and delight in himself, in his eccentricities, his unaccountable ways, even his ignorance.

"Anyhow here we are pressing on to Lakka or we were a page ago before I started carrying on about something I know nothing about." All this coyness and self-infatuation is the motive force behind the desperate casualness and flair with which he controls the protean nature of experience. It is no different when he approaches the subject of classical myth (despite the dust jacket). "For those without Classical Education, Icarus and his dad, Daedalus, flew with wings (sic) from Crete to escape the wrath of the king and poor old Icarus went too near the sun, which melted his wings (sic) so that he fell plop into the sea."

The book divides into equal portions of vanity and condescension bound together by the ligature of chronic dissimulation and confirmed in the predictable development of its theme, which is nothing other than the domestication of Arcadia. On first setting eyes on his newly-built house: "You see, why I am going on so is because it's never happened to me before. Things exactly as you imagined them, I mean . . . . How rarely the reality comes anywhere near the expectation." Which it does, of course, on Paxos. The book concludes with the indispensable sunset, summoned expressly for the occasion, the hero standing meditatively by his house on the cliff and considering with cinematic *profondeur* "the magic of a dream come true."

It all sounds like the jazzy, with-it commentary to the pop revival of a TV detective thriller; that is, it reads exactly like a spoof, as if it were burlesqueing the conventions of travel writing. The amazing thing is that he is blithely and ethereally unaware of this deflationary aspect of his writing, and the result is a devastating bathos. When one's work reads like a deliberate parody of the genre in which it is embedded, when it approximates satire, but is in fact seriously intended to be accepted at face value, in this case, as a comical, lighthearted and ebullient description of the Merry Prankster's adventures on a Greek island, then one can only ascribe the clash of modalities to a condition of terminal adolescence, the absence of latitudinal awareness. The impression one gleans from this book is that of an astigmatic, essentially harmless but jejune and quixotic teddybear obsessed by his own furry perspective on the world. The work itself is unredeemingly frivolous and vitiated by the mutual annihilation of categories, of deliberate comedy and involuntary farce, of narrative and travesty. As for the man, I guess he would have made a stalwart drinking buddy and a wonderful clown, but he is the most insufferable of raconteurs, possessed by the chattering demon of his own embryonic self and relying on a borrowed distinction to subsidize a straitened sense of presence.

Further, when it comes to plot and character, he writes like a souped-up, customized version of A.A. Milne. Paxos is his Hundred Acre Wood. Nikos the Fisherman, to whom the book is lovingly dedicated, is his friendly and considerate Piglet. Mr. Ypsilos, the churlish and unaccommodating landlord, is Eeyor. And he himself is a kind of profane, trinitarian mishmash consisting in equal proportions of unbounced Tigger (he is "large," exuberant, fun-loving), Winnie the Pooh (he is innocent, cuddly, a gourmand), and Christopher Robin (he is slightly detached, incredulous and superior). It is his compound destiny to experience many absurd adventures and to find, upon subsequent reflection, that all has providentially worked out for the Leibnizian or Poohian best. What has been left out of his account, clipped by the unconscious censor that prohibits imaginative honesty, is the sinister reality of *Animal Farm*, which is one of the parishes in this Hundred Acre Wood. Accuracy, as well as pith, requires that Orwell impinge on Milne, if only to some small extent in Paxos, to right the fantasy/reality balance.

Forty years ago Greece was an occupied country. Thirty five years ago it was cloven by a civil war whose ferocity and magnitude inflicted wounds that continue to fester in its lustral politics and its daily journalism. Lenin, albeit a watered-down version, is at least as prominent a figure here as Alexander Small. But Peter Bull writes of Paxos as if it were the private fiefdom of Pirandello's Henry IV or a sprawling Hollywood set. One can just see the British thespian striding and declaiming amidst a throng of dazed and admiring inhabs. Even his friend Nikos, who comes in for so much praise and gratitude, comes out no better (to change the analogy) than as a sort of Greek Friday, resourceful, trusting and agreeably primitive, while our latter day Robinson runs about subordinating all complexity to the primacy of Ego and dominating an island by means of an invincible superciliousness.

What makes Peter Bull so interesting to me, and is the reason I have invested so much ink in squidding out his innocuous libretto, is the iconographic quality he possesses, the stamp and watermark of a representative mentality. In him we can detect the peculiar debasement of the modern imagination, the imperial revery of the disenfranchised and the powerless. He dreams of an empire his ancestors once commanded but which he, in himself, is incapable of justifying, preserving or augmenting. Dignity has become bluster; strength, technique; and joy, mere distraction. As was once and still is, *mutatis mutandis*, the case, the metropolitan bankrupt can always repair his fortunes in the colonies. This has been the fate of the imagination in the contemporary world — the ephemeral solvency of a colonial degradation. Here we encounter one more facet of Arcadia, which is nothing more than the product of vertiginous slumming and the terrible premonition of disinheritance. We invent what we can no longer discover.

Karin's critique of Peter Bull and his book is styptically brief: "All that vanity, the contrived fun. He must have been an awful bore." Yet everyone liked the man. Spiro Petrou remembers him fondly, indicating his occupation as a writer by turning his fingers into little dancing fantocinni performing their pirouettes over the keyboard of an imaginary typewriter. Suzy, the lively and astute wife of a local entrepreneur, applauds his innocent and good-natured flamboyance. Sotiris, one of the islands five taxi drivers (or Taxiots, as Bull might have said), is deeply impressed by the existence of a book on Paxos, which he has never read and yet which he solemnly maintains is a scrupulous and comprehensive muniment of the island. The hijinks and spectacles with which Bull entertained the inhabs have become legendary. Everyone regrets his passing.

In a way I do as well, for I would have like to meet him. I even concur in his opinion on the shooting habits of the islanders. "The air is horrendous with the sound of gunshot and many's the guest who has had the bejesus scared out of him as a bullet or a bit of flying shrapnel goes whizzing past his head." But he is too much the great Panjandrum for my taste, the dispossessed, belated aethling for whom an island jaunt assumes the proportions of the Seafarer's legendary wanderings. It is probably clear by now that Peter Bull is also myself, the inner antagonist with whom I am in a state of perpetual conflict and who constantly threatens to overwhelm my fragile sense of discipline and integrity. He represents the insidious temptation one always feels to surrender to the operatic and self-indulgent dimension of the Ego, to identify Lotus-land with the 'kairos' or with Blake's Jerusalem. He is the busy man of the world who moonlights as the shepherd prince of Arcadia, and this is precisely why I bring whatever invective I may possess to bear against him. Because he is the century in which I live and which lives in me, talented, versatile, prodigal, and like the river he describes in Lefkimmi, too shallow for anything but vessels of limited displacement.

Went down to Lakka last night. The town was deserted and Spiro's cafeneion unwontedly empty for a Sunday evening. It seems all the rummy and tavli experts were in political conclave. A PASOK meeting had been called to discuss the usual obscurities and subtleties of Greek politics. I remember two years ago in Gaios reading a PASOK signboard in the square excoriating the latest hyphenated conspiracy: the American-Jewish-Turkish connection. It was the time of the Israeli incursion into Lebanon and the ruling Socialist party, with infallible sagacity, had penetrated the shifting miasmas of global malevolence and descried the real features of the composite enemy. The ancestral foe, the Turks, are naturally behind every act of Levantine belligerence. The Americans are everybody's scapegoat: without America it would be necessary for nations to become politically responsible. And the Jews, whether Israeli sabras or European Zionists, also serve an indispensable function: they explain America's political behaviour. So the complexity of world events is duly simplified and everybody is happy except the Lebanese.

Greece is a politically unstable nation and I fear will always remain so. The Greek character is too theatrical and captious, too variable, to permit even the rudiments of stability to enter into the social equation. Nothing ever factors out in this country. I referred a few pages back to the 'lustral' politics of this nation. Every five years in Rome a period of lustration and catharsis was proclaimed. Similarly, in Greece there is a coup or revolution or some kind of social cataclysm every five or seven or ten years without fail. When I was in Hydra in 1967, the country was more or less peaceful and centrist. Awakened one morning by the brass cacophony of military music, I descended to the port for news and found it swarming with policemen. I went to Pireaus and the first thing I ran into was a tank.

Soon my friends were being clapped into jail and I was being followed by the Asfalia (Security Police). Greece was now a Simon-pure, stentorian, right-wing nation. Some years after the fall of the junta, Andreas Papandreou who, during the interregnum, had enjoyed asylum in the United States and Canada, was elected as prime minister to the almost universal acclaim of the newly-liberated Greeks. Greece was now a socialist nation veering ever more to the Left in the ensuing years. America was progressively denounced and alienated. (Canada is defended by its anonymity.) I am convinced that in a few years time Greece will be once again centrist, Andreas will be rich, and the country will gradually prepare for the right-wing or left-wing takeover that is bound to follow sometime in the nineties.

Meanwhile the crack rummy players and tavli virtuosi are huddled in caucus in the corner house where the Olive Association meets. Cigarette smoke hangs thickly over their intensities like a Paxiot thundercloud, ready to burst with a sort of meteorological rhetoric whose inundations seem necessary to fecundate the Greek personality.

In moments of occasional delirium I see myself savouring pralines on the terrace of a coconut hacienda or happily chinging away in the Pachinko parlours of the Orient. Lately the Grenadine islands have become a cherished fantasy. To have gone there rather than come here would have meant, in my latifundian imaginings, having the sun at our constant disposal, swimming daily all through the winter in our Caribbean jacuzzi, watching friendships blossom between Hannah and the local children in various flavours of English. We would have sailed on John McKeating's yacht and visited St. Vincent every weekend to shop or take in a film or enjoy a change of scenery. Instead of hibernating in an icebox whose interior temperature should be measured on the Kelvin scale, we would amble around the verandah of our large, comfortable manse or luxuriate in the perennially-accessible outdoors. Whereas here we remain forced to endure the depredations of four-year-old Anthia because she is Hannah's only friend. Anthia arrives promptly at ten, proceeds to kick the cats, aiming always for the head, destroys Hannah's crayon markers by pressing too hard on the nibs, gathers all the chairs, blankets and pillows and piles them in a heap in order to play house, is either catatonically silent for three hours straight, refusing to respond to a single question or suggestion, or screams insanely the same word over and over such as "Rocky! Rocky! Rocky!", the name of our neighbour's dog, till I am driven from my writing table, Alki from his morning studies and Karin from her wits, or shatters the fragmented remnants of our composure with a monotonic, staccato laugh whose complete lack of inflection or tonal music argues some profound inner deficiency. After pushing Hannah off the table, scattering her lunch to the ground, clanging the gate repeatedly, hopping in the back seat of my rented car, stomping on ants and spiders and throwing walnuts at imaginary passersby, she is finally induced to leave for home. Hannah retires exhausted and happy for her afternoon nap and Karin sags on the wooden bench — the local equivalent for a sofa — her nerves vibrating like bouzouki stings in high arpeggio. After such a morning I tend to dream passionately of my Caribbean island, until I suddenly remember the sinister blandishments of Utopia, the tenacious Elysian paradise which is always located elsewhere.[5]

For the Grenadines must have their share of carrion-eating mosquitoes, scorpions, tarantulas. In spring when Paxos is exfoliating in lavish sunlight, the Grenadines are turning into brisket. No doubt the sea is teeming with Portuguese men o' war and limb-devouring sharks. By this time we would certainly have gone stir crazy, wandering disconsolately along the shoreline dreaming of Paxos and "the blue honey of the Mediterranean." Hannah would have been tied to a mango tree by the local kids and left to blister in the sun. And I would have been busy demythologizing Arcadia.

Revisited Vassilatika and the 'Algerian' fortress. We worked our way through the bracken along the smooth-faced mosaic of the ancient revetment and emerged at the top of the precipice overlooking the sea, an almost vertical drop of two or three hundred feet. The cliff wall is scalloped out so one cannot see the rocky strand, which should be directly beneath one's feet. The knowledge of that enormous concavity in the limestone plummet produces an intense feeling of insecurity and vertigo. We edged along the cliff through clusters of nettle and Christ-thorn and thick, squat, bunched-up ganglia of pine and ilex trees to a small door in the stone wall, which had been left unfastened. Now we could explore the grounds of the fortress, several acres of terraced groves, communicating walks of hewn stone, rock escarpments, ruined watch-towers, a small, round bartisan-like structure, something that resembled an oubliette, and everywhere eroded lettering incised in the rocks. The emblem of the radiant sun appeared frequently and a skeletal Grunewald-like cross. I found a few shards of plate with the six-petalled flower or rosette glazed on the rim. One has silly thoughts in such circumstances: to close one's eyes, touch a corner of wall, and see the events of the last three hundred years as if unrolling on a reel of film: the 'Algerian' raids, the Turkish devastations, the indigenous feuds. For a moment everything wavers and grows hazy, colours fade and sounds are muted. There is a sense of real menace and strangeness in the air, then it passes, like a wind from the beat of a bird's wing. We returned with a few holm acorns, bits of pottery and a mixed feeling of oppression and exhilaration, to be so time-blinded and yet to sense that one has had a momentary glimpse through the dark glass of the present tense into the turbulent if indistinct past.

Karin's insight about Paxos, as opposed to the general run of Greek islands, strikes me as valid. On most islands one must perform a kind of prescinding operation in order to accommodate oneself to the place. For example, on Alonissos the people are a surly and irascible lot and the pillbox architecture of the last thirty years is offensively psoriatic. *But*, one says, the *island* is beautiful. This is true. The island is genuinely magnificent, especially the views from the ancient capital (now rebuilt after the earthquake and largely in foreign hands) towards Turkoneri and Megali Ammo on the ironbound western side and the stippling of smaller islands towards the cloudy pinnacles of Evia in the east. The trouble is that in order to enjoy the island one must first cut the people and the local architecture out of the picture, cultivate a blind spot, as it were; once all the social clutter and aesthetic vulgarity is bracketed off, one can begin to appreciate the untrammeled beauty of the island itself. The same was true within limitations for Hydra in the late sixties and must have been the case in Mykonos even earlier.

In Paxos, the editing process is less acute, less violent. The people do not *impose* themselves as they do on some other islands and the architecture is comparatively tasteful and discrete. Builders and renovators still tend to adhere to the traditional designs that work well and do not affront the landscape. Chimneys continue to wear their rhomboidal caps with the flues perpendicular to the roofs, an efficient way of dealing with the rains as well as aesthetically appealing. Occasionally the new walls are still constructed according to the old pattern — stone placed on stone in an oddly delicate, tessellated arrangement rather than glued together with rivers of cheap, time-saving cement. Of course Paxos comes in for its share of tawdriness and ostentation but the imagination need not exhaust itself scraping away the outer memoranda of the island palimpsest in order to read its authentic and underlying script.

Notes on travel writing

There is a sense in which all literature, or at least fiction, is travel literature. The country to which and in which the author is travelling, which he is describing and probing, is not a nation or a people or a landscape in the ordinary sense, but a *concept*. That is, he is travelling in the realm of ideas, and the territory which he marks out for study may be in its essence something abstract or impalpable, at any rate, non-geographical. The subject may be, for example, 'growing up,' as in the traditional *bildungsroman*; or the complex nature of human relationships, most prominently, love; or the lunar configurations of the mind, as in Kafka; or most often, the multifactorial nature of human experience, including the eternal theme of the relation between the individual and society. In every case we are travelling into a new country or the same country seen from different perspectives.

Is this equation reversible? Is travel literature an inverse form of fiction-writing? Are all travel books really novels?

What are some of the general types or categories of travel writing?

1) The tourist booklet: simply information for the sake of convenience. Not literature in any sense of the term.

2) The mere record of personal experience in foreign climes. Such efforts should be considered as diaries with an exotic flavour, interesting only if the recording sensibility is also interesting.

3) The genuine travel book, in which elements of the former types are encysted, but which also describes the *culture* of a people and the personal responses of the writer to the strangeness and depth of what he confronts. The features that distinguish the genuine travel book are:

a) the style, which is the reflex of sensibility;

b) the degree of perception, which is the reflex of sensitivity;

c) the accuracy of description, within the limits set by the informing and contextual imagination, which is the reflex of sincerity. There must be a significant absence of special pleading, sentimental extravagance and personal foregrounding. The genuine travel book contains a kind of ethnological value or relevance which, for example, *Le guide bleu* does not. (Cf. Barthe's essay).

Now the question is: what is the writer actually describing? He is, of course, describing (i) the people among whom he moves; (ii) the landscape in which they move; (iii) the political, social and cultural systems which they have evolved (literature, architecture, folkways, etc.). All these correspond to the objective side of his portrayal or critique.

But he is also depicting the curious and hitherto obscure *terra incognita* of his own personality. In a sense the objective record which he is compiling is also a pretext for the discovery and revelation of his own interior landscape, and naturally this would correspond to the subjective aspect of his inquiry.

Here we have the two irreducible components of all serious literature, and it might be appropriate to apply the canons of traditional fiction to the travel book:

a) Is there a kind of 'plot'?

b) Is there, if not so much development, at least the *presentation* of character?

c) Is there something that can be identified as a *theme*?

d) Finally, is the world which is delineated, for all its apparent documentary status, essentially the embodiment of an *imaginative* vision, a world which exists and does not exist; that is, is it, whether overtly or with imperceptible subtlety, a prescription for conduct or a projection of an ideal or desired condition?

If the travel book satisfies these criteria, then it must be considered as one of the categories of literature and specifically of fiction.

(Among the moderns: Durrell's Greek books, Lawrence's travel writing, Miller's *Colossus*, Chatwin's *In Patagonia*, Naipaul on India, Theroux's train books. Earlier moderns: Fermor's *Roumeli* et al, Byron's *Oxiana*, Stephenson's Yucatan volumes, Doughty's *Arabia Deserta*.)

Note: important for my own efforts. To study the ways in which the subjective side of the enterprise modifies, overwhelms or cancels the objective side. In the best travel writing, the objective receives genuine respect and is not scumbled or obliterated in the author's desire to privilege and foreground his own obstreperous self.

Question: degrees of possibility? To what extent does my own deposition fail?

In the light of the foregoing, Peter Bull's pixilated and gawky account of life on a Greek island does not qualify as travel literature. One could perhaps make a case for the existence of characters — all Greeks are characters by right of birth, and the author was himself a noted character actor; but there is no thematic current and nothing which might remotely attain to imaginative vision, either in terms of the analysis of motive and conduct in the name of a controlling ethical design or in the noble attempt to attest to the immanence of miracle, the act of bearing witness to what, after all the explanations have been exploded or forgotten, remains mysterious and irreducible and essentially *memorable in itself.*

One could do worse than go back two thousand years to evoke the figure of Aulus Gellius, the Roman seigneur wintering in a friend's house on the outskirts of Athens and recording in his monumental *Attic Nights* the recollections, events, aperçus, characters and thoughts with which he diversified and enhanced his interlude of Greek expatriation. This is probably the first and archetypal travel book, the great torrent of reflection and observation of which all subsequent specimens of the genus are more or less worthy tributaries.

Poor Peter Bull comes in for a real hammering in these pages. The casual reader would probably be hard put to believe that I have never met and have absolutely nothing against him, so incessantly do I keep pummelling away at his naive and departed spirit. But as I have already indicated, Bull has taken on an importance far beyond that merited by his flimsy, dandiacal book. He is an extreme case of the contemporary Arcadian and as such an emblematic figure of the first magnitude. In Peter Bull I recognize myself, though I have none of his talent for caricature and impersonation and considerably less *joie de vivre.* Yet in his innate shallowness, the unremitting tendency to the maudlin and the facetious, and that terrible fear of loneliness to which he frankly confesses, I see the familiar profile of my own flawed sensibility.

If one capitulates to this denial of the self and its constituent rigors, and blunders away its constantly diminishing reserves of awareness and austerity, then one's entire life assumes the proportions of a dedicated flight from reality: what the analysts might diagnose as false or negative cathexis. And where do these exiles and fugitives go? At the other end of the round earth's imagined corners awaits the blissful land of Arcadia to receive its Boeing-loads of visitors and tourists. But it should be remembered that Arcadia is also portable and, like Cavafy's Alexandria, always comes along as a natal part of one's own interior climate and geography. All that Paxos or the Grenadines do is objectify, with varying degrees of success, that internal, utopian topography. "All travel," said Saul Bellow in *Henderson the Rain King*, "is mental travel."

This is an insight that Aulus Gellius had in the auroral epoch of cultivated travel and one with which we must continue to brace and refresh our memories if we are to affirm the laborious and complex world in which we live. Otherwise travel will remain escape, experience a systematic hallucination, and what we call the self a strategy for critical avoidance. This is exactly why, as I've said before, we are obsessively driven to register on tape and film the entire pseudo-saga of our travels: to convince ourselves of the reality of an experience we have done everything in our power to evade, counterfeit or misconstrue, and to persuade ourselves at the same time of our own indisputable existence. Look, that's me leaning on the column, standing beside the statue, dancing the *hasapiko* with Nikos the fisherman!

❖

A day out of God's picture book. The house flooded with sunlight and the air almost balmy. Karin busy for hours shaking out and hanging up sheets, towels, sweaters and rugs to burn off the month's accumulated dampness. Took Hannah to the doctor in Bogdanatika this morning: she has a persistent bronchitis like wet radio static in her chest. (She too has to be dried out). Returned with a whole pharmacopoeia of medicines. Typically, everything is as complicated as possible. The antibiotics are in powder form and must be mixed with water. The vitamins come in huge glass ampules — Hannah thought they were batteries — which must be sawed through at both ends and their contents poured into a cup. The liquids are fulvid, sweet and plentiful, especially the cough syrup which for taste and consistency seems pure ichor of baclava. As I write the afternoon is beginning to cloud over and the air is once again cold and damp.

I remember an expression that used to be very popular in the sixties: to be "bombed out of one's gourd." This describes graphically what happened to Hannah as a result of that explosive remedial compound she swallowed yesterday. She soon became completely unrecognizable to us, undergoing a personality change so extensive and profound that I thought we had a classic case of possession or schizophrenia on our hands. It was really quite terrifying. For the rest of the day and a good part of the night she was transformed into an inordinately loud, ill-mannered, disobedient, peevish and destructive little kid, very much like Abdullah in the Tintin comics; in fact, her behaviour was an exact replica of many of the local children who love to torture animals, defy their parents and fill the air with a constant laryngeal barrage of shrieks and wails.

We did then what we should have done immediately instead of trusting to the doctor's instructions — we began to decipher the labels on the medicines we had administered. It turned out that the glass ampules we had been told were vitamin supplements were nothing of the sort. They contained something called *durobion*, a substance consisting largely of malate acid which is a noted antidote for psycho-intellectual depression and somatic asthenia. In the case of adults it is meant to combat memory loss, chronic inattentiveness and the reduction of intellectual activity and alertness; for children, it functions as a kind of alexipharmic or restorative against serious prostration, anorexia, infectious diseases and, once again, profound depression. Hannah was perfectly correct: these ampules *were* batteries. Time bombs, brain-busters, neuronal detonators.

Thank God the effect was temporary. Hannah is her amiable and perceptive self this morning, only she is debilitated by the ordeal she underwent. As for the doctor, he enjoys the implicit confidence of the islanders. At first we were aghast at his incompetence but, after thinking it over, realized that he had undoubtedly prescribed *durobion* regularly for enfeebled youngsters with satisfactory results, because what we interpret as aberrant or neurotic behaviour is in fact the norm here for healthy, boisterous, well-adjusted children. When I took Hannah down to Lakka yesterday evening, I was shocked by her bratty convulsive behaviour, but everyone we met was charmed and delighted. Agapi, the sweetshop lady, handed her a chocolate, old Haralambos in the grocery store a ladleful of almonds, Spiro pressed a macaroon on her, and so it went. She had become a happy and exemplary Paxiot child.

The Ace Cafe in Gaios

A pokey hole in the corner resembling an excavation, soon to become the magnetic centre of the town, as it contains in its dark, clammy interior a small bar and four video games. One of these is called Phoenix. On its screen appears a gigantic Star-Wars-type mother-craft planet-killer and a busy multitude of midget rocket launchers that move rapidly back and forth along the bottom of the screen in typewriter-carriage fashion. Suddenly the whole ensemble mutates into a flock of ferocious aquiline birds that must be destroyed by an arsenal of warheads. This is obviously the most popular game on venatic, bird-crazy Paxos. When the birds have migrated on and the hunting slackens, the youth of the island repairs to the Ace cafe to vaporize electronic *trigonia* and exult in feathery carnage. The real advantage, so far as I am concerned, is the absence of cartridge litter, which now forms a thick stratum of the island's topsoil.

❖

> who are these thousands entering the dark
> Ark of the moment, two by two . . .
> — James Merrill

I recall two years ago in Gaios, when we lived directly across from the verdigris statue of the young Paxiot who reputedly set fire to the Turkish flagship during the War of Independence, the daily shiploads of English tourists who paused before the monument with cameras at the ready. Margaret would hold the Minolta while Edward mounted the stone pedestal and gazed nobly at the lens, a military adjutant in Byronic pose. This act was repeated a thousand times an afternoon for two months. The crisp mechanical clicks of the cameras became one of the elemental and component sounds of the island, along with goatbells, donkey brays and the diesel chutter of the fishingboats. I grew to hate the quiet insidious clicking more than the amped-up mosquito whine of the unmufflered Zündapps and Lambrettas that wreaked acoustic havoc on the days. And I began to fantasize, imagining the statue gradually eroded by the harsh, abrasive glare of the cameras, or hearing each click as one more elfin hammer-stroke on the small psychic casket in which each man's experience of reality is enclosed and nailed tight.

It was then I began to understand that for the majority of visitors, "Paxos" was the contemporary version of le Petit Trianon in which, like Marie Antoinette and her maids playing shepherdess with indolent, Theocritean elegance, they affected the roles of strolling millionaires, parvenu industrialists and Promethean heroes, imposing a celluloid rescension or construction on the surface of the real world, and so by various techniques of *trompe l'oeil* and imaginary montage entering into the elaborate fiction of significant life. Meanwhile all authentic feeling and perception was conveniently suppressed and obliterated. These people I observed from my terrace every afternoon knew nothing about the Greek War of Independence to which they contributed their proleptic sympathies and theatrical postures, and probably less about the sensuous and kinesthetic quality of the very island whose coasts and beaches they were systematically promenading. What, then, was "reality"? They reminded me of certain stereo-freaks who are experts in the suave complexities of sound systems, who know everything there is to know about woofers, speakers, amplifiers, balance, treble, and so on, yet remain in a state of relative ignorance with respect to the *Fifth Symphony* or the *Brandenburg Concerti* which their complex equipment is meant to render with absolute technological fidelity.

The same applied to the hordes of tourists who drove me from my terrace with their barrage of exhalations, commentary and camera-static. They knew more about their Canons and Minoltas than about the scenes they were presumably recording. It seemed as if the adoration they felt went out to their instruments and not to the ostensible experience they were in the act of preserving.

There is a subtle distinction to be made here. Arcadia is not abstract. The critique which is usually leveled by poets and sensitive sociologists against the meretricious nature of contemporary "reality" is that people tend to live in a galloping abstraction which spirits them away from the concrete vitality of experience. Life is becoming more and more abstract. This assessment of our current malaise is an oversimplification. Experience is as concrete and empirical as it ever was, only it has been *deflected* in another direction. What has happened is that our sophisticated instrumentation has intervened between the individual and his experience of the world in such a way that the individual now enjoys a more intimate experience of his instrument than he does of his world. His experience remains concrete, but the object of his perusal, attention and love has changed dramatically. He knows the sound system, not the symphony. He loves his camera, not the wave or tree or chapel or heather-purple hillside he is photographing. In the same way, but at a transitive remove, he is delighted by the stereotype, not the person he is apparently encountering, as he is seduced by the image he projects and which his accompanying technical apparatus facilitates, rather than disciplined and instructed by the imperatives of self-authentication. The point is, his experience is just as concrete and sensuous as it theoretically was prior to the acquisition of that battery of intermediary devices for rendering and recording, but it is now a concrete experience, not of the world as it impinges on the senses or the spirit, but of the instruments with which he filters, mediates and censors that receding and elusive world. In short, *Arcadia is not an abstraction, it is a deflection.* Or more precisely, it is a pretext, a transposition, the sensuous and spiritual residue of a falsifying modality of perception. And the Arcadian personality is one that has allowed itself to be instrumentally deflected away from the world it has betrayed in the direction of that fictive, embroidered and skimmed-off pseudo-world which consists in equal proportions of inner theatre and outer instrumentality, of a rampant and untutored subjectivity in a milieu of technological intercessions. The Arcadian sensibility is hyphenated and duple. It is in love with the object which has become for it the embodiment of a perfect intervention. And it adores the figment of an unsponsored and unearned heroism which it identifies, in an act of idolatry which eclipses the philistinism of all the past ages taken together, with the obscure, laborious urgencies of the self. All that is cryptic and strenuous, mysterious and resistant, is ruthlessly expurgated from its paraphrase of the world.

Arcadia, then, is not only a deflection, it is also an *evaporation of reality* and a docetic effigy of man himself. In its name the rape of the human personality is daily enacted, justified and celebrated.

We have entered the realm of what the French philosopher, Jean Baudrillard, calls the "hyperreal," that contradictory state in which the distinction between the real and the imaginary is erased. The problem, Baudrillard writes, "is that of the satellization of the real . . . the process whereby *reality is contaminated by its own simulacrum.*"

✥

The snail which reposed on our pillar-gate is no more. He had sealed himself up and webbed himself in and seemed prepared to spend the rest of the winter in a state of blissful hibernation, but he failed to reckon with the spontaneous yet methodical destructiveness of four-year-old Anthia. She noticed him for the first time this morning and his fate was immediately decreed. In a burst of irrepressible enthusiasm she flattened him to the concrete, pulverizing the thin shell to smithereens, and left the mangled corpse to coagulate into a brown, soggy smudge on the ground by the threshold. I recollect Peter Van Toorn's translation of the Issa poem about the snail which clung to the gate like a miniature lock. For Anthia, as for so many of the children and adults in this land, the lock of privacy must inevitably be forced and smashed. The snail is, obviously, the incarnation of privacy, and as such is an affront to the medieval temperament which still flourishes here. The concept of a private life is entirely alien to this people: everything from reflection to infidelity is rigorously con-trolled and generally prevented by the age-old technique of perpetual and reciprocal surveillance at close quarters. Even the simple disposition of the houses makes freedom and privacy impossible, and nothing is permitted to hap-pen without the entire village, and the island as well, knowing about it with superluminal instantaneity.

The Greek temperament is, at bottom, archaic and despotic. In fact, it is the direct antithesis of that buoyant, anarchic and euphoric fiction generated in the pages of tourist brochures and in much of the travel literature. The relation of the modern Greek to the Western world with which he is coming into more and more extensive contact, through tourism, emigration and the Common Market, cannot be understood if the confusion and resentment he feels at the spectacle of freedom on parade is not taken into account. One side of the Greek soul wishes to emulate the foreigner — disco music and nude bathing are becoming increasingly popular; but the other, darker side wishes to smash the harbinger of personal autonomy and self-sufficiency like a snail fastened to the Pillars of Hercules. The foreigner is generally ignorant of this bitter dialectic and persists in taking the Greek at face-value, or rather at mask-value, as the noble savage of the modern world, like Diderot's unspoiled, eighteenth-century Tahitian.

Family relations are teetering "on the dangerous edge of things," to quote that paragon of contentment, Robert Browning. Hannah has become practically unmanageable, catered to as she must be during her illness. She refused to drink her antibiotic last night, whimpering, complaining, raising a howling face contorted with the arrogance of dissent. She is really pitting her will against Karin's, which has been going on for some time now. I had reached the end of my emotional tether after a day of acrid quarrelling and entered the room to administer the medicine myself, beginning by clutching Hannah's hair the way a nursing cat lifts her kittens with her teeth by the furry scruff. This was a tyrannical gesture and I should not have made it, but at that point I was a tired, seething cauldron of frustration and animosity. Karin seized my wrist in a vice of hatred, transfixed me with a glance of pure malevolence, and uttered some steely imprecation that brought images of divorce dancing into my head. This kind of behaviour just doesn't square with the ideal of marriage I carry permanently around with me like a paradigm of happiness or an infectious disease — I have never been able to decide which. Are people really meant to be happy together? The great poet, Osip Mandelstam, diagnosed the quest for personal happiness as the characteristic infirmity of the modern mind. "Why do you think you should be happy?" Mandelstam used to ask. And his wife Nadezhda comments, "The concept of happiness for all seemed to him the most bourgeois thing in the whole intellectual baggage inherited from the nineteenth century." In fact, the central theme of her book, *Hope Against Hope*, is that "the pursuit of happiness can lead to disaster."

The intellectual part of me, tremulous and insecure as it may be, is in complete agreement with this evaluation. Yet the emotional man resists, argues, denies. A man is intended to get along with his wife, as Milton knew when he wrote that no worse fate existed for a man than to be "wedded with a fell adversary." And the naive and primitive voice that speaks through me claims that she is meant to be by nature what the Anglo-Saxons called "the peace-weaver," soft and conciliatory, and to display the virtue that Rabelais praised in his description of the female guests of his Thelemite monastery, who were to be "sweet-tempered." And Swift quotes with what appears to be approval the Lilliputian domestic maxim, "A wife should always be a reasonable and agreeable companion, because she cannot always be young." For myself, I am convinced a woman has no right to behave like Virginia Woolf, unless, like the lady in question, she has genius as well. The question I am posing to myself now is: does my opposition to the subversive duplicities of Arcadia require me to accept the shocks and buffets of outrageous reality? Is the notion of happiness, as Osip Mandelstam suggested, irreparably utopian? (Did not Thomas More's Utopians require "modesty and a respectful attitude toward themselves" from their women? "A pretty face may be enough to catch a man, but it takes character and good nature to hold him.") Chaucer's lovelorn knight, Sir January, is afraid that the happiness he will experience in marriage will prevent him from suffering enough to merit the indemnifications of heaven. He is assured by his brother that there will never be enough happiness in marriage to stand in the way of salvation.

No travel book on Greece, be it the meanest tourist guide or the elegant discriminations of a Durrell or a Fermor, can aspire to any degree of completeness if it fails to

mention the most popular activity, competition and entertainment in this country, which is nothing other than
spitting. Unless he has been dried up by the cosmopolitan
life of Athens or Thessaloniki, he will spit at will, copiously,
thunderously, frequently, and with unerring accuracy. The
true pastime of the men on Alonissos, more so than tavlis
or rummy, was to sit outside Nina's cafe and engage in
spitting competitions, the object of which was to hit the
mulberry tree in the square not only dead centre and from
a respectable distance, but with an air of unstudied casualness that befitted their natural and effortless sense of
personal dignity. And the spitting tournaments on
Alonissos were only the smallest part of the general inundation. People spat all the time, the women too, from their
terraces and windows, along the cramped paths and lanes,
at the tables in cafes and tavernas and restaurants (indoors
or out made no difference). I used to be awakened in the
mornings by a tympany of hawking sounds (like the gunshots up here on the mountain) which accompanied the
sunrise. The path to Maria's *pantapoleion* used to be
irrigated by the morning shoppers, turning a muddy,
lateritic red-brown, and the cobblestones were slicked
and glistening.

Everywhere one goes in this country one is in danger
of being spat on or at least of receiving a few droplets of
lateral spume. I remember sitting on the deck of an island
ferry unwrapping my lunch and uncorking a bottle of
wine; one of the deckhands sauntered by and delivered an
enormous gob which narrowly missed my sandwich but
made a cloudy, ambiguous elixir of my retsina. This was

obviously a gesture of friendship, a conversation-opener, which at the time I was still too callow and squeamish to appreciate.

Paxos is not especially renowned for its prodigies of expectoration. Public spitting is customary enough but nose-picking and snot-flinging is perhaps a more developed art. Last night I watched with utter fascination as an elderly gentleman, standing in the middle of the plateia, dug into his nostril with a finger as thick and crooked as a boat-hook and after much concentrated labour extracted a pea-green pellet of olfactory substance which he proceeded to regard with deep satisfaction, flourish like a kind of trophy to a group of men drinking coffee at an outdoor table, and then with a powerful flick of thumb and index finger propel it halfway across the square where it came to rest in an empty ice cream cup on a doorstep.

Spitting is more highly refined and commonly practiced in Corfu. In fact, it was on Corfu that I heard the classic virtuoso performance that surpassed anything I had ever witnessed before in this country for timbre, resonance, sustained fortissimo and contrapuntal intricacy. The event took place in the alleyway beneath my hotel window. It was preceded by a reverberating burp, a bass eructation that vibrated and echoed off the high walls of the Corfiot architecture and promised unexpected splendours to follow. I was not to be disappointed. A deep, retching hack, layered with distinguishable overtones, a brief silence, a stertorous intake of breath, another tense silence, then a species of complex instrumentation that sounded like a tuba and a bassoon in rich antiphonal playfulness, rising to a crescendo of orchestral vehemence accompanied by a reedy, quivering, adenoidal flute, ending in the wet, emulsifying smack of an octopus on rock. The performance engendered two encores of diluvian prodigality and then subsided into the silence of the indifferent universe.

I have no explanation for this phenomenon. Sometimes I think it is simply a way of making one's mark, of establishing one's presence, or of registering an ironic statement in a world in which everything evaporates anyway. In more conjectural moments I interpret these performances as the spontaneous affirmation of an earth-dwelling people: when the fit is on them Greek men seem to expectorate from their bootheels, reaching down to the alluvial depths and refructifying the cobblestones and pavements with the zeal of their agricultural forebears. I no longer consider the custom as a sign of raw vulgarity or peasant crudeness. It is too elaborate, too catholic, and too perfected to pass as anything but a defiant metaphysical assertion of man's place in the cold, mute cosmos that made even the civilized and eloquent Pascal shudder with terror.

Travelled *en famille* to Corfu to see Karin and Hannah off on their annual visit to Karin's family in Berlin. A cold, blustery morning, everyone gathered about the *Kamelia* in earnest speculation about the weather and the possibility of the crossing. The ritual trope rising like a Kyrie Eleison in the celebration of this huddled, secular Mass was: *Pende*

Beauforts. Five Beauforts of wind out there. Two summers ago we had spent seventeen hours languishing in the harbour of Ios because the captain of a ship many times the size and seaworthiness of the *Kamelia* refused to sail in a six Beaufort gale. Pende Beauforts, departure unlikely, was the general consensus of the veterans of Corfu crossings, solacing themselves with great draughts of morning cognac in the bleak cafe by the docks. We waited almost an hour while the Captain deliberated. Hannah vomited the dregs of her antibiotic and while we were mopping up we heard the cough and stutter of the ship's engines and everyone rushed to the door in a crush of luggage, execrations, groans and prayers, two fat matrons wedged in the doorway and blocking traffic while the crowd surged and heaved behind them. I stood and watched with a vomit-soaked rag in my hand and recalled suddenly Forster's limpid phrase, "the losses incidental to an oriental embarkation."

The voyage was surprisingly calm and uneventful. A few huge swells had the ship yawing and shuddering at first, but then it settled into a lulling, pleasant, hammocky rhythm that mingled with the general feeling of relief and exhilaration. Nobody was seasick. The women sat and gossiped, occasionally peering out the salt-streaked windows and crossing themselves mechanically. The men collected at the bar under the faded Delial advertisement and the picture of the pipe-smoking, blue-vested old tar who always struck me as a peculiar hybrid figure, half 'John Player' and half Captain Haddock, with whom I tended to identify. The atmosphere was raucous and convivial and by the time we reached Corfu everyone was steeped in generous quantities of no-star Metaxa.

We made our way to our customary hotel whose name should have occurred to me earlier in these pages for its ironic drift and implication: the Arkadion. We had tried out a number of hotels on the island, including the ostentatious and prohibitive Corfu Hilton: five days in Kubla Khan-like splendour followed by three months *in statum paupertatis* paying off Chargex. The Constantinople, a sprawling, ochreous tenement in the old port, flavoured our occasional shorter visits with the fragrance of paint, cleaning fluid and Turkish coffee. But the Arkadion had become our regular *pied à terre*, partly for its uncluttered modesty (though breakfast is a skimpy, drab affair) and partly for its pleasing location on the Esplanade. That I should find myself writing a book whose real subject is the romantic detoxification of Arcadia while at the same time staying over frequently in the Arkadion hotel on the pastoral sward of the *Spianada* with its Rue de Rivoli arcades, its cricket field and its outdoor cafes, makes me wonder about the plausibility of the entire enterprise. Arcadia always finds a way of re-establishing itself in one's life, even after it has been demolished, razed and salted over. A further confession: these hortatory, anti-Arcadian paragraphs are being jotted down in a room with a fine, bosky view and a comfortable balcony in this same Arkadion hotel. *Et in Arkadion, Ego.*

Visited the church of Aighos Spiridon, the island's patron saint. Pleasant conversation with the sacristan, an amiable and untidy man named Alekos, who was convinced that he detected certain spiritual leanings in me toward the Orthodox faith. He regaled me with stories of converted foreigners who had abandoned wife and children for the erimitic life of Mouth Athos. Afterwards, duly softened up, I joined a file of worshippers in the small chapel to the right of the sanctuary where the remains of the Saint repose in an elaborate reliquary. Though he died shortly after the Council of Nicaea in 325, the body is largely intact and exudes the odour of sanctity, a veritable miracle which has to this day resisted the theories and analyses of delegations of visiting European savants. One sees only the feet, encased in tasselled slippers, and the face, contorted with the centuries, the mouth curved in a clown's rictus and the skin a mackerel grey. (It's curious to note that the expression of the lips paradoxically resembles the so-called 'archaic smile' one sees on the face of Chrysaor, the Gorgon's son, in the archeological museum in Corfu. The resemblance is unmistakable. The figure of Chrysaor dates from the sixth century B.C.) The priest intoned solemnly and pompously in tenorial plainsong while I clasped my hands in a facsimile of religious anguish and felt like the coarsest of interlopers. When the ceremony was over I met the priest in the sacristy. The transformation was instantaneous. He dropped his canonical pants, as it were, flashed a gap-toothed urchin's smile, and became the shifty, inquisitive, viverine descendant of the wily Odysseus. He had seen me deposit a five hundred drachma note in the votive coffer, which was more than the entire congregation had donated. I did not explain that this was conscience money, but answered his quick, curious questions regarding my origins and accepted a fragment of ribbon shorn from the Saint's slippers as a memento. (The slippers, of course, are constantly being replaced.)

When I left the church something in the order of a small miracle occurred. A white pigeon detached itself from the flock wheeling over the rooftops, dived steeply and skimmed the furze of my sailor's cap. For a moment I expected a message from the Saint in the form of a well-aimed globule and was greatly relieved when the pigeon flew immaculately off and became a real bird again, just as the priest in the sacristy had vailed his intimidating solemnity and become an actual man once more.

Women with the name of love keep cropping up in my life, as if to tempt and mortify me with their unavailability. There was Madame Venus, a live carving of ebony voluptuousness, whom I met on Ste. Lucia. She was the star performer at the hotel where she performed the belly dance that had made her famous throughout the Windward Islands. We met one evening on the hotel grounds and after a little conversation in which it was tacitly established that the night was yet young, went together to Lucifer's disco. It was clear that she was waiting for me to propose an alternative, but as Karin and Hannah were in the hotel room and I knew no one on the island, and as she could not bring me to the family home in Castries, the evening ended with an Eliotic whimper. I bade her a tame goodnight and she smiled back with faintly disguised contempt. I discovered next day that she was sixty years old and her fame rested as much on her preserved youthfulness (like Saint Spiridon) as on the suppleness of her abdominal convolutions.

Then there was Madame d'Amour whom I spoke to on the telephone back in Montreal in connection with renting out my house before leaving for Greece, a kindly, amusing, sprightly woman I would have relished meeting. I prolonged the conversation as long as I could until there was nothing left to do but say good-bye, hangdog and anticlimactic. And in Lakka the local sweetshop is run by another of these *donna angelicatas*, a woman of about forty with a smile that contrives to be both shy and intimate and the kind of body Huxley would call 'pneumatic,' whose name is Agapi. There is an erotic undercurrent between us of which she is well aware and which, in speech, look and gesture, she deliberately promotes, but she is married and Greek and unassailable. She might as well live in a Petrachan sonnet, remote and virginal, or locked up in one of her own glass display cases, for all the promise of her temptations.

And now, Aphrodite. She is perhaps the loveliest woman I have seen on Corfu: fine, clear eyes, a smile that would melt the heart of an Albanian, and a body best described by the Yiddish 'zaftig.' She speaks a fluent cultivated English no doubt honed and perfected over the years in her job at a travel agency. I have dealt with her may times, most recently yesterday morning to pick up Karin's ticket for Germany. Today as I was ambling along the corniche after seeing Karin off at the airport, there was Aphrodite sailing into my life on a bicycle in a high wind, labouring up the slight incline, hair streaming out behind her as if painted by Botticelli in a frolicking mood. She stopped, she balanced on one leg, we exchanged banalities, she remounted her bicycle, she pedalled off again. All the tiny, puffing, Cherubic zephyrs dancing in my imagination sagged and collapsed, as Aphrodite scudded out of my life to join the mythical sorority of promise and disappointment that haunts my craving for miracle.

There are a whole fleet of igneous candidates for Odysseus' petrified ship. (The people here all refer to it as 'Odysseus' ship.' It was, of course, the ship of the Phaecians returning from its errand of mercy that Poseidon turned into stone.) The Paxiots claim that it is *Exolitharion*, the split-rock formation off the northern headland of the island. The Corfiots advance several pretenders of their own into this crowded mythological harbour, chief of which is *Ponderikonisi*, the famous Mouse Island near Perama that embellishes all the postcards. There has arisen, however, a sect of modern iconoclasts who assert that Mouse Island derives its name from its shape, which from above putatively resembles that of a rodent. This assumption is neither here nor there as, with a little imagination, one can stretch and pat and mold the island into practically any reasonable shape one desires, like a lump of playdough. Recent skeptics have plied a different tack in the direction of realism: the island was once infested by rats (probably during the plagues from which St. Spiridon delivered the Corfiots), and though the rats were expelled, the name in its milder form remained. But the pawky Greek temperament is never at a loss for an answer. "That may be so," the zealots retort, "but the rats were those from Odysseus' ship." How can one not love this people?

With Karin and Hannah off in Berlin, the rhythm of time has changed quite palpably. The days appear to pass slowly in the immediate moment and yet quite quickly in retrospect. When I bed down in my sleeping bag for the night, it seems as if I had unzipped it only a minute or two before to stagger into the cold rain or unaccustomed sunlight. The mornings are spent pottering about the house or going down to Lakka for a little shopping and conversation at Spiro's cafeneion. In the afternoon Alki and I generally set off on longish rambles to the eastern or western extremities of the island. Yesterday we explored the "lighthouse beach" on the northwest coast, a strip of shingle bordered on one side by a prow of limestone that projects about fifty metres into the sea and shelves on down the seaboard to a place just under the cliff of Vassilatika. We negotiated this rocky margin as far as we could, at one point clambering over a narrow, sloping, pebbly trail, perhaps eight inches in width, the granite rising almost vertically above us while below a sheer, dizzying plunge to a dragon's jaw of broken rocks. It was probably the most foolish thing I've done in years, especially as this thread of path consists mainly of loose, jingly shale that crunched and slid underfoot. The slightest miscalculation and the ridiculous melodrama would have become fact. Today we played it a little smarter and hiked down to Lakkos, a small beach on the eastern side and a mite south of Apergatika. This may become one of my favourite swimming places in the summer, not just because it is a hospitable spot but because the eye is relieved from the perpetual grey-green, clinkered, gauzy light of the relentless olive trees and welcomes the flood of darker green from the forests of cypress and pine that encircle the cove.

Most evenings supper down at Myro Mourtis' dreadful restaurant which reeks of garlic and sweat and possesses the peculiar squalor associated with old linoleum and dusty windowpanes, though last night we ate at home, Alki having learned from Arete how to bread and fry *keftedes*. A few pages of reading, three or four glasses of cognac, the medullary cold of 11:00 p.m. and the nerving up for the ordeal of undressing, and another day on the picturesque island of Paxos comes to a shuddery, prosaic close.

Dipping into a number of booklets on Corfu, my favourite being the badly-printed *Tourist Guide of Corfu* by Kostis Dafnis, a mixture of pidgin English, inflammatory rhetoric and dreary sentimentality. Some of the phrases are choice sweetmeats of transliterated malapropism and more than justify the three hundred drachmas I shelled out for it. We learn, for example, that "in spite of the oppressions and the persecutions of the English, the struggle is evolving with an admirable national palpitation," and later on, switching from the political to the aesthetic mode, that there began in the eighteenth century "the Greek theatre that generated the notorious theatrical reputation of Corfu." In order to appreciate the floral abundance of the island we are urged to visit Perama and Krissida, "suffocating from an orgiastic vegetation." The celebrated Spianada is described as follows: "All streets converge to this incomparable square, which constitutes the diadem and blood-donor of the beauty of Corfu." Poetry recovers its share of patriotic obeisance as well. At Ermones, for example, "was coming frequently for being inspired the poet C. Mavilis" (at Ermones today, the cove where, according to one reading of the Odyssey, the briny seafarer met the princess Nausikaa, there is a cyclopean 500 room hotel and a funicular railway that connects it to the shore); "In Spianada of Corfu, Solomos slapped on the face a man only because he was ugly" (Solomos is the author of the Greek National anthem); and in the Muses garden of the Achillion, we encounter Lord Byron who "absorbed in his meditations, seems to compose his epicolyric master-pieces." Finally, after several of the miracles of St. Spiridon ("who taking a cross persecuted the plague, which resembling a phantom tried to save itself. Some men testified that they heard its frightened moans as, going away from the town, escaped the implacable persecution."), we come to a description of the various festivals and are informed, under the rubric 'Procession of the Palm Sunday,' that "It is the most pompous."

Reading books of this sort is a good way of improving one's Greek, for the locutions which strike one as quaint or spooneristic are often direct calques and transliterations. All one has to do is transliterate straight back into Greek and one is practically guaranteed of proper phrasing and grammar. At the same time they are like X-ray films of the island personality with its love of florid detail, its lyrical articulations and its passion for declamatory rhetoric. Despite one's amusement, it is sometimes hard to resist the contagion of influence.

Life down in Lakka has opened up a crack with the appearance of a lanky, eccentric Italian named Luciano. He runs a small pasta-and-pizza restaurant on the other side of the square from Myro Mourtis, catering to the influx of Italian tourists in July and August, but has arrived early to make repairs and arrangements for the approaching season. Alki and I have eaten there two nights in a row, but Luciano refuses to accept payment. The suppers are really convivial gatherings, a collation of three foreigners accompanied by two Greek sisters, Soula who is in love with Luciano and plays waitress during the summer, and the younger Magda. The conversation is in three languages. Luciano manages a bumpy, exiguous English larded thickly with Italian; Soula, having lived eight years in California, dimples along charmingly in English; Magda speaks only Greek; and I repeat everything twice, in Greek and in English. This Babel of tongues is richly illustrated by a profuse and enthusiastic Esperanto of gesture, and the whole resembles a mad glossolalia of humorous desperation in which everyone finally understands everyone else perfectly.

The sisters do not interest me much, though they are sweet enough in company for an evening. A tension has arisen between us that will never quite dissolve, owing to the misfortune of a drunken challenge. After a first meal together, I suggested facetiously that we all go for a swim. As it was past midnight and the windows were rimmed with frost, I didn't expect to be taken seriously. But Soula decided it was an excellent idea and prepared to leave for the beach. Taken aback, I tried to wriggle off the hook by stating the obvious: I had no bathing suit. "Is okay," said Soula, "I sweem in my leetle pants." "But I am not wearing leetle pants," I confessed, somewhat abashed. "Is okay. No problem for me. Is problem for you?" Bundled up in sweaters and jackets, teeth chattering, we trudged off to the beach, borrowing a towel we found hanging on a line by a shuttered house along the way. When we arrived, Luciano, Magda and Alki stretched out shivering on the stones while Soula and I stood barefoot in what felt like subarctic waters. "I sweem in my clothes," said Soula, reneging on her commitment. I refused to comply, having by this time taken off my shirt. A deal is a deal, I reminded her, and as I had no intention of swimming in my clothes and was not wearing underpants and would therefore have to swim naked, I expected no less of her, or was at least willing to make the concession of the "leetle pants." She objected. I re-objected. We stood in the water arguing back and forth with equal obstinacy and righteousness, our feet turning blue with cold. Finally we backed anti-climactically out of the water and began putting on our socks. Then Soula made her fatal mistake. She began to taunt, half frivolously, half derisively. She was ready to take the plunge but I had funked the challenge from shyness and cowardice. "Come, Soula," I said, "time for a swim." "But you not sweem," she cried, "if I not take off my clothes." The issue had now left the realm of play and entered that of pride. "Is no problem," I said, "you sweem with clothes," and proceeded to strip naked and walk into the sea up to my knees. Soula had no choice but to follow, clothes and all, until she had reached the level of her knees as well. Whereupon, trembling and crestfallen, she returned to the shore. The contest was over. We made our way back to the restaurant, Magda seething with anger and indignation, Soula very pale and obviously shaken, and Luciano diplomatically telling funny stories in some rhyth-mic and incomprehensible dialect of his own. Luciano opened a bottle of Greek champagne to try and liven up the atmosphere but the bottle exploded with a resonating cannonade and drenched half the restaurant and its star-tled occupants. "Well," I said, "we sweem with clothes." But Soula and Magda did not appreciate the comment and the symposium fizzled out like wet kindling, gloomy, dismal and silent.

We ate together again last night and though the mood was cheerful and upbeat, the knot of tension was always there. Soula had been stripped far more naked than I, a fact for which she will never be able to forgive me. But the supper proceeded amiably on the surface and the conversation ranged over politics, the crusades, Robert Guiscard, Parsival and the Holy Grail, and the origin of the Sarakatsan nomads in the Thesprotian mountains. Luciano impersonated the titanic and heavily armoured Robert Guiscard being unsuccessfully winched out of the sea into which he had absurdly fallen, reducing the tragic episode to the scale of satyr-like burlesque. On this level the talk went smoothly enough, but as soon as anything of historical import was mentioned, Luciano or I would be forced to stop and explain it to the bewildered Soula and her sister, though both were bright, vivacious and well-educated by local standards, and Soula had spent many years abroad into the bargain. Luciano could not suppress the occasional gesture of annoyance. They had not heard of the Holy Grail. Parsival may have been an English or German tourist for all they knew. Robert Guiscard meant nothing to them, though he gave his name to the popular harbour of Fiscardi on the neighbouring island of Cephallonia. The Crusades need never have occurred for all the historical clangour they generated in the memory. When the talk veered toward politics, Soula admitted to crypto-communist sympathies because she resented the taxes she had to pay when working in the United States. All this is one reason that Luciano, though he likes Soula immensely and appreciates her sprightliness, cannot reciprocate her unconcealed love for him.

Another reason is that Luciano is in love with the great-granddaughter of Jules Verne with whom he lives for eight months of the year. "She is crazy," he says, "we fight, we fight, bouf, boom, all the time fight, but she give me power." For Luciano love is the apotheosis of human selfishness. He entertains no sentimental illusions, no purfled and decorative fantasies about the complex nature of human love. It has nothing to do with charity, kindness or compatibility. It is a mystery rooted in the hunger for power and identity, in the passionate necessity for discovering the sources of one's own interior dimension of self. In fact, according to Luciano, this *is* love. "When we are together, I am how you say I am *strong*. Fight, fight, no important. I find my power. I anything can do. Is not woman, is yourself you love." Love, as Nietzsche would say, is ipsissimosity.

Luciano spent several years as a dedicated agitprop secretary for one of the conventicles of the Italian Communist Party. Disillusioned, he abandoned his left-wing idealistic wife after one week of marriage (though he retained his Stalinist moustache), repudiated the Party, and doing a complete volte-face, started an independent advertising agency which after four years threatened to make him inconsolably rich. One day he attended a convention of businessmen in Como and as he walked into the room, he saw himself, a chuckling, dark-skinned southerner amidst a conclave of serious, fair-haired northern industrialists and walked right out. He had saved enough money to live for a year or so without working, making frequent visits to Paris, to gain strength and power, presumably, from the moonstruck great-granddaughter of Jules Verne. "But is very expensive. After five months, poof, is money all gone." For the next two months he incubated in a small room, giving himself up with total absorption to painting. "But is big problem. No can draw one line on the canvas." For the following seven months he worked in a restaurant, where he conceived the idea of going to Greece and opening his own establishment. "I have big dream," he explains, "but little money." With nothing to lose he approached an older friend, a wealthy notary in Bari with whom he had transacted business in his affluent days, and received a substantial sum of money as an outright gift to invest in his dream. Shortly afterwards he found himself in Lakka, negotiating with the Cappodistrias family for the licence and premises of his restaurant which led, some months later, to a court suit for default of payment. This was how he met Soula, who with sublime illogic was testifying against him, since she had not been paid by Cappodistrias (for whom she had formerly worked) on the pretext that Cappodistrias had not been paid in entirety by Luciano. Luciano cited the revalued drachma as the reason for his breach of contract. The issue has not yet been settled and probably never will, this being Greece. But Soula was charmed by Luciano's insouciance and humour and immediately, when court was adjourned, asked him for a job in his beleaguered restaurant. This was two years ago and the 'partnership' is flourishing though the relationship promises to remain partial and one-sided.

Luciano, despite his droll and casual attitude to life, his whimsical irreverence, has his tenebrous side as well. He keeps a loaded pistol in his drawer. "Is my freedom," he confides; "if one day I want to go away, is very simple. But I *love* life. Is not contradiction. Is because I love life I keep loaded gun in my cabinet."

Luciano tells me that salvaging his career as a restaurateur is only half his dream. The other is to buy a fifteen-meter yacht whose expense can be partially defrayed by chartering. I ask him if he knows Pierre-Paulo, an Italian acquaintance of mine two years ago in Gaios, a skipper by trade. "Yes," he smiles reluctantly, "I know. But is two kinds sailor. One love the sea. For other sea is profession. I am the first. Pierre-Paulo . . . ." The Greek sisters enter. Luciano switches on a cassette of traditional music. Magda does one of the erotic oriental dances the Turks left behind along with the coffee, the baclava, and a considerable portion of the *demotiki*. Luciano begins breaking plates on the floor. "Is okay. No wash dishes tonight."

I have grown to resent the olive trees. I never imagined this could happen — after all, the olive has been the source of life and one of the few roots of stability in Greece for a good part of recorded history. Moreover, it is not only a sacred tree but a magnificent tree as well, pushing into all kinds of fantastic shapes, bulging into great knurs and burls and bulbous configurations of gargoyle-and pumpkin-face, or twisting upon itself its veined and gnarled musculature as if shouldering the heavens. But I have grown to resent them with a resentment of mythological proportions and if I could have my way I would fell and lop every last one of them. For they are chiefly responsible for the marrow-jelling cold we suffer here, as their linked reticulations of leaves over whole square miles of landscape screen out the sunlight like a gigantic, never-folding parasol. Walking along the west side of the island where the olives are sparse and the sun strikes full on, we are forced to shed most of our clothes. Off goes the fur-lined jacket, the thick woollen sweater, the heavy shirt, and finally the t-shirt as well. We trek to Vassilatika or Ipapanti dripping with sweat. Returning to the house, we pile everything on again, plug in the electric heaters, and as the evening grows darker and damper, resort to our last line of defense, gloves and shawls as we sit at the supper table, and finally sleeping bags and blankets in the 'living room' for a bit of reading. We have no way of estimating accurately, but the temperature differential we experience on any given day must be in the region of 20 degrees Celsius or more. This is another factor contributing to the illusion of scale and magnitude on this microdot of an island where there are at least two and probably three climactic zones to be found in its one-and-a-half-mile width. In the same hour we move from the pleasant, amber warmth of early fall to a moist, rheumatic cold to the teeth-rattling gelidity of deep winter. The feeling we are sometimes left with at the end of the day is of having travelled at high speed in a short time over vast sections of the globe, though we have merely spent a leisurely afternoon walking to Vassilatika and back.

What I especially like about Luciano is the rare ability to regard his misfortunes and reversals as the material for comedy. When he narrates the series of misadventures of which his life mainly consists, he is frequently compelled to stop in a paroxysm of incredulous laughter. Speaking of his friend Lorenzo: "Lorenzo is crazy. I give him my car to take from Corfu to Italy. Spend all the money so leave car in customs at Brindisi. Two months car stay in customs. I must pay fifteen hundred dollars to take car out. No can pay so no have car anymore. Lorenzo is crazy." And he crumples in his chair at the Horiatis Pub, shaking his head and sneezing with laughter at the absurdity of it all. I ask him why he cultivates such friends. His response is typical. "Is only crazy people are interesting. The others poof like dead." He mentions as further confirmation his friend Luigi whom he hired as a pizza chef last summer. "Luigi is big problem. Nine o'clock and restaurant full. Luigi, he decide he must take douche. People wait and wait, but Luigi? He singing in douche upstairs." Another fit of uncontrollable laughter. I had met Luigi briefly at the end of September, at eleven o'clock at night in the Lakka parking lot as I was starting the car for home. Bleary-eyed, unshaven, a desperado if ever I saw one, he knocked frantically at the window to ask if I could transport a dog to Gaios, where an acquaintance was waiting with a boat to ferry the animal over to the coast of Albania. It seems the dog, a particular friend of his, had been teased and provoked by one of the local children and had responded by taking a chunk out of his tormentor's leg. The village was up in arms, literally; several men were presently searching for the animal, which Luigi had concealed in his house, with loaded shotguns. After some hesitation I decided to assist Luigi in his errand of mercy, but I had neglected to fill up the car for the last week and had only enough gas to drive to Gaios but not back to Lakka. The one filling station on the island was closed at this time of night and as we could not find a litre-drum of gas anywhere in Lakka, I had to beg off. Luciano informs me that Luigi managed the coup more or less successfully and is presently wintering with his dog in the Epirot mountains near Albania.

I notice that my spoken English is beginning to deteriorate alarmingly. A heavy dosage of Haralambos and Luciano over several months is enough to knock the bottom out of anyone's grammatical heritage. Alki reports that he has just washed yesterday's dishes and I automatically reply: "Is okay. Is good boy." This morning I had some errands to do in Gaios and decided to take Alki with me. "Come," I said, "we going Gaios for shoppings." This sentence flowed naturally and was not intended parodically. And Alki himself has been more than marginally influenced by Haralambos' speech habits. "Ees alright. No problem. Naatheeng," is his most frequent locution.

The Paxiots are incapable of getting along with one another. The internecine tensions might serve as a model of discord for the rest of this logomachic country. The population of the island hovers between two and two-and-a-half thousand, yet there are something like eighteen hundred telephones in operation, which boils down to about three or four per family. Why so many? The most plausible theory is that the Paxiots are in love with mechanical appliances: Japanese well-pumps, mini-calculators, television sets in abundance, cassette-players and ghetto-blasters, Yamaha motorbikes, Suzuki jeeps, blenders, washing machines, quartz watches, bidets and telephones. It is a perfect example of the medieval mind seduced by the proliferation of miracle. But there exists a second hypothesis to explain the inundation of telephones, which is equally cogent, namely, that several telephones per house enable family members to complain and inform on one another to the police with a mixed assurance of convenience and propriety. They hate one another with such ardour, such rancour and vituperative delight, that it is indistinguishable from love. The people from Gaios consider their compatriots in Lakka as a vulgar, unenlightened peasantry. The residents of Lakka conversely regard the Gaians as a tribe of inveterate misers and buccaneers. And a man from Boikatika dismissed a fellow Paxiot as "a stranger. He is from Fontana," which is less than a mile away.

Now the islanders wish to form a joint-stock company to purchase a large ferryboat to facilitate travel between Paxos, Corfu and the mainland. Such a venture is absolutely necessary, as the island is cut off three days a week from the major centres of trade and supply, and even scheduled travel is at the mercy of the weather considering the size of the *Kamelia* and the even smaller *Anna Maria*. But the *koinotita* of Gaios demands a fifty-one percent share of the projected company while the rest of the island, resenting so invidious a claim, is holding out for parity. The chances of acquiring a new and profitable ferry service are, in the most generous assessment of the issue, approximately nil. Though people toot their horns vociferously at one another on the road and embrace fervently in the cafeneions, the feeling of tension and uneasiness in the air is at times distressingly tangible. There are moments when I find myself *embarrassed* without knowing the precise reason at the instant or how to dispel the strain, the sense of subliminal anxiety that infects the atmosphere. Yet the Paxiots, I am convinced, would be a miserable and abject lot should the spectre of a transient harmony ever darken the horizon of their relationships with a winter of content.

Pocket calculators have become the new Cabieri of the Greek islands. Though these leprechaun-like divinities flourished only on Samothrace in pagan times, they have in their modern guise of mini-calculators achieved a pan-Hellenic diffusion and influence. No respectable shop-keeper on Paxos is to be found without this article of iconic reverence on the counter before him to perform its miracles of computation at his bidding. The simplest arith-metic operations are religiously transacted twice over as if the postulant derived a kind of sacred pleasure from his oracular consultations and a feeling of vicarious power from so effective and instantaneous a manipulation. A kilo of ground meat costs 500 drachmas. We bought a kilo and a half from Yanni the butcher this morning. He accordingly multiplied 500 by 1½, achieving the predestined result of 750 drachmas. He then cleared the tiny screen of his calculator and performed the operation a second time with a look of inexpressible satisfaction on his lined, dignified countenance as the identical number reappeared in red, digital print. Chaos had been staved off; the world admitted of continuity and duration and was guaranteed by miracle. The owner of the small stationery shop in Gaios retains a more sceptical attitude to the dominion of the transcendent. After totalling the appropriate items on his calculator and attaining the magical result, he invari-ably adds everything up again with pencil and paper as if verifying the diktats of the praeternatural. Most of the shopkeepers do it the other way around, the laborious operation of simple addition afterwards confirmed by the electronic Tom Thumb on the counter. The stationer remains an incorrigible heathen, prompted no doubt by the nature of his trade which requires him to affirm the predominance of writing materials over the shadowy realm of silicon phantasms. I think in this connection of the magisterial hand of the Pantocrator raised in benediction, fingers poised in the mystic sign. Today these same fingers would fall daintily, still arched, on the buttons of the minikin control panels of the myriad calculating devices flashing and coruscating beneath them.

Visiting Corfu

In most of the books on the Ionian islands and especially Corfu, Paxos receives only the most glancing and perfunctory of references, if it is mentioned at all. Its historical importance is negligible; its geographical position on the rump of Corfu is disconcertingly haemorrhoidal; mythologically it figures in only one brief allusion in Plutarch, albeit a significant one; economically, it is an appendage to the larger island to the north and a part of the same administrative nome; aesthetically (what the guidebooks call 'natural beauty'), it clearly cannot compete with the opulent splendours of Corfu; and architecturally, it is entirely undistinguished. Its status in the official accounts resembles approximately the void expression on the face of the American woman I met last night. I lived on Paxos? Where, she wished to know, was that?

In my imagination, however, the situation is precisely reversed. Paxos is the principal island of the Eptanisi and sometimes, in moments of lucidity or presumption, I am convinced it is the Ptolemaic centre of the whole wheeling cosmos as well. Corfu is merely an elaborate hoax, a smokescreen and stalking horse, under whose thick and distracting cover (to quote Thomas again) Paxos continues to work its sly dissimulations. When the tourists bubble and swarm over Corfu in the summer, they are really making their annual pilgrimage to Paxos. From the perspective I am taking, Corfu, with its pelican sunsets, its gold-dust beaches, the towering battlements of Mount Pantocrator, its intricate Venetian architecture, its lakes and plains and lush lemon-flecked and orange-lit vegetation, its gambling casino in the Achillion built by the melancholy Elizabeth of Austria, and the labyrinthine massiveness of the Old Castle dominating the wide bay of Garitsa is nothing other than Paxos itself. Fotis Lappas, in his runcible booklet on Corfu, dwells lovingly on "the traditional classic carriages" which offer "endless rides through beautiful places as long as the visitor can coordinate the rhythmic gallop of the horse with the beauty and musicality of the place so that he can be brought back to a romantic season away from the reality even for an instant enjoyment." This is exactly the global function of Paxos, which it exercises through the intervening media of these roseate and brocaded Corfus. In this way the modern appetite for beauty, peace and harmonious communion with nature is both stimulated and sated while remaining at the same time on the level of a collective hallucination, utterly devoid of substance. We abandon our unreal reality in favour of an all-too real unreality. This is called recreation, a word flavoured with the tumeric of irony as it paradoxically denies its component meaning, re-creation. Thus Corfu pursues its career as a flourishing and expanding colony of Paxos, which retains its mythological hegemony.

Corfu Itinerary

Arrived yesterday morning and put up at the Arkadion. Went to the Emboriki bank where, after an hour of shunting between wickets, desks and counters, managed to open an account. Afterwards walked along the Spianada and around to the Archeological Museum, only to find it closed. More desultory strolling. Stopped at the statue of Thomas Maitland, the infamous King Tom and first governor of the protectorate, all boarded up in its peristyle, lavishly disfigured with graffiti. On one pillar the word 'chronos' in thick, black crayon strokes. Approached by a portly androgyne of forty who wanted to know if I was alone, what hotel I was staying at, did I like Greece, and so on. I was fascinated by the molten gleam of spittle on a gold incisor. I shed him as politely as I could and explored the crumbling acres of the Old Castle, which is now used mainly as a kind of test track for motorbikes and scooters, one of the acoustic blights of modern Greece. Afterwards returned to the hotel, where I received a call from Luciano who is on his way to Italy. Arranged to meet at an obscure place called 'The Barley Stone' which, after some fruitless searching, I discovered was 'The Bar Liston.' Supper and conversation, chiefly about women. "I do not love the woman," Luciano insists, "I need the woman." Soon joined by a friend, Spiro, a marine engineer absolutely fluent in Italian, French, German and English. More talk about women, the insolubility of marriage, and the definition of courage. I proposed Ernest Becker's: 'Courage is the ability to live in a state of contradiction.' Luciano defined courage as the strength to live knowing that degradation is infinite: to live without pulling the trigger. Spiro proffered no definition of his own, but I should imagine if he had it would have been something like: the ability to translate other people's definitions in five different languages, without losing heart. Got very drunk on very little and staggered back to the hotel, bitten by the gadfly of lust for the wide-eyed, Junonian, big breasted American woman who had not heard of Paxos.

For an ephemeral moment this morning, ambling along one of the *kandounia* of the old town, I almost believed I was in Greece again. A sharp twang of bouzouki music pulsated in air and vanished among its own tremulous overtones and I was back in Hydra in '67, in Lesbos in '73, in Amorgos in '81, where people looked and acted as if they were 'Greek,' sending bottles of retsina careening around the tables, dancing their solitary meditative *zebekiko* or the linked intricacies of the buoyant circle dance, breathing dense basilisk-fumes of wine and garlic through cries of 'opa!' and the rhythmic hisses accompanying their steps, with their flaring and unreliable friendships, their impulsive promises soberly retracted in the *lendemain* light of amnesia and remorse, and their extravagant disdain of the material future. This was the 'Greece' I once knew, the archipelagian realm of the spontaneous gesture, shattered not by the Turk or the German but by solvency. The modern Greek is scarcely 'Greek' any longer, if one discounts the language and a few residual predispositions. These people remind me of home. They wear designer jeans, casanova lapels, punk haircuts that emphasize jug-handle ears from which small gold pendants twinkle. They drive Honda and Yamaha motorbikes at breakneck speed in unmufflered pandemonium through the mazy streets of their medieval towns. They scribble erotic graffiti on every available column, statue, stele, obelisk and peristyle. They listen to disco music incessantly, jerking their tall epicene frames in ghastly parody of their fathers' disciplined and laborious dances. Under the vaults of the Liston where their aristocratic predecessors enjoyed the daily promenade, they loiter in black, ruffled boots and leather costumes, consulting digital watches as if they had somewhere to go. What could their domestic lives possibly be like? Dorian Lambley, in his discussion of eighteenth century Cofiot social life, remarks that many people with pretensions to nobility or pre-eminence would dress the part in their obligatory appearances on the Liston while living mean and impoverished lives at home.[6] Is the same true of this punk generation that struts and caracoles in the porticos of the coffeehouses, all glitter and ostentation, retreating when the lamps are extinguished to hovels and tenements, *kalivia*, in the warren of the old town? Or are they the offspring of the kelp wave of tourist entrepreneurs lapping on the stones of Anenomylos and Kardaki? How disillusioned would the pages of the Grecophile historian, Ferdinand Gregorovius, who wrote toward the end of the last century, now read should he return from his presumably undefiled grave — Gregorovius who eulogized the Homeric characteristics of his beloved Greeks, "their divine endowments, their innate politeness, the grace, the behaviour, the democratic and social ideals . . . ."

"Politics," a young Serbian friend once said to me when I was in Belgrade many years ago, "is for old men." He belonged to a generation which tolerated Tito with benign indifference and spent its time and energy recording pop and disco from the short-wave radio in clandestine and parodically subversive nocturnal sessions. There is still an intellectual minority in Greece, affiliated with the universities, that believes in the efficacy of political ideas and gives its allegiance largely to the Left, but the overwhelming majority of the youth in a country which every day grows increasingly to resemble the coast of Spain and the south of France has corroborated the maxim of that Serbian 'revolutionary' and become part of a new generation of tinselled and beribboned epigones, shallow, derivative, and most of all, noisy. As Patrick Leigh Fermor wrote in

1966, with the prescience of a man whom love has not blinded to fact, "Greece is suffering its most dangerous invasion since the time of Xerxes. Bad money may drive out good, but good money, in this case, drives out everything." Tourism, of whose virus we are the inadvertent carriers, has taken Gresham's Law to its logical and inevitable extreme. Fermor stands mortified as he regards the vision which assembles its malignant shape before his eyes: "the shore is enlivened with fifty jukeboxes and a thousand transistor wirelesses. Each house is now an artistic bar, a boutique or a curio shop; new hotels tower and concrete villas multiply." Less than ten years later this same vision would find its cinematic equivalent in Cacoyannis' harrowing film, 'The Day That The Fish Came Out.' The moving finger, with its black crayon extension, writes *chronos*, and having writ, moves on to the next Ionic column.

The spirit of Corfu town is incarnate in a strange, composite figure out of the *commedia del' arte*, a woman of about sixty, under five feet tall, wearing a floppy red *mandilla* on a trapezoidal head, red and white striped legwarmers, particolored shorts, florescent sneakers, and a fluttering gonfalon of a shawl. Her eyebrows are entirely shorn and painted over in broad white arcs, her mouth daubed in oily blotches of deep carmine lifting over the top lip like a chevron or circumflex and extending along the jawline to the ear. Her cheekbones are chimney-smudged in black mascara. She carries a large empty shopping bag stitched together with patches of canvas and plastic and other unidentifiable fabrics. She is also crippled. When she begins to walk, she rises straight up in the air like a pogo stick, hovers briefly, then lunges forward and down like a human roller coaster except that the nadir of her trajectory is interrupted by a momentary yawing motion which reminds me of the *Kamelia* plunging into a trough. At this point, bent and contorted, her midget stature is even further reduced. One step at a time is her locomotive utmost. She pauses, stares directly ahead muttering inaudibly, and slowly disengaging the locked segments of her spinal column, prepares for the next complex series of kinetic ambulations, jerk-pause-lunge-yaw-pause, to compass a distance of perhaps a foot and a half, which is precisely the Greek way of doing things, maximal performance in the service of minimal results. All jink and whiffle and lollop and skew, somewhat like Pantagruel riding his hobby horse, "which he made to prance, leap, curvet, plunge, and rear at the same time," a farcical and harmless version of Solomos' 'Woman of Zakynthos,' with the 'small, misshapen body' and the breasts 'like tobacco pouches.'

Visited the Archeological Museum yesterday and the Collection of Asiatic Art this morning with, as Baedecker might say, very little profit. Simply couldn't work up the proper contemplative mood to appreciate the magnificent

Gorgon pediment which once decorated the west facade of the temple of Artemis, or the enamels and porcelains of the Asiatic trove. It would have been impossible in any case owing to the obtrusive presence of the watchmen. In the museum the man who has been assigned to dog my footsteps persisted in jingling his keys, *koumbaloi*-fashion, as energetically as he could. I found myself wishing the Gorgon on the pediment would petrify him with her sightless eyes. Everywhere the rusty clangour of the key-chain until I was driven out of the place and back to my room where I could examine the coloured illustrations I had bought in relative privacy. Same business this morning at the Asiatic Collection. My attendant suffered from a racking cigarette cough mingled with an explosive nose cold. From one wing to another I was accompanied by the sound of retching, sniffling, and reverberating sneezes along with a fluid spate of bronchial cursing. I adjourned to a small cafe to consult the booklet of illustrations but the television was blaring at full volume — the shrieks, grunts, and gravelly imprecations of a typical domestic comedy. Back to my room again where the traffic noises, comparatively speaking, diffuse the sweetness of Brahms.

During the last days and weeks I have experienced enormous difficulty in committing words to paper. It is as if my vocabulary has shrunk to the size of a Paxiot olive or a Corinthian currant. Words I have been long familiar with cut me dead as they pass along the vaults of the Liston for their evening stroll, so that I have begun to feel like a verbal outcast, a poor lexic mendicant. Giving birth to a single written perception involves me in agonies of frustration and ineptitude.

I suddenly recall the shopkeeper in Gaios, a small auburn-haired man with lips like a sharpened adze. I met him for the first time when I entered his shop to buy Hannah a trinket of some sort. He said nothing as I examined his wares, did not respond to questions, refused even to quote prices. When I left the shop I vowed never to return, so cold and truculent he seemed. Months later I discovered in conversation with friends that he was mute, and moreover, a man of consummate shrewdness who had amassed a comfortable nest-egg over the years, no mean feat in a country where volubility, rhetoric and gesture is the *sine qua non* of social life and commerce. As I myself live in Moungelatika (literally, as previously mentioned, 'the village of the mute'), I conceived a reluctant sense of identification with this man whom I had so grievously misconstrued. That psychic equation has never seemed more apt than at present, only I do not possess his vaunted shrewdness and enterprise or, for that matter, his legendary frugality. My hope is that, with luck and patience, *i megali ipomoni*, I too will manage to amass a fortune despite my pedestrian stammering.

If one wishes to experience the quintessence of the Greek sensibility, the best place to go is to a bank. As the rent is due any day now, I decided to drive in to Gaios this morning and cash a traveller's cheque. The first hurdle is the usual prolonged wait, like buying a ticket in an Indian railway station. The clerk was busy paying out a wad of thousand-drachma notes, a slow, fumbling, much-disrupted procedure since Greek tellers rarely count with a moistened index finger, like a bicycle sprocket propelling a chain, but shove the bills upward with blunt and spatulate thumb, like bitches muzzling puppies out of a crowded litter. Finally my turn came round, but as the bank on Paxos is also a hardware store, I had to wait for another lengthy interval while the teller helped collect the scattered contents of a bag of nails a customer had dropped on the floor. Back in his chair behind the cluttered counter, the clerk looked up at me inquiringly. I reiterated my intention to deposit a portion of a traveller's cheque in my account and retain the rest in cash. This necessitated a call to the head office in Corfu to establish the rate of exchange. The immediate problem, however, was to disentangle the receiver cord from the telephone wire, which slowly and inexorably developed into the thirteenth Herculean labour as the clerk doggedly wound, rewound, unwound, tugged, pushed, spliced, unknotted and eventually cleared the two wires from what had begun to seem inextricable confusion. The call was then placed but now the line was occupied. Another customer entered and engaged the clerk in an interminable search for a piece of weather-stripping. Then another try at the telephone, this time successful. But my trials were far from over. The rate of exchange for every currency in the world had to be duly jotted down into the fat, black ledger which is also used as an album for loose photographs and a repository for laundry-chits, and afterwards the entire bordereau of figures demanded verification. This operation accomplished, the clerk now proceeded to write out in triplicate the amount of my deposit, followed by a strenuous scrutiny of my ink-smudged bankbook. When all the figures had been tallied and recorded, added by hand and ratified by calculator, the papers shuffled, earmarked, and diapered up with a safety pin, O then, in an upsurge of relief and gratitude, I attempted to withdraw the sum in cash I needed for the rent. For the first time since I walked into the bank immemorial eons ago, the clerk manifested a twinge of impatience. Money? Impossible! He opened the drawer in his desk and revealed a bare, Mother Hubbard till. The last of the cash had been paid out, but a shipment of new money was expected from Corfu this very evening. However, as the bank is closed after 2:00 p.m. and as tomorrow is Christmas day and the day after everyone will be sleeping off the vapours, perhaps I could try again in three days time.

When I left the bank, the morning, so bright and full of promise, had petered out into a typical, rainy, disconsolate Paxiot afternoon. I remembered the Englishman I had met in this same bank three months ago who had cashed a Eurocheque in a Quonsat hut in the Nigerian bush in — he looked at his watch as if to underline the luminous and mythic nature of the transaction — fifteen seconds.

❖

Received a Christmas Eve visit from Areti and Yanni, armed with a box of honey-macaroons freshly baked by Agapi. We should have heeded Cato's apt warning, but inveterate innocents that we are, settled our neighbours as comfortably as possible on the banquette, served up glasses of mulled wine, and made a heroic attempt at conversation. I showed Yanni the new chess computer Karin had brought from Germany to enliven Alki's solitary hours. Yanni wanted to know how much it cost. That subject exhausted, Yanni next inquired into the comparative level of Canadian wages with respect to Greek, which led into a discussion on the price of bread, the size and weight of the loaf, and the nature of the ingredients. There followed a longish pause in which we busied ourselves with all sorts of inane activity to give the impression of happy, unself-conscious bustle. Yanni next wished to know what a Nissan pick-up truck cost in Canada. Much intense calculation to arrive at the correct sum in Greek currency. The conversation guttered and went out. Yanni and Areti then proceeded to sit like hieratic figures painted on a wooden iconostasis and to stare fixedly at Karin as she wrapped presents and fluted out the ribbons in loops and petals with the cap of a ballpoint. After a time Yanni turned his stern, pragmatic attention to our new petrolgaz heater: how much, he inquired gravely, did it cost? There passed another half hour of increasing nervous debility and frantic efforts at doing nothing in particular, in which Karin's ribbon-petals began to droop alarmingly, Alki challenged Mephisto the computer to a game on level 6, and I grinned benevolently on all till my cheeks began to hurt. An hour passed and then another, broken only by Mephisto's urgent beeps, reiterations of *kalo kalo* to the replenished glasses of mulled wine, and Rocky's rain-muffled barking in the yard. Rocky! A new subject of conversation energetically hurled itself at the front door. How much, I asked Yanni, did Rocky cost? Finally, at around midnight, our guests rose and prepared to leave, Areti commenting on the cabriole swirls of the bench frame and Yanni praising the humble arborite table beside the frigidaire. When they had gone, we discovered we were all profoundly drunk on immense quantities of mulled wine. When we tried to speak our syllables staggered and fell and I had a visual impression of words lying in a sodden heap on the table beside the box of macaroons.

I still cannot fathom what our neighbours were after. An hour would have made a pleasant and sociable visit, but three hours of cataleptic gazing and sporadic talk merely snapped the bonds of hospitality and turned an encounter into an ordeal. Were we objects of anthropological wonder to them? Why, for that matter, did Haralambos, after a five hour meal in which he was regally served and entertained, go off in a huff of estrangement which has lasted for a quarter of a year? And why did Mitzo one morning in Alonissos invite us for that same evening to a feast of grilled lamb and when we appeared with several *gallonis* of wine at the stated time, regard us with an expression of barely suppressed bewilderment? There was no misunderstanding, the arrangements had been emphatically clear and thrice-affirmed, but in the twelve hour interval between the intention and its consummation, an entire cosmogony of revery, practical activity, and evolutionary amnesia had slowly and ineluctably transpired.

I have been reading Fermor's *Mani* which, although distinctly inferior to his subsequent *Roumeli*, is adorned by a flush, plutocratic style and a deep and intimate knowledge of the Greek people, their history, art, religion, and the palette of assumptions and premises with which they paint their many-hued, iconographic picture of the world. With the possible exception of Robert Byron, there is no matching Fermor in the annals of twentieth century travel writing, and especially writing about Greece. Durrell is too precious and rococo, too *Durrellian*, to render an accurate depiction of Greek history and psychology. Miller is a volcano of poetic eruptions and the lava-flow of his rhetoric, astonishing in itself, hardens and conceals the outlines of his nominal subject. Fermor has his weaknesses, too. Whereas *Roumeli* is a mature, balanced, profoundly informed and ever-fascinating account of his wanderings among the crags and massifs of the Greek sensibility, *Mani* is in many places disingenuously ornamental and amblyotic with unexamined love. The Greeks, for all the narrowing of perspectives over the centuries, the invasions and occupations, the derivations of speech and custom from other peoples, are nevertheless regarded as the *ne plus ultra* of courage, sensitivity and creative effulgence. "I think that the restless, dispersed and unharnessable but indestructible Greek genius, released at last, will produce something which will astonish and enrich the world again beyond all our imagination," the scholar-gypsy avers.

Fermor's opinions and convictions are to be respected as those of a man who has fought in this country as a guerilla leader, has crossed the entire length and breadth of its rugged surface many times, speaks the language with enviable fluency, and has eventually settled down here, much decorated and admired. Moreover, he has mastered all the available literature on the subject of Greece and is familiar with its poets, novelists and academicians. This makes him the reigning English-speaking authority on the history and psychology of the Greek people. Nevertheless, he is as fallible as the rest of us, at least on occasion, and in this particular book (unlike the later one) he has succumbed to the strabismal occlusions of excessive love. His analysis of Greek reality and character trembles perilously on the edge of uncritical adoration, as if he were writing more out of a sense of blood-kinship and clan-solidarity than from the passion for lucidity and scholarly proportion which valorizes the wonderful *Roumeli*. The unfiltered reverence of the earlier book underwent a sea-change into a spry and ironic and appreciative sense of amusement, and amusement is always more to be trusted than reverence. But in *Mani* his appraisal of Greek manners, customs and psychology borders on infatuation and idolatry, a perfect example of the heart even in its Pascalian severities clouding the arduous discernments of the intellect. For the contemporary Greek can by no means sustain the weight of homage and veneration which Fermor heaps indiscriminately upon his demythologized shoulders and must inevitably collapse under the burden of so much borrowed glory.

On Rereading *The Colossus of Maroussi*

The first time I visited Greece in the winter of 1967 I knew almost nothing about the country except what I had gleaned from the novels of Kazantzakis, the anecdotes of the singer-poet Leonard Cohen who had bought a house on the island of Hydra, and a passage from Henry Miller's *Colossus* reprinted in a selection of his voluminous writings. This passage seemed almost providential in that it treated of his arrival in the straits of Poros through which I would have to pass in order to reach my destination in Hydra. Prompted by Miller's vivid and exuberant description of these uterine straits and the hanging-garden atmosphere of the town, I eagerly awaited the revelation of Simiramian beauty as the ship rounded the headland. "Suddenly the land converges on all sides and the boat is squeezed into a narrow strait from which there seems to be no egress," writes Miller. I craned about desperately trying to confirm this impression but all I could see, about half a mile across, was the little town of Galatea on the Peloponnesian mainland. Miller continues: "The men and women of Poros are hanging out of the windows, just above your head. You pull in right under their friendly nostrils. . . . The beards hanging down over your scalp from the inhabitants suspended above you . . . envelop and entrance you." Looking up I saw nothing but the fuming smokestack, the kippered rigging and the snapping blue and white flag. The balcony-loungers who so impacted on Miller's sense of raw, cardiac propinquity could be clearly discerned with the aid of a pair of binoculars. The town

163

rose up and away from the port on twin hills that impart both a sense of softness and distance to the scene. The port itself was like almost any other island harbour, neither closer nor farther from the side of the docking boat. It was then, at that synoptic moment of recognition and disappointment, that I began to distrust Henry Miller in particular and literature in general, or to put it differently, began to understand that the actual subject of poetry and fiction was inevitably the author's own sensibility and that the world being described existed mainly for the sake of its mythopoeic refraction. The naive reader, which is what I was at the time, invariably mistakes ostensibility for reality but for years I considered Miller an arrant and egregious liar.

Miller wrote at the outset of the Second War when Greece was a very different country from what it is today. Miller's experience sailing through the isthmus was tantamount to a rebirth: "To sail slowly through the straits of Poros is to recapture the joy of passing through the neck of the womb." What revived his partially jaded and exhausted imagination too many years in France was "the palpitant breath of friendship, sympathy, guidance . . . until you are blown out like a star fulfilled and your heart with its molten smithereens is scattered far and wide." It was in these same straits a year ago that Antonio, an Italian charter skipper whom I met at Luciano's restaurant a few weeks back, ran aground on a sandbar. He hailed one of the myriad *varcas* that taxi between Poros and Galatea to tug on the hawser and haul him off the bank, which would have taken perhaps a half minute at most. The *varca*-captain was more than willing to offer assistance, provided Antonio was equally willing to pay the thousand drachmas required for the service. Antonio, shocked, then disgusted at this flagrant breach of marine etiquette, refused. Another *varca* pulled alongside and its pilot offered to perform the task for the more reasonable sum of eight hundred drachmas. Soon the yacht was surrounded by a flotilla of small boats and the air filled with prices, exhortations, discounts, pleas, penultimate offers and final comminations. As time passed, the prices started to go up, the remaining *varcas* churning like piranhas around their prey. To his great relief, Antonio succeeded in freeing the yacht under its own power, but he himself is now stuck on the private sandbar of distrust and antipathy with regard to the country that Henry Miller considers the embodiment of friendship and sympathy and Fermor extols as the *fons et origo* of uncalculating fellow-feeling and spiritual largesse.

What many writers seem to forget, especially those with the gift of unstinted eloquence and promethean vitality, is that in literature one must tell the truth, not only about oneself but about the world as well. The world is not to be used merely as a springboard or trampoline to propel one as high as possible into the prismatic and aerial regions of one's own personality. The world is also to be respected, that is, to be rendered candidly as what it is before it has been smelted down and molded anew in the smithy of a generous if overheated imagination; otherwise the residue of literature is really nothing but a small, precious bibelot perched belletristically atop the enormous slag-heap of reality at its most disappointing, since one has come to demand more than the world can be fairly expected to give. Had I not read Miller's effluvious account of Poros, I would have responded freshly and with unblemished joy when I entered this identical harbour. As it was I saw no beards I could reach up and pull like bell-cords to signal my jubilant, authorial arrival.

Why am I so fond of this infernal, backward, self-destructive country? The sea is now medusa-infested as if it had become the junk heap of a discredited mythology. The islands, with a few doughty exceptions like Kastellorizo and Kassos, are scummed over with the effluence of modern tourism. The nature of the people, broadly speaking, does not correspond to the glowing and polychromatic character given it by the writers I have been discussing, whether hacks like Peter Bull or acknowledged masters like Patrick Leigh Fermor. My own experience of Greece, since I first arrived on Hydra in February of 1967 to the present moment, New Year 1985 in Paxos, has been persistently ambivalent, dyadic and fluctuating. My relationship to this country has not been superficial, except inevitably at the beginning, never entrepreneurial, and rarely ventriloquial, as is distressingly the case with Henry Miller.[7] Maybe this is the problem. I could never remain the impervious tourist nor was I "privileged" to undergo the baptism of blood during the bitter fighting of the Occupation in order to achieve that degree of imaginative emigration which would have made me partially Greek.

But in this way I may have been spared both the myopia of close-up intimacy and the blindness of casual indifference. Consequently I could never love Greece with the passionate enthusiasm of the compatriot nor ignore it (or misconstrue it) with the egoistic introversion of the mere hedonist. All this explains to some extent the volatility, the stop-and-go aspect of my relationship to the people, and the fugitive exaltations I sometimes feel for the country in general.

I have left Greece forever, never to return, at least a dozen times. After being cheated, abused, exploited, lied to, defamed and betrayed by landlords, shopkeepers, hoteliers, taxi drivers, acquaintances and friends an incalculable number of times, I came to the reluctant conclusion that there was something labile and quixotic in the Greek temperament which the foreigner might neglect only at his peril. Yet I have had so many bizarre experiences here that, mixed up with my scepticism and misgivings, there is always that feeling of grudging affection born of amusement and incredulity.

Where else but in Greece, Lesbos, to be precise, in the summer of 1975, when Greece and Turkey were preparing for war over the issue of oil-drilling rights in the North Aegean, could I be awakened early in the morning by the cicada-like scraping of many shovels, and open my kitchen door on a company of soldiers burying landmines in my front garden? For two hours I argued vehemently with the lieutenant in charge of the operation, citing the insubordinate fact that I had three children who would be immediately blown to bits the moment they stepped off the kitchen stoop. The lieutenant contended that as the Turkish mainland was only five kilometres directly across the straits from the coast where my house was situated, this would make a favourable spot for an amphibious invasion. Finally he consented to move the mines into the back yard with slender lines of white thread marking the path to the outhouse and the red, triangular, tin *narkai* signs imprinting a sinister warning on the air. To add to the lunacy, when the Turkish sabre jets started buzzing our house (the Greek army having encamped in the neighbouring field), and I wrote to the Canadian embassy in Athens to inquire into its evacuation plans, I received a postcard-size Canadian flag with instructions to fly it from the roof in order to deter hostile jets in the event of strafing and bombing. The flag was barely visible from ground level; moreover, passers-by thought it was a fragment of bunting left over from a festival or party. Finally I could never figure out what the mines were doing there in the first place. They could never aspire to be more than a minor irritation to an army invading in force (apart from the likelihood, amounting to near certainty, of the soldiers forgetting to remove the warning signs and the white thread marking the corridors.) The only effective deterrent to an invasion by sea would have been a chain-mail net of sea-mines tightly corsetting the island but this would have meant scaring off the tourists for whom swimming was the significant attraction. As it was, those tourists who remained avoided the mined terrain — the major beaches and hotel property were free of such impedimenta — and the island maintained its fighting posture while attempting to preserve its tourist-generated prosperity. But a Turkish attack would have rolled over this thin zodiac of landmines in a matter of fifteen minutes. The crisis eventually blew over and the Greek population of Lesbos (according to local reports) counted twelve dead, including a child and an elderly lady collecting *chorta* who plucked a flower and detonated a mine. I keep very few postcards and snapshots to remind me of Greece during the long Canadian winters, but I cherish the two *narkai* signs I pilfered one night when, slightly intoxicated, I slipped past the sleeping sentry, tiptoed through a field of metal tulips with a wandering flashlight, and made off with this mnemonic plunder.

Or when I think of "Greece" I ply back to the summer and fall of 1969 in Crete, where I had moved from Hydra with my newly pregnant wife to take up a post as an English teacher for the Hambakis Institute in Hania, the capital. At that time Greece was in a state of renewed political turmoil. Unknown to the foreign press, the Greek navy, based chiefly in Crete with its NATO installation at Suda Bay, was contemplating an act of secession. Accordingly, the military junta had flooded the island and especially Xania, a mere two or three miles west of Suda, with its Security myrmidons, the hated *Asfalia* (a popular estimate had it that one out of every four people in the capital was a security agent). I was in my mid-twenties and still considered myself proof to the threat of history and politics, and so made a complete fool of myself every evening in the tavernas spouting anti-junta sentiments. After a while I began to notice two men in brown suits and dark glasses sitting at the next table in every taverna or cafeneion I frequented. A short time after that, I became aware that wherever I went, a big white Chevrolet was sure to go. It followed me through the narrow streets of the New Town, waited at the curb whenever my wife and I went shopping in the Agora, parked across the street from the restaurant we usually ate at, stopped at the corner with engine idling when I visited the post office. Soon an agent was stationed beneath the chestnut tree in the courtyard of our house where he would often remain overnight.

At last I was summoned by Mr. Nikakis, my Superior at the school, four days before the start of the new semester. I sat before his desk while he coughed and fidgeted and turned the pages of a thick dossier which, he informed me, had been compiled by the police and contained the record of my activities during the last month. He had no choice but to dismiss me as of that instant, considering that I had comported myself in a manner unbefitting a professional. Thereupon he shut the folder and closed the subject. I found myself on the street without a job, without a drachma to my name, and with my wife expecting our first child in a couple of weeks. Then I remembered that my visa was about to expire and, given the current state of affairs, I could not look forward to anything so mild and idyllic as simple deportation.

During that time we had become friendly with a young sailor named Alexis who often visited the house for supper and accompanied us on our travels around the island. I had also lent him a considerable sum of money which he was always on the point of repaying. His father, he assured us, was an admiral in the Greek navy and a substantial allowance cheque would be arriving as soon as Alexis senior returned from naval maneuvers somewhere in the western Mediterranean. When Alexis heard of my misfortunes, he brightened up at once: he had just had a telephone call from his father in Malta. Nothing could be simpler than to get in touch with the admiral and have him communicate with the central police station in Hania where I was daily expected to regulate my visa papers. Two days later Alexis appeared for breakfast — our larder was now being stocked on credit from the greengrocer in Theotokopoulou Street — buoyant and unabashed. All was well. He had spoken with his father who had immediately telexed the police station commanding that I be given the red carpet treatment. As the rendezvous had been set for ten o'clock this very morning, I could hardly believe my good fortune. Brimming with confidence, I sauntered at my most leisurely through the town and entered the station half an hour late for the appointment. Without knocking I walked directly into the small glassed-in 'Visa and Passport' office, reclined in a castored chair, put my feet up on the rim of the wastepaper basket, and smiled benignly. The Visa officer seemed too surprised to say anything, but merely regarded me with an air of total stupefaction. I produced a pack of cigarettes and offered him one, which he accepted mechanically, but I made no movement to follow up with a light. After a moment of obvious perplexity, he reached into his pocket, took out a box of matches, and leaned across to light my cigarette. I don't know what got in to me, but smarting from my humiliation at the hands of Mr. Nikakis and basking in the protection of a high-ranking naval officer, I behaved with unforgivable insolence, making disparaging comments on the collective acumen of the Security Police and its tendency to melodramatic absurdities, and ranging pejoratively over the topic of Greek politics in general. After a quarter of an hour I made a show of consulting my watch and gave the official to understand that I was shortly expected for lunch and would appreciate getting on with the business at hand, whereupon I dropped my passport on the desk and leaned back in the chair, blowing smoke-rings at the languidly-rotating punka. In two minutes the job was done and I was ambling homeward, feeling privileged and immune. A few weeks later, as we prepared to leave the island with an infant son (and an airplane ticket arranged by my father-in-law), I discovered from another friend that Alexis' father had died many years before and that his mother worked as a waitress in a restaurant in Athens. How I had contrived to renew my visa, considering that I was blatantly *non grata*, unemployable, living on borrowed money, and in imminent danger of detention — pluming myself on the guardianship of a non-existent authority, was beyond all rational comprehension.

But then, this was Greece, where reason conceded to drama, calibration to bravura, and matter to performance. This was also fifteen years ago, and I am afraid that the habit of pettifogging calculation and furtive hoarding so prominent today has largely banished the redemptive flamboyance that once made Greece the compelling and magnetic and seductive *idea* which has haunted the western imagination for centuries. For Greece is no longer "Greece": it is a small, Balkan economy feeding parasiti- cally off remittance cheques from America and Australia and shoring up its currency through rampant tourism. And the people who endured and survived invasion after inva- sion, who remained intact after hundreds of years of ruthless Turkish domination, who ran into the fields with pitchforks and awaited the German paratroopers, are succumbing daily to the petty, rapacious, accounting spirit of the modern world. The young are a different breed entirely from their klephtic ancestors. They have little of the generosity, courage and grandeur of soul one reads about or even dimly recollects. Their leisure hours are filled with television programs, scooter races and soccer games, and their professional lives are devoted with unswerving attention to the amassing of money and the accumulation of material goods. They are in love with the products of a foreign technology which they have inducted, like the rest of us, into the service of a banausic and insipid conception of life. The beautiful old dances are slowly dying out and in their place one finds the electrocuted frog-spasms of the increasingly popular *s'ake*. The disco revolution is in full swing in the Thesprotian mountains, the Outer Cyclades, the Northern Sporades, Chalkidiki and the Seven Islands. Beside the temple of Apollo in the port of Naxos, near the sacred plot of ground from which vine-wreathed Dionysus raised the abandoned Ariadne, a garish new discotheque built into the cliffside spews out its mindless cacophony. Without a shot being fired, Greece has fallen to the infidel. And this time, I am convinced,

173

because the conquest is actively desired and collaboration is ardent and ubiquitous, the damage is irreparable. What we mean by "Greece," despite its fabled resilience, is irremediably lost in the pleasures of a feckless and insubstantial generation.

✛

Among the many Greek cookbooks that have begun to saturate an oleaginous market in recent years, one of the most notable (as Karin assures me) is Rena Salaman's *Greek Food* (Fontana, 1983). Recipe collections are not part of my standard reading fare but this one interests me partly for thematic reasons and partly because I remember Mrs. Salaman from our Alonissos days. In fact, it was her house we rented sight unseen in the summer of 1977, our first on the island.

As we had made all the arrangements by letter, the inevitable omissions of detail should have been expected. I assumed I was to bring my family to a Greek village more or less like any other: clutter, noise, children, and the basic necessities. I knew there had been an earthquake on the island twenty years before but had no inkling of the extent of the devastation. The letter, concerned mainly with specifications of domestic detail and the *gemütlich* quality of village life, had left the larger picture somewhat blank.

The brute reality proved somewhat different from the bright epistolary image we had treasured. We docked in June in the port of Patatiri, one of the ugliest island towns we had ever seen, disfigured by too much of that raw, instant, concrete architecture to be decently absorbed and hidden away. We left immediately for the village on the mountain several kilometres distant, eager to settle in and begin life in our new surroundings. On the way up I asked our driver how may families lived in the *choryo*. "About six," he replied. I thought I had misunderstood. "You mean sixty," I corrected. "No, six, as I said."

We stopped by the dusty cenotaph in the carpark at the base of the village and looked about us. We could not believe our eyes. The devastation seemed almost total, tumbling ruins everywhere, shattered walls, collapsed roofs, gaping holes, bushes of thorn and prickly pear shoving and jabbing like Roman cesti in our faces, and a vast, pervading silence that seemed almost praeternatural until it was torn by the melancholy bleating of a distant goat. We were in a state of collective shock as, led by our driver, we stumbled over broken steps and dislodged stones to the house on the lee side of the mountain. "How many families used to live here before the earthquake?" I asked. "Three hundred." "Where are the remaining six?" I wanted to know. "There is one next door," he pointed to the house across the skewered cobbles, "but they are not in now. The others . . . ." He indicated with a vague sweep of the hand the tilted panorama of the lower village which lay before us like a monstrous jawbone studded with loose decaying teeth. The children had started to cry as the truth dawned on them and the silence closed in with the gathering twilight.

That was how our first, inauspicious and most difficult summer on the island began. The loneliness turned out to be the least of our problems. The children soon learned how to amuse themselves constructing bottle-cap villages and playing hide-and-seek in the ruins, and in the ensuing months a few people drifted through so that Karin and I enjoyed occasional company. The immediate dilemma was shopping. The village was a necropolis and provided nothing except a few leathery eggs, and as there was no public transportation to be had (three years later a taxi materialized and a year after that, a bus) we had to haul everything up from Patatiri by foot. We became our own pack animals. But the gravest problem was the lack of water. The house had no built-in sterno to collect the winter rains, an absolute necessity on this island, and the tap-water pumped up from the port trickled into our pipes once a week when it came at all for a period of ten or fifteen minutes. We would stand sentinel by the kitchen sink waiting for the gurgling and whistling sound that announced the long-awaited advent, and fill every bucket, bottle, jug, mug and glass we could find, working silently and frantically until the last drop hung disconsolately from the faucet and the hissing and sucking of the empty pipes announced another week of drought. The water we managed to coax and plead out of the tap rarely lasted for more than two days, and for the rest of the week I would have to lug a huge *bidoni* of 'borrowed' water from a German neighbour who had bought and restored one of the ruins and added a sterno (he was the first of the Biedermeier wave that would swamp the village in the coming years) or, since our benefactor was only there for a short time, drag buckets of water up to the house from a deserted sterno at the bottom of the cobbled path. The results of this ill-fated source I detailed earlier in these pages.

But the island itself partly made up for the difficulties: green, herb-scented, ruggedly beautiful, plummeting views and dappled seascapes, and in those early years, the sea clean and invigorating, providing us with the best swimming and diving we have ever enjoyed in Greece until, that is, a tidal wave of jellyfish appeared on the horizon and tightened like a vast colloidal net around the island. Many years later we still bear some of the nematocyst burn-marks on our skin.)

Drawn by the beauty of the island and by the emotional investment we had made, we returned, but took care to rent another house, considerably larger and equipped with the indispensable sterno, which happened to overlook the Salaman cottage. One morning, two years after the initial misadventure, the Salaman family arrived. The village had filled out, approximately fifty or sixty houses had been purchased and restored, two cafeneions were now open, and the taps functioned twice a week, although with occasional lapses. The water shortage was no longer as critical as it had been in the first year. We watched from our balcony as the Salamans moved in amid considerable bustle and neighbourly ceremony, swept out the house, unpacked their luggage, and fussed endlessly over two small white-frocked children who ran in and out and threatened to fall off the low-railed terrace. "What will they do for water?" Karin asked. The answer to that question came several hours later as the Salamans repacked their belongings, rounded up the children, and moved precipitously out, obviously down to Patatiri. The following day two workmen arrived, and during the next few days a drum-sterno was mounted and affixed to the roof. After it was filled, the Salamans reappeared.

It would be ridiculous to subject a cookbook with no pretensions to literary sufficiency to a prolonged and rigorous critical analysis. Let the recipes be good and the writing intelligible — one could not fairly expect more. If a national cookbook places its material in a cultural perspective, treating food and its preparations as a tangible expression of customs, traditions, relationships, that is, of a particular attitude to man and the world, it is also performing one of the essential functions of its medium. After all, for Lévi-Strauss food preparation is a primary anthropological category, and for Roland Barthes, magazines treating food and its display are eminently suited for semeiotic exegesis, revealing the basic presuppositions of the social classes to which they appeal.

One does not have to be a literary specialist to respond gratefully to a clear and limpid style, which impresses me as somewhat more than a mere garnishing or an aesthetic presentation of ingredients. Joyce Stubbs, for example, in her *The Home Book of Greek Cookery* (Faber, 1963) writes lucidly, crisply and unpretentiously. There is a persistent temptation to anecdotal bias in cookbooks served up with a *parti pris* or a sense of mission, prerogative and authority. Mrs. Stubbs, however, presents the reader with the prefatory reminiscence and leaves it at that; the rest of her commendable introduction is neatly arranged on a bed of historical exposition. A touch of wry humour flavours her aperitive preamble as well and places the reader in an appropriate frame of mind, informed, entertained, relaxed, to get on with the serious business of cooking well and authentically. There is no beating of the cultural drum, no rhetoric of salvation, no mystique of personal election, which are the condign and besetting vices of national cookbooks, often prepared by those who tend to regard themselves as custodians of cultural values or exponents of cultural purity. If, hypothetically, there were room for only one Greek cookbook on the shelf, the Stubbs' "cookery," for the reasons suggested above as well as for the excellence of the recipes, would probably be our choice. Karin considers it the "basic" cookbook, the one which provides the foundations on which to build, which is a trifle ironic when one considers that Mrs. Stubbs is not Greek (and what is even worse from the point of view of cuisine, she is English). In one sense her non-Greekness may be an advantage, as the book is free of the peril of creeping chauvinism that often mars the presumably more authentic compendia. As for her being English: *mirabile dictu*. (The same for Jane Grigson and Elizabeth David.)

Cooking the Greek Way, by Anne Theoharous (Magnum 1979, Methuen 1983) does not occupy a prominent niche in our culinary library. The recipes are there in minute and circumstantial detail but the tone is that of an entrepreneurial middleman writing largely for an expatriate audience equipped with all the latest gadgets and the preconceptions to match. Results are often "out of this world." American friends, returning from a Greek visit back to their home in Connecticut, construct "a permanent, electrically rotating spit," which is activated on Easter weekend when "we celebrate . . . all over again in the tradition of a very small Greek village." I tend to boggle at such readily exportable 'authenticity.' In comparison, *The Best Book of Greek Cookery* by Chrissa Paradissis (Efstathiadis, Athens, 1971) seems preferable. There is a plain, straightforward, uncluttered account of Greek cuisine. Attempts at stylistic embellishment are kept to a minimum and one is not offended by that peculiar ornamentation or embroidery of the sensibility of which cookbooks form such a natural vehicle. A lengthy introduction, written in transliterated English, furnishes a wealth of historical data to establish the independence of Greek cuisine from its Roman, Turkish and Italian tributaries. The voice of personal exultance is refreshingly absent; instead the reader senses a legitimate pride in cultural accomplishment and originality. The recipes are then presented with a minimum of rodomontade. One gets exactly what one needs.

Rena Salaman's cookbook, *qua* cookbook, merits serious and respectful attention, especially as it collects a number of rare or unusual recipes with which to vary one's cuisine. There is a touch of the exotic, the cryptic, the elusive, the refined, the subtle, all attesting to culinary erudition of a high order. Stubbs for the basics and Salaman for the elaborations would make an appropriate tandem.

But Mrs. Salaman's book interests me for quite other reasons, that is, for reasons of tone, style and attitude, which do not properly pertain to a cookbook as such but nevertheless tend abundantly to illustrate the central thesis of my own cultural affidavit. For *Greek Food* is an Arcadian text, an excursus in imaginative pastoral. I discount the puerilism of the style — for example, the dinning repetition of "So" (doubtlessly the Greek 'lipon') and the insistent reiteration of "a lot," "quite a lot," and "a lot of," which reminds me of the student termpapers I grade for a living — in order to concentrate on modal imponderables. Mrs. Salaman appears to be doing two things apart from purveying recipes. First, she is preserving a cultural heritage of which she gives the distinct impression of being its anointed recipient or chosen vessel. Greekness is not only stressed but glorified, magnified, at the cost of a certain tangential distortion. For example, it seems evident that Mrs. Salaman is not overly fond of Germans. A German neighbour on sampling a particular dish "got terribly impressed and overenthusiastic." There are frequent references to the "long German occupation" and the excessive suffering it caused, but no indication of the Greek dictatorship of 1936, of the fact that Greek neutrality had been reaffirmed in 1939, that Greece did not enter the war until it was itself attacked, and, more to the point, there is only one brief citation with regard to the period of the civil war which was just as vicious and bloody, perhaps, as the Occupation.. But this unpalatable truth must be omitted or diluted in accounts of the recent past that wish to establish the inviolability, the grandeur and uniqueness of the Greek nation.

Collaterally, the author is engaging in the dialectics of self-invention and self-election. The tone is patrician throughout. The attitude is one of intensive ego-sanction and cathartic purity. And the psychic impetus which powers the whole is the need to construct a congenial, proprietary fiction in which a privileged self, somehow vestal, incorruptible and pious, moves in an ambience of gracious bestowals, exemplary friendships, an adoring family (as in the pleonastic introduction: "For my mother / and for Graeme and / our lovely daughters, / Alexandria and Sophia"), splendid and immaculate landscapes, nourishing reminiscences, and effortless access to the gastronomically delphic. All is blissful and hieratically ordered. The disturbing element, like the Athenian "mafioso" who appears on the scene, is reduced to the status of anecdotal divertissement. As with Peter Bull, I feel once again that I am in the Hundred Acre Wood, or that I have been permitted a precious glimpse into the lacustrine splendour of Neverland.

For the world Mrs. Salaman evokes is a world I have never yet been privileged to find or enjoy. Her 'Alonissos,' which my five year old boy at the time called "a loony's house" and which I thought of as "a lonely house," is generally referred to in locutions such as "on the island" (the iteration of the definite article suggesting its specialness, as we say "at the house," the "the" accentuating the missing possessive), or "in our village" or "in our village on the island," although Mrs. Salaman as the book informs us was born and bred in Athens and now lives in London. Friends and acquaintances are presented in the best possible light, neatly expurgated, as if in epitaph; in fact, they resemble the foodstuffs Mrs. Salaman had observed in the Xania market in Crete: "the most beautiful collection of vegetables I have ever seen; perfect specimens of an almost utopian dream." Festivities are lucullan; locations are expertly manicured. Through it all Mrs. Salaman perambulates, dispensing grace, collecting recipes, welcoming friends, serving up Edenic reminiscences, fostering all that is good in life, building up a mythology of self and place that is ineluctably Arcadian. It is almost irresistible and almost complete in itself, except for one omission: reality.

Alonissos, the *locus amoenis*, is also Paxos. It is an island whose inhabitants are not only gentle and hospitable, as Mrs. Salaman observes, but shrewd, hard and rapacious. One of my Alonissos informants disclosed that before the Queen arrived to inspect the damage left by the earthquake, many of the villagers put the finishing touches to the disaster, knocking down walls and pulling down roofs, to impress the royal visitor with the degree of their plight. The ploy apparently worked and a state-subsidized village, the Nea Chora, was erected on the fringes of Patatiri — a dun-coloured emplacement of concrete pillboxes of which the best that can be said is that it makes Patatiri look like a model village in comparison, but which the beneficiaries did not object to. I have no way of verifying whether this allegation is mere rumour and defamation or is piquantly close to the truth: after five summers "on the island" I tend to suspect the latter. (Though in Greece, as I have been at pains to point out, there is no clear line between the veridical and the apocryphal. I am reminded in this connection of Italo Svevo's character, the lovable Zeno, for whom a story began to be true the moment it became impossible to tell it differently.)

When the tourist earthquake struck in 1978 the village that Mrs. Salaman immortalizes, transforming nostalgia into fact, disappeared almost entirely. As more and more tavernas and cafeneions opened their doors, the pervading hum of the electric generator banished the natural harmony of quiet and birdsong from the summer evenings. And as more and more foreign families bought up the ruins and proceeded to renovate them, the island took on a distressingly schizophrenic character with Greek being spoken in Patatiri and German, English and French in the village of Alonissos itself. Then the village split into two factions, one contending for the development of electric facilities and the other striving to keep it kerosene-lit. Tempers rose and resident foreigners cut one another dead in the streets. One lady, a presbyter of the foreign colony, took to wearing the authentic island costume (dying out with its original weavers), organizing refuse clean-ups which left the village choking in a pall of dust, and presiding over the gossip klatches. After a six month reign of terror she was spirited away by a long-absent husband and placed in a European asylum where she gradually recovered her modesty. Then the village united temporarily in a paroxysm of collective indignation against another foreigner who had built a new house on a knoll outside the village, thereby obscuring a segment of the original, unblemished view. Meanwhile prices rose steeply, even insanely; local workmanship grew shabbier and hastier (how often was I summoned to mediate between startled and uncomprehending foreigners who found their cesspools disgorging through the kitchen tap and their roof-sternos askew in the wind, and the irascible local workmen gesticulating a bewildered innocence, which in fact masked a thorough and systematic incompetence!), tourist dances proliferated, wandering bands of rucksackers plundered the gardens, and native cookery deteriorated markedly. Nothing of this granular, discontinuous reality survives the fine Salaman sieve. For if it did the myth of Arcadia in which she has invested would become instantly and flagrantly indigestible.

There can be no doubt that Mrs. Salaman moves in an elevated, iconographic latitude, in which lesser mortals are occasionally permitted to visit. She observes the hieroglyphic figure of the thresher working "in complete silence; a silence, uninterrupted even by the cicadas, that feels ripe and impregnated with life; an image that can grip a spectator and keep him captive with its soporific spell for hours." The reader is introduced to the archetypal family in its discretionary, prandial setting. "We choose our fish in the early evening, usually 2-3 *skorpines*, and then we stroll a little further down the harbour for our ouzo and succulent charcoaled octopus . . . ." It is the sort of description which hankers to be read in a parodic, nasal, mock-elocutionary way. When it comes to the flavour of stuffed squid, we transcend the sphere of gastronomy entirely and enter the domain of the aesthetic-sacramental: "It instantly evokes an image of brilliance . . . . One can hear the sea-murmur and feel the salted slightly iodized breeze mingled with the scent of pine trees at the magical hour of translucent sunsets, when the iridescent waters reflect . . . in an almost solitary apotheosis . . . ."

Revelation succeeds revelation. The exquisite portrait of the heroine is completed in a coronation of special effects, of which the culminating moment occurs near the end of the book. Reliving her grandmother's tales of swinging in a pine tree, the author speculates that this particular recollection may have "made me become an air hostess later, in my quest for 'touching the sky'." It is like one of the ceremonies of the *indigamenta* in ancient Rome, the installation of a new divinity. Amid a rustling scripture of recipes, the emblematic figure of the protagonist consummates her ascension.

Thus the realm of pastoral has been firmly annexed and absorbed, partially by having been uncritically *assumed*, naively taken for granted in the first place. The Greece we explore with our reminiscing cicerone is fundamentally a collection of *objets choisies*: a round, blue table, a pot of basil, a meal served "by a simple peasant family," a white, cubic house by the sea reflecting the cerulean light, "droopy-eyed fishermen (joining) the choir of the new day" (presuming they are sufficiently awake to lift up their voices), and "the solitude of a mountain village." The technique that is applied, as in all Arcadian fantasy, is based on the principal of reduction or exclusion. (Witness the popular series of contemporary Greek postcards which feature a blue-painted geometric window-frame but censor the garish, plastic-braided iron chair that infallibly rusts beside it.) The language in which it communicates is thus, inevitably, the medium of nostalgia and yearning and the 'truth' which it seeks is the impeccable lie of perfection. For Arcadian fiction is really a species of hagiography in which the author, the dreamer, the imaginer is unconsciously intent on canonizing or transforming his or her own unavoidable human insignificance. It is a question of personal focus and is these days usually performed with the aid of the epidemic camera or, in intervals of literacy, with the compliance of the quotidian diary.

Evidently I am approaching Mrs. Salaman's book from my own special and congenial anti-Arcadian standpoint. The majority of its readers (it has apparently sold quite well), seeking authoritative instruction in the intricacies of Greek cuisine, would probably respond in a completely different vein, although they might possibly find the book a little too windy, a little too much on the chatty side. The relative proportion between personal reminiscence and the amplifications of preference on the one hand, and the actual itemized recipes on the other, may tend to appear somewhat unbalanced and misconceived. But once *Greek Food* is understood as something over and above a cookbook, that is, as a kind of quasi-existential document as well, in which an idyllic, unprecedented past, centred on the legendary figure of the wise grandmother, is gradually being evoked, and an ideal, bucolic present is being artfully constructed around the prelapsarian family in its matutinal dominions, exempt from the rude demotics of everyday life, from the quarrels, misunderstandings, resentments, and the myriad tiny despotisms that cloud the relationship of parents and children, then the anti-Arcadian perspective begins, I think, to seem reasonably justified.

The author tells us, for example, in another of her innumerable allusions to her Alonissos summers, that sometimes a bottle of olive oil, accompanied by freshly picked plums or peaches, "is left on the front steps or at the table in the garden . . . ." This is a delicate, homey touch and is perfectly inoffensive except that I lived in that house for one summer and passed it almost every day on my way to the beach during another four, and have no recollection of anything that might reasonably be construed as a garden. There was, to be sure, a narrow stone porch in front of the house decorated with a few straggly potted plants and maybe a bush or a clump of flowers. Perhaps in the two years that separate my last visit to the island and the publication of Mrs. Salaman's book, a garden had been miraculously engendered, although I couldn't for the life of me say where it might have been scaped in so cramped a property. Or perhaps during the interim the Salamans moved into more ample premises. The impression one gets, however, is one of continuity, of certain events having proceeded in a certain way for an extended and uninterrupted period. I can only conclude that a miracle has transpired, that a flagged porch not much wider than a companionway and not much longer than a vestibule has suddenly emerged through the *fiat* of Mrs. Salaman's pages as a "garden," a bower of neighbourliness, much as the straits between Poros and Galatea had been imaginatively transmuted in Miller's *Colossus* into a kind of uterine contraction responsible for our voyager's mythical rebirth.

These are the precise mechanics of the Arcadian transaction between the common and habitual world in which we are condemned *nolens volens* to live and the nostalgic, dream-haunted, cinematic imagination dedicated to the metamorphosis of daily experience into heroic tragedy or lyric pastoral. In this way even a cookbook can become an involuntary *confiteor* and a recipe for a personal *A la recherche*, a quest for meaning and significance. For the medium is charged with commutative power as raw experience is cooked into the sublimely memorable, the bread and wine of the daily, often uninspired menu transubstantiated into the stuff of mystical nourishment, and the ordinary, humble self gradually heightened, progressively redeemed, and ultimately eucharized.

The collective attitude toward garbage in this country serves as a prime cultural indicator. The interiors of the houses, even the poorest and least pretentious, are always scrupulously clean: the windows rubbed and breathed on, the oilcloth tablecloths set with intricately crocheted doilies, the coffeecups sparkling. The gardens are equally immaculate with their raked gravel beds, whitewashed petroleum drums that double as flowerpots, and laundry lines sagging with the weight of a perpetually drying wash. But where the ordered domestic cosmos ends at the metal gate or chickenwire fence, primeval chaos in all its turbulence and confusion begins. Broken bottles, rusty tins, shards of pottery, containers of all sort, soggy cement bags, mouldering rags, splintered chairbacks and amputated table-legs, old shoes, aspirin cartouches, koumbaloi beads, faded cameos, synthetic flowers, and the inevitable nude dolls encrusted in a pink-and-white magma of plastic suppurations collect in a heap of archeological tawdriness and squalor until, sprouting a pelt of shaggy grass and bound together by a twisting infiltration of tree roots, a growing hummock of marl and humus shoves its way into the skyline. I have noticed this phenomenon everywhere in Greece and especially on Paxos. We have visited and inspected hundreds of houses on our daily walks and in almost every case we have had to scale these artificial tumuli before crossing the cosmological line into the universe of property. The Greek housewife marches to the end of the garden and heaves the broken coffeepot into the quagmire of chaos. Her husband tosses his used razor-blades and empty lighters into the same primordial swamp. Ten years later there is a small mountain at the door.

It is an attitude that is hard to fathom, given the obsessive cleanliness of the average Greek household with its armamentarium of deodorants and sterilizers, incense cones in the outhouse, the air reeking of detergents and aerosol sprays, until one remembers that for the ancient Greek the civilized world ended at the frontiers, beyond which tribes of prehensile semi-humans roamed, procreated, and grunted in barbarous speech; and indeed the precinct of cosmopolitan refinement was often thought to be coterminous with the city limits themselves. Each *polis* on its mountain eyrie or in its crag-defended valley was the terrestrial mirror of transcendent perfection and symmetry: all the others were inferior models, tarnished specimens of diving ordonnance. Hence all manner of treachery and aggression was countenanced and even justified. The political, economic and social junk pile began in the next valley or adjacent mountain.

It seems to me that this archaic predisposition has survived in the apparently paradoxical attitude of the contemporary Greek to cleanliness and dirt. William James defines dirt as "matter out of place." The refuse mound which disfigures the approaches to so many houses on this island is clearly not regarded as a deformity or an eyesore; in fact, it is scarcely even noticed at all because it is discarded matter in exactly its proper place, outside the locus of custom, order, legislation and meaning.

There is little feeling for communal responsibility here. Greek fishermen have dynamited the Aegean clean of fish roe and now bemoan their dwindling catch. The Greek landscape has been largely deforested and farmers complain of the lack of topsoil. There is almost no intimation of life as a common enterprise founded in temporal continuity, as an intimate partnership even in the same small village, which is generally riven by fratricidal hatreds, envy and resentment. The dwelling which must be kept spotless and the family which must be raised free of reproach are the centripetal expressions of form, relation and propriety. The seethe and welter of chaos starts on the other side of the wall, where it is thought legitimately to belong.

❖

I write down my itinerary of this last day of the year, not because it has any intrinsic significance, but because it helps me to savour the irony of my Greek sabbatical and to observe the prosaic truth of the writer's existence. I find myself experiencing an indefinite series of typical days that bear an oppressive resemblance to the present one, which plods and shuffles as follows.

awaken at 9:00 in a dark, shuttered room, curled up in my amniotic sleeping bag for its pittance of carminative warmth. Hannah is piping in the next room.

dress hurriedly, get the morning ablutions over with, empty Hannah's potty and rinse it out with Sunsilk shampoo and replace it under her night-table. Meanwhile Karin prepares the little princess' breakfast and brings it in on a tray, plugging in the electric heater to thaw out the room.

plunge into the kitchen and wash up the stack of last night's dishes. A quick cigarette and coffee. Afterwards the trial of getting Hannah dressed, which can take anywhere up to half an hour. Each item of clothing has to be dried at the heater from the night's damp.
now it is time to drive to Gaios for shopping and other chores. Bakery. Butchershop, where we are cheated on the cut of the pork chops. Grocery store. Bank, where I manage to withdraw money with comparative ease, a mere ten minutes though I am the sole client. Laundry. Gas station, where, because the Super pump

ran dry a week ago, I have to mix my quarter tank with another quarter of Regular. Next, the garage to inflate the flat, wobbly front tire, but it is closed. The proprietor is off on a card-playing binge and will not be back for three days.

drive back to Lakka to complete the shopping and to try and locate a foot pump. No luck on the latter score. Finally, return to Moungelatika and unpack.

while Karin is preparing lunch I endure my daily shower, from which I emerge clean, refreshed and chilled to the bone. Lunch. After, it is time for Hannah's bath and hairwash, which I administer as briskly as possible. A partial success, as no suds get into her eyes, but she complains bitterly that her 'bagina' hurts. Karin appears to staunch her tears and apply liberal quantities of Penaten cream. I set the heater going to warm up the icy room for Hannah's afternoon nap. Three o'clock.
Karin has the plujiis today. She is lonely, homesick, bored, and walks about looking grim and pallid. I inquire into what is troubling her as if I were conducting an inquest. She sputters like a half-drenched fuse. We have short a quarrel. Later I speculate that maybe I am the one who is sometimes difficult to live with, and feel a trifle exalted by this bit of modesty.

smoke my tenth cigarette of the day. Clean up the bathroom. Wander about disconsolately for a minute or two, looking at the sky which is grey and flaky, almost deciduous. Tonight we are due at Soula's for New Year's supper, an invitation I'd like to renege on but can't think of a convincing excuse.

four o'clock. Sit down to scribble these scanty paragraphs. It is now seven hours since I struggled out of my sleeping bag to meet the demands of house, larder, family, climate, and the impending obligations of neighbourliness. At 5:00 Anthia will be over and I will assume my supervisory role. At 6:00 we will drive to Manasatika for supper with Soula, Magda and the children. At 9:00 or 10:00 we will return home. At 11:00 I will try and slip an hour's desultory reading into the day's crowded schedule. The maxim by which I regulate my life is called the domestic imperative.

4:15. Karin has just come into the room to invite me for a walk. I will now lay down my pen and live, I hope, to write another day.
Moral. As time goes on I will have to mix more and more Regular with my Super.

Q.E.D.

I need not have been so apprehensive. The New Year's dinner at Soula's turned out to be a roistering success. The food was plentiful and undistinguished: two roast chickens that fell apart at the touch of the fork, a huge Gorgon's head of gluey, writhing carbonari, a potato salad Soula spent two hours preparing and then forgot to serve, and a mess of hamburgers which I was responsible for scorching and charring beyond recognition but everyone was too drunk to notice. Captain Spiro (often called Spiro Amerikanos, as his father had been a boxer in the United States) whom I spoke of some pages back, was the guest of honour, and with his bountiful good humour, laughter-squinched eyes and besomy St. Nicholas beard, joyfully dominated the table, imposing and abdominal. When the meal was over and the guests had adjourned to the kitchen for coffee, Spiro and I remained in the dining room, drinking Corfiot wine, smoking pipes of Sobranie, and discussing his old friend Haralambos who only yesterday had greeted me effusively for the first time in months. Spiro insisted on speaking French, which in the general hubbub of Greek and English fibrillating through the house, gave his conversation a quality of detached urbanity and loftiness, as if he were settling the fate of nations or indulging in philosophical discriminations of exceeding subtlety.

What he was telling me in confidence was that the attempt to probe into Haralambos' motives and ideas amounted to a prohibitive waste of time. Haralambos had devoted his life with heroic assiduity to the accumulation of a fortune. After twenty years in Africa, where he was involved in banking, film distribution and other unspecified enterprises, he returned to Paxos and "il a construit cette veritable bordelle d'une maison en Lakka." But in the pursuit of affluence and freedom, "il a devenu esclave a son propre independence" a nice, quasi-Sartrean turn of phrase. Big Harry had become a casualty of his own emancipation; his relentless pursuit of security had left him permanently out of touch with himself and equally incapable of genuine relationships with other people. In effect, one would fail to understand the basic Haralambos if one did not see that he was the archetypal, the quintessential, the irreducible petit-bourgeois, the 'poujadist' of Roland Barthes. Of course Haralambos succeeded in camouflaging the truth by mantling himself in his congenial gargantuan style. But beneath his "phallocentric manner" beat the timid, farouche and suspicious heart of the inalienable petit-bourgeois. Thus Captain Spiro.

Afterwards, we went on to discuss the perennially fertile subject of Greek politics. Spiro's affiliations are vaguely syndicalist, but his years in Belgium and Germany had delivered him from the raw, journalistic passions of the Greek political temperament. "Moi, j'etais civilisé en Europe." His summation of the Left in this country is succinct: it is a question of winter communism supplanted by summer capitalism. In the off-season Lenin comes into his own. Stalin and Mao assume their places in the Pantheon. But in the summer the good middle-class communists are too busy making money to exhaust themselves in the rhetorical advocacy of the millennial society. Politics here are an inflammable mixture of talk and violence, incendiary emptiness, vanity preening itself on ritual insurgence. The poor, regardless of their political persuasions, are always betrayed. As for Paxos, one must always remember in analyzing its political sentiments that they are largely a seasonal phenomenon.

After an hour or two of conversation, we moved back to the kitchen where Spiro donned a straw-mesh hat and performed a raucous belly-dance to the great delight of the children. Soon the time came to leave. We returned home just before the bells and fireworks: Hannah to bed, Alki down to Lakka to attend a party at Spiro's cafeneion, and Karin and I sharing a quiet bottle of champagne by the petrolgaz heater.

Paxos in Winter: *An Inventory*

- a cracked, orchre pisspot leaning against an olive tree, where it must have been flung years and years ago.

- the cortical wither of the same cauliflower in Spiro's mini-market. It has lain there in its box for several weeks, like an anatomical specimen.

- breath fogging the bathroom mirror, making shaving somewhat risky.

- the *skoupithi*-heaps in which Karin digs and scrabbles for shards. She has been hunting for a *kantaros pillinos*, a clay kitchen-urn, glazed egg-yolk yellow on the inside, uncountable fragments of which festoon every mound and tumulus on the island. These *kantaroi* are rough-hewn and beautiful objects dating from the last century, but the people threw them indiscriminately to shatter on the junk piles, victims of the plastic revolution.

• the magnificent view to the south when the tramontane vacuums out the atmosphere: the distant, sweeping ranges of the Epirot coast, the camel-hump of near-peninsular Levkada and the hazy shimmer of Kefallinia thirty miles away to the south-west.

• hailstones golfing down on the ceramic tiles of our suspect roof; wind hammering at the door as I write, straight from Porlock.

• the icy cold in the house, kept marginally at bay by a battery of petrolgaz and electric heaters.

• conventicles of idle men playing rummy in Spiro's cafeneion, slapping the worn, greasy cards with a resounding thwack on the tabletops.

• the slather of oily grey light dripping and spreading over a desolate landscape.

• the eternal quest for warmth: cognac, wood, kerosene, barricaded rooms.

• homesickness, like a cramp in the gut.

✣

Shard collecting with Karin this afternoon. She approaches her avocation with the rigour and discipline of a professional archeologist. First she stations herself at the wall of some (preferably) abandoned property and measures off what she calls the "throw radius," by which she means the likely trajectory of a discuss of pottery hurled by a short-armed but muscular woman of dwarfish stature. This leads her inevitably into an olive copse which testers the inescapable tumulus. Then she performs a bit of private trigonometry to calculate what she calls the "ricochet factor" — she goes bevelling off at an angle from the matted tell and infallibly returns clutching a small shard-like piece of polished tektite. For heavier pieces she computes the "catapult force". Sure enough she returns with massive fragments of water urns and flowerpots. Sometimes I lose sight of her altogether among the groves and terraces and webbed and cluttered hummocks. I find her ten or fifteen minutes later in a small coomb on her hands and knees digging up the roots and decaying matter of ancient compost. She has the gift of artifactual rhabdomancy and an interesting and growing collection of flower-printed chips, glazed parings, scraps and flinders of all colours rescued from the detritus of a century. What fascinates her is that the ubiquitous flower-print that blossoms on potsherds all over the island is different in almost every case, as if it were painted or incised by hand: what M.I. Finley, if I recall correctly, denominates as "compulsory originality," the lack of precedent compelling novelty in art and life. The modern garbage heaps are instantly recognizable by the invariable sameness of their contents:

the same blue plastic *tsantas*, the same standardized plates, the same *Fanta* bottles and cheap, gilt-rimmed coffee cups, the same sameness in every part of the same un-differentiated stratum.

✣

I have been asking myself what sort of traveller I really am. Real travel, as I was considering earlier, is always an analogue of psychological faring and corresponds to the semi-mythic journey into the terra incognita of the self. It is a species of introspective picaresque, a measuring of one's own interior possibilities, and a discovery of states of mind and conditions of feeling that are generally aver-aged over and washed out in the repetitions and familiar-ities of daily living. The rule here is that of correspondence. Sights, landscapes and encounters that carry the patina of unexpectedness function essentially as correlatives or vehicles for inner recognitions. As Novalis writes in *Heinrich von Ofterdingen*:

'Wo gehn wir denn hin?'
'Immer nach Hause.'

Ordinary travel holidays, vacations, tours, programmatic visits to far-away Xanadu do not count as travel in any authentic sense. In fact, this kind of nosegay-picking is the very opposite of travel in that the profound compulsions of the self, the dual needs of discovery and creation, are religiously evaded in the Prospectus of systematic escapism. Here the rule is not correspondence but avoidance. Travel becomes a diversionary tactic, the feint of aborted adventure; ultimately, a form, not of psychotherapy, but the physiotherapy of the psyche. One returns from one's holiday tanned, fit, and lugging a portmanteau of canned memories, but totally unchanged in any significant way. The same person, slightly toned up and orthopedically restored thanks to the prosthetic miracle of a modern Lusiad turns up at work ready for another year of methodical futility.

Laurence Sterne in his amiable and leisurely manner distinguishes between the different kinds of travellers. The two most populous categories, which flow from a brace of major causes, namely, "Infirmity of body" and "Imbecility of mind," reductively encompass the following six species: idle travellers, inquisitive travellers, lying travellers, proud travellers, vain travellers and splenetic travellers. Sterne makes it amply clear that he is none of these. There is a third category he calls "Travellers of Necessity," which apparently subsumes the delinquent and felonious traveller, the unfortunate and innocent traveller, and the sentimental traveller, "meaning thereby myself." Sterne informs the reader that "with study and reflection hereupon he may be able to determine his own place and rank in the catalogue — it will be one step toward knowing himself."

Of course the eighteenth-century usage of the word 'sentimental' like that of the word 'artificial' is almost diametrically opposed to its current pejorative sense. By 'sentimental' is meant something like 'sensitive,' the ability to feel, perceive, discriminate and empathize, and it is precisely at this point that external travel impinges on the interior region of the sensibility. Travel 'educates' although in the platitudinous extension of the phrase such education becomes synonymous with the mere accumulation of facts and experiences for their own encyclopedic sake. Travel in this sense is just a more rarefied form of materialistic acquisition or social remuneration. Travel 'broadens' in the same way that shrewd investment enriches or diligent application generates a surplus. This is clearly not what Sterne intends by 'sentimental' or what the word 'educate' genuinely implies.

The value of travel contends Alvarez in his introduction to *A Sentimental Journey* is "not in stunning adventures or strenuous sightseeing or exquisite views exquisitely rendered back into prose"; it is, instead, "in the traveller's receptiveness to feelings, and the flair and subtlety" of their expression. What Alvarez neglects to take into consideration is the obvious rejoinder of the sedentary man: surely such affective receptivity is not the monopoly of the peregrine man. People who remain at home are not thereby disqualified from enjoying the fruits of receptiveness and sensitivity. Perhaps it is only the blunt, callous and saurian individual who needs to be shaken up in a *desobligeant* between Calais and Amiens for the scales to fall from his eyes and the thick coagulations from his heart. The truly perceptive and imaginative person need only stroll around the block, or perambulate once a day beneath the clock in Konigsberg, to compass marathons of creative accomplishment. After all, Kant's longest journey was a matter of fifty miles.

There is no answer to this objection. Great books have been written and great thoughts entertained by sedentary people. And there is no valid means of determining whether these are the exception or the rule. At this point I must fall back, *first* on my own experience, and assert that the oddest encounters, the most interesting events and the most startling recognitions I can recall have unfailingly occurred on one or another of my travels. Travel is the sworn enemy of habit, and although Englishmen may persist in taking tea at four o'clock in Singapore and German families in turning a Greek village into a *Schrebergartenkolonie*, thus converting travel into an exotic way of staying at home, the odyssey on which the authentic traveller embarks operates by the dislocation of the personality, the puncturing of expectations, the infliction of loneliness, anxiety and disorientation on the suddenly exposed and all-too vulnerable self. If habit calcifies, travel dissolves. Travel must not be construed as the purveyor of mere novelty. On the contrary, by throwing us back upon ourselves and shearing away all the social and customary props which have sustained our fragile sense of personal identity, it educates as it terrifies in revealing to our astonishment what patched-up, dependent, hyphenated creatures we really are. It shows us our place in what Ernest Becker calls the Cultural Plot or fiction and, if we are truly receptive, urges us to *construct*, not fabricate, a real and unalloyed identity, a kind of stratigraphic integrity as we renovate from the instinctual cellars upward to the roof-tiles of consciousness. Travel is a form of benign madness.

Secondly, circling back to the beginning of this excursion, if the classical emblem is correct or appropriate and life is to be conceived as a voyage, a journey *in partibus infidelium*, a periplus round an unexplored continent, an odyssey among snares, pitfalls, enmities, resentments, delights and revelations, then all travel is ultimately a species of analogy and metaphor, of establishing concordances between potential stirrings of self-awareness and realized, expository images. Which is to say, travel is the art of correlating the profound or chthonic self, often embryonic and confined, with its ideal reflection among an alien people or its natural embodiment in climate, landscape and atmospheric influences. Travel is the magical technique of transforming a destination into a destiny. The direction is perpetually towards the source. Novalis is right, one is always travelling home. Familiarity only disguises the central fact that our natural condition is one of exile or banishment — we are *unbehaust*, as Heidegger poignantly says — and deadens the awareness of the enormous distance we have put between our false self and our 'true self.' It is the *desire* to close this distance that is the real homesickness. And it is the *attempt* to close this distance that is the aim and prescription of real travel.

Drove to Vassilatika to replace a small *kantaros* we found last week by the wall of a shed where it had obviously been discarded. We decided to rescue it, the last, apparently, of its kind, before a stray cat or a gust of wind should reduce it to smithereens and render the species extinct. But conscience does make cowards of even the greediest expatriates and so we delivered up our booty to its shardy fate. In a month or two we will return to collect the fragments, but meanwhile we can revel in the anomaly of Paxiot rectitude. We have despoiled no one, not even the indifferent housewife who threw away the piece of pottery which Karin cherishes and has been hunting high and low for.

As we parked the car, an elderly man whom we had never seen before stepped out of the bush with a double-barrelled shotgun in the crook of his arm. Sturdily-built, dressed in black, coarse-featured, with eyes like the narrow gunslits in the 'Algerian' fortress which towered behind him, he barely returned my greeting. Instead, he planted himself squarely in the middle of the road and slowly raised his rifle, aiming it directly at our heads. He held the pose for ten or fifteen seconds while we stared back in utter disbelief. Then, in an elaborate slow-motion gesture, he cracked the barrel and unloaded two fat red cartridges, snapped barrel and stock together again, slowly lowered the gun and slipped the cartridges into his pocket. But he stood where he was and continued to glare at us, raising the empty rifle again and pointing it in our direction. Finally he shambled off toward an immense villa on our right that had been empty since the summer. Obviously a Corfiot landlord re-visiting the ancient manse and enjoying a spot of bird shooting.

Oddly, we did not feel offended, his sullen and rebarbative action blending so harmoniously with the grim, oppressive air of olive-gloomy Vassilatika so as to form a kind of aesthetic whole. It was as if churlishness was a thing to be anticipated, part of the funereal chill of the place, the weird, aquatic light, the toppling walls, the ruined fortress and collapsing hovels surrounding it like over-grown, paleolithic barrows. We replaced the *kantaros* and left, having gleaned a new adjective for our Paxiot voca-bulary: *Vassilatikan*. As in: 'Let me be, I'm in a Vassilatikan mood today'; or, 'the weather has turned Vassilatikan again.' Which is indeed the case.

Walked to Apergatika and veered down a fork to the further limits of the community past the spruced-up *prika* houses and the newer eyesores of yellow cement with grids of red paint supposed to simulate brick. We were approached by an old woman who turned a gap-toothed domino smile on us and croaked, 'Elate, thelo na sas gnoriso.' 'Come, I want to know you.' We followed her into a small, tumble-down house and sat in the living room examining family photographs while she prepared the coffee. An odd coincidence — her son, Thomas, has been living in Montreal for the last twenty-three years where he runs a pizzeria on Laurier Street, not far from our own house. The face was strangely familiar. I must have passed him innumerable times on the Main or seen him at one or another of the Greek tavernas thickly sown all over that quarter of the city. Kyria Panoraya had visited Montreal four times but had no recollection of the city, which consisted for her exclusively of the restaurant on Laurier Street and the residential suburb of "Brossa," by which she meant Ville Brossard south of Montreal. Her experience of Montreal symbolized the wacky, disembodied nature of modern travel in which the world is edited out of our sensuous (one might almost say textual) awareness. For Kyria Panoraya, travelling to Montreal from Paxos meant taking the *Kamelia* to Corfu; from Corfu, the plane to Athens; from Athens an Olympic Jumbo to New York and Montreal; from Montreal, a Buick Skylark to "Brossa." And the Brossa-experience consisted in remaining pretty well encysted within the prefabricated walls of an over-sized lego-house in a sprawling, fenced-off development on the edge of the Eastern Townships autoroute. Montreal was nothing more than a far-flung extension of the shabby airport lounge in Corfu town and had about the same degree of substantial reality as the film shown on the transatlantic flight.

There was, in effect, very little panorama for Panoraya, the beneficiary of modern travel in which one is scooped up, preserved for a time in limbo in a state of quasi-anaesthetic suspension, and then *deposited*. Scenes flicker and alternate like movie stills. One is here, then one is there. But what happens in between is factored out of the travel equation or is replaced by a pseudo-experience, an illustrated vacuum or synthetic ellipsis in which time is not something to be *endured*, that is, felt, absorbed, digested and slowly integrated into one's being but is rather an inconvenience to be circumvented or, as the expression goes, killed. Modern travel is the murder of time. *We are all taken hostage from ourselves.*

Naturally, I said nothing of all this to our hostess as we looked at her photographs, praising the handsomeness of the grandchildren whom I have seen a thousand times sitting baffled and resentful in my poetry classes. Those who have stayed behind in Paxos are not altogether to be pitied, even though most are bursting to get out and escape the confinement of island life. The girls here retain a certain dignity of face and carriage, a sense of stature, and a kind of virginity that has nothing to do with the flesh. They can be quite fierce and interesting beings. The men, venatic, shrewd, lazy and rhetorical, have resisted the pressures of anonymity. They are not forgettable.

Kyria Panoraya, like Kyria Maria in Boikatika or old Kyrios Demosthnes who gratefully shakes my hand and strokes me paternally on the back of the head whenever I give him and his dog a lift to Aghios Nikolas, represent the best of what is to be found here: a candid sociability without diffidence or evasiveness, and a disproportionate sense of gratitude considering the smallness of the favours they receive and the unstintedness of their own generosity. But they are ineluctably dying off and when the last of them is censed, buried and forgotten, reduced to a faded daguerreotype hovering ectoplasmically on the walls of rented rooms and villas, then Greece will have irretrievably vanished.

❖

Yesterday was the festival of Aighos Yannis Theologos, St. John the Baptist, and every Yanni on the island was busy celebrating his name day or having it celebrated for him. (In Greece the name day enjoys the same status as the birthday in what people here call the 'Angliko systema.' Birthdays are regarded with almost complete indifference. What counts is the baptismal day, which is often delayed for as much as a year or even longer after the birth of the child, unless he is feeble or sickly and stands in immediate need of spiritual indemnity.) We were invited to Myro Mourtis' restaurant to join in the festivities for his younger son, but when we entered the crowded premises, there was no sign of Yanni. Haralambos was holding court, wedged behind his corner table. Relatives and friends were milling about. In another corner, engaged in strident conversation, were Barbara, the bossy, voluminous woman who runs the diving club in Lakka, and Raoul, the East-German heroin pusher who is eking out a perilous and impoverished asylum on Paxos. He looked harried, edgy, hectic, gesticulating wildly and laughing convulsively at every second word. Suddenly he stood up and frenziedly announced that tomorrow he would be leaving for Djibouti and then South Africa. We went upstairs to the family quarters to find Yanni and present our gift. In the front room Myro, wearing a shiny seersucker suit but still unshaven, lay on the bed dozing lightly; in the back room the immediate family were eating cakes and drinking ouzo, fussing over Maria's baby and discussing the weather. Yanni was nowhere to be found. We deposited our gift in the corner and sat somewhat ill-at-ease on the couch.

Marina served us cognac in glasses no larger than thimbles and when we took our first sip, Karin and I linked glances: the cognac had been cut with water and laced with a soupçon of almond-extract to give it body. Typical Mourtis, we thought. Not a tumbler of cognac but a thimble of cognac-flavoured water, which reminded us of our last meal here three weeks ago: mucid spaghetti and three cremated porkchops which cost us eleven hundred drachmas and two days of nausea and stomach cramps.

We departed an hour later, having paid our respects to the family and shared in the *mezes* of pastichio and retsina with Haralambos. On our way home we stopped for a moment at Spiro Petrou's cafeneion, and whom should we see comfortably installed behind his dark glasses and neckwarmer beard, passionately involved in a game of rummy, but the elusive celebrant himself oblivious to everything but the spreading fan of cards held close to his chest, too absorbed to acknowledge my congratulations. I will never get to the bottom of Paxos.

After an absence of several days, Adonis has returned bloody and dishevelled. He is so huge that we have inflated his name to Adonis Kolokotronis, but his size is in inverse proportion to his prowess and ferocity. He is too dim to run away from the feints and thrusts of the unbounced Rocky, merely sits on his thick haunches and gazes benevolently at the ninety-pound retriever, and so brazens his way inadvertently out of trouble. But every kitten and fruit rat in the neighbourhood takes a chunk out of his perpetually bleeding muzzle. He is one of the presences I most appreciate on the island: mild, puzzled, trusting, and endlessly amiable. The moment he sets eyes on you, a thunderous bronchial purr emanates from the massive engine of idiot love within him, as if he interpreted the merest recognition of his existence as the most energetic and affectionate of caresses.

I have been reading Gavin Young's *Slow Boats to China* and am mightily impressed by the sheer professionalism of the book. His years as a war correspondent for the *Observer* have clearly served him in good stead: his writing is crisp, economical, wire-taut, no-nonsense, ruthless toward sanctimoniousness and truculence whenever he meets them, acrid and resigned in the face of the Grand Guignol of the political theatre whose productions clutter the globe with horror, fustian and melodrama, and always appreciative of what are for him the cardinal virtues, kindness and individuality. To his great credit he has avoided the pitfalls of journalistic prose, the inveterate shallowness that goes hand in hand with the affectation of omniscience and the pose of condescension to the rest of poor, benighted, ignorant humanity. I think what I most admire about his writing is the simple and apparently effortless ability to get from one sentence to another: sentences which remain somehow invisibly linked, without an excess of moralistic cartilage. Without ethical or declamatory ballast to weigh it down, the book is still and essentially a humanistic document, a paean to the vanishing quality of distinctive personality, of cheerful and robust individualism. The world today is organized around the collective and the aggregate. In politics, life is seen as a perpetual confrontation over issues which inflame whole peoples and reduce them to the level of partisanship, slogans, monolithic hatred, grand and sweeping oversimplifications, in which 'thought' consists of nothing but manipulated opinion and extravagant conceits of national pre-eminence. Left to themselves, people tend to get along, like the Chinese and Malay crewmen on the *Perak* plying between Singapore and Kuching (though Young is too sophisticated to fall back on the bromides of official Anarchism). When it comes to the realm of travel, once again it is the individual who suffers at the hands of the complicated apparatus of travel agencies, immigration moguls, and customs regulations geared exclusively to the processing of the ubiquitous *group*. In today's world, the individual has become supernumerary cargo: without luck, without contacts, without friends in unlikely places, he is doomed to quarantine. Only if he is a member of a group which has, of course, booked in advance can he expect an unproblematic transit; otherwise he is in imminent danger of being strangled by an ever-tightening noose of red tape, suspicion, and pure incomprehension. Even the mode of travel is growing increasingly featureless and anonymous: air travel by jumbo cattlecar.

All this is implicit not only in the content of Young's book but in his succinct and curiously visual style. He is a master of the definitive image. Rounded balconies are like breasts in an aristocratic decollete. Smoke from a steamer's funnel stands straight up like an angry cat's tail. The smile of a black boy is like a pair of dentures in a coal scuttle. On almost every page there is an image which fixes a scene or an event and renders it memorable, which is to say that even the images he lavishes upon the reader partake of that sharp and luminescent individuality to which the book bears such loving and abundant testimony.

This said, I must in the interests of frankness register a certain misgiving or hesitation about the organizing principle of the work, which strikes me as somewhat arbitrary and mechanical, perhaps even a touch derivative. Paul Theroux scored a great success with his two train books. He, too, writes well and has the gift of vivid characterization, but one can see him searching for a construct, an architectonic, to give his work the semblance of unity and the feel of inevitability. So he settles on the deictic fiction of the train which will take him from station to station and, as an apparent by-product of his journey, from chapter to chapter as well. But the spin-off effect is really the raison d'être of the entire procedure. The train is basically a contrivance, a way of imposing a discretionary and automatic consistency upon the work, rather than allowing it to be an expression of internal coherence, of a guiding, intrinsic and personal vision of life or of what Coleridge called 'the shaping spirit of Imagination.' As a result all of Theroux's trains from the crack express to the rickety wooden boxes swaying over the Andes bear a disconcerting resemblance to the toy trains in the basement of some fanatic hobbyist. They exist in order to be played with, to be speeded up, slowed down, shunted from line to line, taken apart, reassembled, and ultimately put away at supper time. They are not really trains; they are action-binders and chug through the pages of the book like shuttles in a loom whose reason for being is the eventual rug. Similarly, Gavin Young's boats are essentially a means of crossing the channels, bays and expanses of open sea between one chapter and another in order to convey the impression of unity. And they are, apart from that, vulnerable to the charge of derivativeness. The vista of successors is endless. *By Helicopter Through the Greek Archipelago. Big Jets to Bali: Pacific Crossings.* Or in another hundred years, *Shuttles to Mare Imbrium.* In literature, as in life, the chief desideratum is always order, and there are, it seems, only two ways of achieving it: one is to impose it, and the other is to discover it. The discovery and exfoliation of a latent order is the work of authentic imagination, but the imposition of it from outside or above is a function of either tyranny or helplessness. Or to put it once again in Coleridge's vocabulary, of mere Fancy. And the latter smacks inescapably of the mechanical, the aggressive, the peremptory. Instead of the obstetric coax-ings of the imagination, we have the rigid and arbitrary Caesarian of the will cutting out its pre-ordained shapes.

And such is the great temptation of all travel literature, to rely on the good offices of some technical device, some providential stratagem, some fortunate coincidence to produce a facsimile of order and cohesion from beyond the strict frontiers of the self rather than enunciating a moral and imaginative vision of life whose source is, to use the discredited word, spiritual. That is why Paul Theroux's writing for all its occasional scintillation is regrettably jejune. It lacks both depth and authority. Gavin Young's book, while subject to analogous criticisms, is rescued by its informing as opposed to informative spirit of sympathy and warmth, by its redeeming humanism. And though it is never mentioned explicitly, the book is graced by the presence of a *theme* — the rare and endangered species of the individual — which pulls together by a kind of subjective magnetism the tumultuous fragmentation of incidents of which the book consists. Young might have adopted as an epigraph the words which Kierkegaard wished to have burined on his tombstone: That Individual.

The passion for card playing is almost universal in this country; certainly on Paxos it is the winter obsession without which its male sodality, deprived of the spring and autumn hunt and living off last summer's tourist ensilage, would probably disintegrate or, even worse, become uxorious. Barba Grigoris tells me there is a mountain village in Corfu which takes its gambling so seriously that the male children are made to sleep with a playing card under their pillows. (Not so long ago in many remote villages, especially in Crete and Mani, it was a burnished knife). Casanova remarked during his sojourn on Corfu that the great passions were unknown on the island, a deficiency which he attributed to the debilitating effect of excessive card playing. The most popular game, almost the only game, is rummy. Gambling *per se* does not appear to be the principal motivation behind this consuming passion, at least not on Paxos; if it were, poker would probably be more suitable. Besides, the scale is always small and innocuous. Marigo complains that she has run out of *talira*, five-drachma pieces, from the incessant petty gambling, and indeed at one point small change had vanished almost entirely from the village tills. It is, rather, the myth of gambling which is invoked with its controllable factors of risk, confrontation and heroic disregard for property in a community in which property forms the binding element in all social relationships. In this sense gambling is a compensatory phenomenon, but also a prophylactic one, restricted as it is to the safe and manageable *taliro* scale. The only real danger is running out of coins.

Just as important, if not more so, is the fact that card playing is an essentially *theatrical* pursuit. The men sit hunched over the rickety, cognac-stained tables, studying their cards intently, murmuring to themselves, casting covert glances at their adversaries, clinching their Marlboros between their teeth. The cards are never simply laid on the table, they are slapped down with sudden, explosive gestures, and as the game picks up tempo it is punctuated by the rapid, staccato crack of knuckles on wood. The men grunt, rumble, spit on the floor, and erupt into furious arguments, hurling their trumps with ballistic force in one another's direction. A stranger entering their midst would assume a feud or vendetta in progress and expect nothing less than bloodshed to top off the proceedings. (I watched a visiting Englishman enter, turn pale, and flee through the still-open door to his car, which he drove at breakneck speed out of the village.) The argument subsides and the winner sweeps in a small heap of five-drachma pieces, gruffly orders another cognac, and the whole charade begins again every day and every evening for five months without intermission. It is a wonderful passatempo, this assumption of mythic gigantism and theatrical grandeur, and better from every point of view than the lilliputian cracking of pumpkin seeds.

We are starting to grow a little discouraged again with life on Paxos. Sometimes I feel like Sterne's 'splenetic traveller' and no doubt often write and behave as one, yet I defy anyone after a year on Paxos to preserve a rosy equanimity or unruffled cheerfulness. "They look at you here," Karin says, "with taxi-metre eyes. You can feel yourself being calculated. When you walk into a shop what they really want to know is: how many drachmas do you weigh?" She is recalling our landlady's sudden attempt to gouge us for more rent, which was a profound disappointment to us. Or the day when Marina Mourtis placed a dish of home-cooked artichokes, which we had not ordered, on the table for us to sample, as a gesture of friendliness, we thought, or as reciprocation for the expensive medicines Karin had brought back for her from Germany as a gift, and Myro included it on the bill. Or yesterday Spiro Minimarket behaving quite insultingly, merely because

Karin had asked for a plastic *tsanta* in which to wrap a fresh loaf of bread. "Why you no ask the baker?" "Because I forgot," said Karin. "Is your problem," came the retort.

Spiro Petrou is one of the few who has made no effort to profit from our stay on the island. He has been unfailingly magnanimous, and I sometimes wish Alki were old enough to ask for the hand of his smiling, sweet-tempered daughter, Tsoula, whose prika-house on the other side of the hill toward Apergatika I would gladly renounce for the honour of the alliance.

As I've said again and again, I will never get to the bottom of Paxos. The method I have been applying in these pages is a kind of poor man's phenomenology — Husserl's technique of radical *epoche* or the bracketing off of all that is merely incidental to perception, of all or *at least as many* of those elements of apprehension which are merely fortuitous, contingent and subjective. Put simply, Husserl's thesis is that once we have performed this surgical amputation of the gratuitous contents of perception the attitudes, assumptions, expectations, intellectual prejudices, relations and emotional connotations in which our transcript of the world is ambiguously soaked, like scented letter paper or newspapers still wet with printer's ink, only then will we enjoy a glimpse of the world as it really is in its pristine and enormously indifferent *giveness*. Seeing the world as it is in itself and not as a manifestation of our contextual subjectivity (the systematic hallucination of 'reality') is like scraping the encrustations from a seashell to reveal the smooth and glistening whorls that lie beneath or like effacing the more recent layers of writing on a palimpsest in order to expose and decipher the original script whose existence may not even be suspected by the uninitiated.

This is precisely the operation I have been attempting to perform on the phenomenon of 'Paxos'; that is, as Conrad said in his celebrated introduction, "above all, to make you *see*." I have been trying to disengage the fictive and chimerical Paxos, the Arcadian deception that fastens on its prey like the legendary and immortal Kraken, from the real, sequestered Paxos whose contours are scarcely visible beneath the folds and convolutions of our subjective revery.

The real Paxos comprises four elements: landscape, history, people and atmosphere — the latter, I am aware, steering dangerously close to the shoals of the private and the introspective. My imagination is primarily engaged by the landscape and the people. After having spent some time here I found myself reluctantly agreeing on the whole with Haralambos' pejorative assessment of the Paxiot character: with the exception of the tottering elders, it presents a rather homogeneous front compounded of surliness, deceit, and accelerating rapacity. And Myro Mourtis had gradually come to assume in my imagination the lineaments of an emblem and figurehead, the embodiment of the island's diverse population, the man who has never bought anyone a coffee, who charges exorbitant prices for abominable food, neglects to procure medicines for an ailing wife, and thins down the cognac he offers his guests on his son's name day with water and artificial essences. He had become a synoptic figure.

Last night we ran out of petrolgaz for our heater, which at this time of the year in Paxos is nothing short of catastrophic. Our life here pretty well revolves around that tiny, focal, sputtering flame at the base of the eerily glowing grate-like surface through which an uncertain warmth emanates. I immediately took Hannah and drove down to Lakka to try and scout up another bottle of the precious stuff, already quailing at the formidable nature of the task. The weather has been filthy for the last month and Captain Lakkis who has the petrolgaz-conveying monopoly, and who, when he is not being lazy, is usually drunk, has refused to make the channel crossing to Preveza where the canisters are filled, with the result that many homes on the island have run out of warmth. For many of the people the shortage is not critical since they have fireplaces, wood stoves, *petrelio* heaters; but for those like us in our windy, rain-strafed, perforated bunker, one day without heating is disastrous. I stationed myself at Spiro's cafeneion and sent out phone messages to every corner of the island: to Irakles' shop in Fontana, to the tavern-general store in Bogdanatika, to Bobby's garage in Gaios, to shops in Magazia. In every case the answer was identical: "Not one bottle." Lakka, of course, has been dry for over two months. After an hour of fruitless effort, as I was dialling still another shop, Myro Mourtis wandered aimlessly in and bought Hannah a strawberry wafer, which so startled me that I put down the telephone and gaped.

When he learned what the problem was, he instantly offered to drive with me to his house in Vassilatika and disconnect his petrolgaz bottle for our benefit, and when I asked him how he would manage to heat his house, he merely smiled and said, "No problem. We will drink tea and wear many clothes." This was the archetypal miser, old Scrooge himself, the money-octopus, offering to drink hot tea so we could enjoy the warmth of which our needs would have deprived him. It was then I felt with renewed force that I would never get to the bottom of Paxos.

Naturally I had to refuse his generous offer and, as it turned out when he consulted Marina on the telephone, the petrolgaz bottle was empty anyway. But I was warmed internally by his unexpected charity and felt humble and ashamed for my private castigation of a man whom I had obviously never understood. Or so I thought.

But my quest for the petrolgaz grail was far from over yet. On the off-chance that I might find a bottle hidden away in some locked and forgotten *apothiki*, I made the rounds of every shop in Lakka and collared every passerby. By now it had begun to rain again, sheets of lightning illuminated the square and thunder rumbled ominously. Having admitted defeat, I was shouldering my way back through the wind to the car and Hannah when I suddenly remembered a small taverna tucked away inconspicuously in the last alleyway of the town near the harbour. I had never patronized it because it always seemed so dank and speluncar but in the light of the emergency I retraced my steps and found it open. Inside the small, weakly-lit room were five or six stubbly, unkempt drinkers nursing tall glasses of ouzo and cognac. When I explained my quandary, one of these men, looking rather more dishevelled than the others with a week's growth of bristle on his chin and a ragged grey toque slipping off his head like a poorly-fitting toupee, positively beamed and said he was sure he could dig up a bottle for me. He owned the three-storey building at the top of the steep path leading eventually toward our house, which was subdivided into five tourist apartments, each with its own kitchen. These apartments were empty now, of course, but attached to one of the five stoves we would assuredly find an undepleted petrolgaz container. We walked up the hill to his house to fetch the keys, then accompanied by his good-natured wife we tried each of the apartments in turn until we found what we were looking for. Not only did Christos insist on carrying the heavy iron bottle down to the car, which I obviously could not permit, but he stubbornly declined to accept payment. We stood for a while arguing in the rain, Christos persisting in his efforts to help and I trying to find some way to reimburse him. To make matters worse, or better, he offered to replenish our supply as soon as it ran out. As I slithered down the hill lugging my golem's treasure, I recalled Kyrios Chrysokopoulos (an appropriate name, as 'chrysos' means gold) in Gaios, one of the more prominent members of the nouveau-riche and the proprietor of a large general store with *two* plate-glass windows. When we first arrived on the island and were not yet familiar with prices and exchange-rates, he charged Karin 1500 drachmas for four small towels — outright theft. Later on, when the autumn deluges began, I bought several pairs of rainboots there, the only shop on the island which stocked this item at the time. I was overcharged 350 drachmas a pair, as I later discovered when Kyria Eleni in Lakka received her shipment of winter drygoods from the mainland. Finally, Chrysokopoulos offered to rent me his much-used Fiat for 50,000 drachmas per month. I rented the excellent little Subaru in Corfu for thirty-one. How my new friend Christos managed to retain the ancestral and noble virtues of *philoxenia*, empathy and munificence in the midst of the almost ostentatious prosperity denoted by the palatial edifice he owned, the largest one in Lakka, is for me one of those mysteries that defy all catechisms. It takes only one Christos (also an appropriate name) to redress the balance of a thousand Chrysokopouloi in the avoirdupois scale of pettiness.

As a consequence of my desperate search for warmth I had read the original script of Myro Mourtis' character parged over by years of habit, and learned to place the Chrysokopouloi of this world in their proper perspective, as clogs and hindrances to sociability but instantly negated by a genuine act of kindness and imagination. This, too, is Paxos.

I have often bemoaned the lack of privacy in Greek life, not only the fact of privacy but the very concept of it. The language does not contain the word for this elusive and Snark-like phenomenon: 'monacho' meaning 'separate' and 'idiotiko,' from which we derive our own derogatory 'idiot,' has an altogether different sense about it, an aura of the freakish and depreciatory, 'removed,' 'withdrawn.' But the close network of mutual surveillance, the tacit contract of public exposure, does bring certain advantages with it. Things rarely get lost or stolen here. Two weeks ago the gas-cap fell off my newly-rented Kadett somewhere on the six mile stretch between Lakka and Gaios. After several days I mentioned the loss to Bobby at the garage just in case the cap had dropped beside the pump. A week later someone found it lying by the roadside near Bogdanatika, left it with Bobby who sent it off to Fontana via the next customer, from where it was dispatched to the mini-market in Lakka, where I retrieved it the following day. The island is small but not that small: counting all the windings, turn-offs, and branching capillaries, there are perhaps thirty miles of passable road, and I had covered much of this circuit on our daily exploratory trips before I even noticed that the cap was missing. A couple of days driving about with a yellow, wet sponge sticking out of the gas tank like Struwelpeter's coiffure was all the loss amounted to. If I had lost the sponge as well, it would probably have been discovered and returned within the week. I find this kind of scrutiny and vigilance gratifying, even reassuring, yet it makes me distinctly nervous at times. One feels like Billy Pilgrim living on exhibit in a cage on Tralfamadore. A delinquent thought entertained in deepest privacy has one peeking apprehensively over one's shoulder.

✢

Walk to Apergatika this afternoon. Passed the 'Corfu Villa' house crouching behind its bulwark of olive trees and its locked iron gate. On top of the high stone wall the owner has cemented needles of broken glass to deter whom? But two metres further on the wall has collapsed, permitting immediate entry. The effect is incongruous and yet typical. Another quarter-mile along the road stands an old and intricately-hewn stone-mosaic construction, obviously a 'sterno' or reservoir but no longer in use. A low channel of clinkered stones, the result not only of immense toil but of love and ingenuity, sweeps in gentle arc from the roadside to a deep, walled pit in which the rainwater collected. When we peered into its depths we saw it had been adapted to another purpose: a rusty iron bedstead, a discarded stroller, jagged sheets of sheared tin, glittered faintly in the anaemic sunlight. A depressing sight. The work and aesthetic foresight that went into this structure was considerable; a generation or two later and it is converted into a garbage dump. I find it hard to imagine such lack of imagination. But this deficiency is by no means peculiar to contemporary Greece; only, because of the stark and relentless clarity of the 'atmosphere,' it seems sadder and more flagrantly conspicuous here than elsewhere.

The rain has finally stopped after two solid (fluid?) weeks of flood and mud, the guttural rumble of thunder and demented glare of lightning, and the wind huffing and puffing at the kitchen door. A towering olive in the next yard was torn out of the earth during a gale and demolished the cyclopean stone wall six feet high and two thick that borders on the footpath leading down to Lakka. Now the air is still and a glum, phthisic sun squints blearily and intermittently through puffy, leprous-hued clouds. The cold is intense, even the local people shake their heads in disbelief and mutter in their shawls, speculating on meteorology. The prevalent theory on the island is that a new ice age is marching on Europe in giant, hyperborean strides. I tell my friends that according to the geophysicists we are not yet out of the last one. What I do know for sure is that I haven't seen my wife naked for three months. We couple like half-blind telluric creatures, covered by a thick pelt of nightshirts and tangled in the pleats and creases of two partially unzipped sleeping bags, then fall asleep snuffling with nose-colds and burrowing in darkness for the trembling illusion of warmth. Yesterday I needed medical treatment for an ear inflammation caused by the draught of cold air that streams from the shuttered and taped-up bedroom window so that regardless how one turns and contorts one is always exposed to some part of the icy current. One fights Paxos with antibiotics and hefty dosages of resignation.

Received a postcard from a colleague envying me my "leisurely and halcyon existence on a Greek isle." I don't have the heart to disabuse him of his sustaining dream.

Halcyon existence? It is so cold the calluses on the side of my thumb from grinding my Bic lighter have split open. We cower in our shuttered hovel and suffer acute cabin fever: the atmosphere crackles with tension, domestic rancor, and a kind of censorious taciturnity. Apart from that, Karin, having more or less recovered from a cold-induced ailment in her lower back that incapacitated her for several days, has come down with a racking cough; I have an inflamed inner ear and am popping three different sorts of tablets at staggered intervals throughout the day and applying camomile compresses in between; Hannah has her persistent bronchial murmur and has begun to regress again. As for our larder, we survive off stale bread, canned milk and dry spaghetti. The island has been cut off so long owing to the weather that foodstocks and other supplies have dwindled alarmingly or been depleted. The baker rations out his loaves, one per family — when he bakes, that is. The only garage on the island ran out of gasoline two weeks ago. My rented Kadett sits and the front gate consuming fifteen dollars a day. The local bus has cut back on its schedule, and Dr. Alexandros, whom I consulted for my ear, tells me that soon he will no longer be able to make house calls. We are still waiting for Captain Lakkis to cross to Preveza for the indispensable Petrolgaz reserves. Now the animals are beginning to fail and even the feisty, discombobulated fruit rats who live in the roof timbers have grown strangely silent. From time to time the generator goes on the blink: being without electricity means for us being without water, as the sterno in the garden is serviced by an electric pump. And, to cap it all, we are running out of clothes. I can't drive into Gaios to pick up the laundry we left in the *Katheroplasteion* several weeks ago and whatever we wash by hand remains dripping on the line. I would like to write back to my colleague and inform him that I have been wearing the same pair of thermal socks for sixteen days; on the colder nights I even wear them to bed. There is, however, an amber lining to the almost perpetual cloudiness of life on Paxos in winter: the abundance of no-star Metaxa cognac. We are in no danger of drought, thanks to the remarkable prescience of tavern-keepers like Spiro Petrou.

My friend, who is an ardent Hellenophile, cherishes in his imagination the paradigmatic figment of life on a Greek island. Apollo guides his sun chariot over the wide, cerulean track of the sky. At night the moon cobbles the sea with blocks of silver light, inviting the observer to stroll across to the next glimmering island. The landscape is clear, stark, glyptic. Each tree shelters its resident hamadryad. The island folk are simple and magnanimous, worshipping the spirit of the past, caring for the stranger in their midst, indifferent to the blandishments and corruptions of modern life. A perfect correspondence exists between landscape and mind: natural grandeur matched by spiritual nobility. The poet wanders from temple to temple, stopping now and then to slake his thirst at the Castalian springs and brooks that flow aboundingly on every mountainside. Life is inexhaustible, vital and fecund. The body is reinvigorated by the elemental intimacy it enjoys, the imagination is braced and stimulated by historical insight and mythological amplitudes, the spirit is strengthened by the examples of courage, dignity and generosity with which it is surrounded. How can one fail to prosper and thrive? How can one not be grateful for the openhanded prodigality one enjoys in this *locus amoenus* where time, nature and myth converge? It must be, my friend concludes, quoting Eliot, an eternal "moment in the rose garden."

All I can reply to this Utopian drivel is that life here certainly has its moments, but they are not eternal and they manifestly do not occur in a rose garden. Of what does dignity consist? Stoically enduring the tenth spaghetti meal in a row. Courage? Working up the fortitude to go to the toilet in the freezing outhouse which even the cats have abandoned. Generosity? Refraining from murdering one's wife and children in an access of frustration, resentment and stir-crazy delirium. As for the imagination, it grows inexorably stagnant and inert as trivialities begin to occupy one's entire mental horizon: how to orchestrate a change of socks is a problem that eclipses the demands of intellectual solvency. And when it comes to the healthful propinquity of the four elements, air is the cold tramontane that has everyone hacking up bile and sputum; earth is essentially mud; water, the cataract of rain that makes it necessary to open umbrellas to get to the kitchen; and fire? fire is the thin, blue dwarf trembling at the base of the petrolgaz heater.

But at certain moments one rises Phoenix-like from the ashes of one's illusions and soars imaginatively to meet the grand, precipitous view from the cliffs at Vassilatika or Erimitis. Only, as I would like to inform my correspondent, it is extremely dangerous to be a bird on Paxos. The winged imagination is a frequent casualty to the jets of reality-grapeshot that stipple the upper air. But if one can survive the perilous banality of this diminished life, the grizzled veteran who emerges in the spring can lay claim, perhaps, to a small pension of haphazard authority in his perceptions and judgments of the local world beneath the Hellenophilic, cosmetic projections which defraud it of its substance.

Karin has now accumulated an impressive array of pot-sherds which, on its backing of white towel, covers half the area of the kitchen table. She is out doing 'fieldwork' at almost every opportunity, digging deeper and deeper into the Paxolithic seams of fused and buckled detritus. Having given up on the irrecoverable *kanteros*, she is now in hot pursuit of discarded fragments of the distinctive island crockery: jugs and plates with the characteristic six-petalled blue flower painted on handle, lip and rim. I wonder if her fascination with shards in general and the blue flower in particular does not derive from her teutonic heritage or at least from her study of the German roman-tics. *Die blaue Blume* is, of course, the pervasive and rhap-sodic symbol in the writings of the German romantics, most notably of Novalis and Rilke, and as it occurs to me now, possibly because he also had a German wife, by cultural convection and in a totally opposite sense, in D.H. Lawrence's 'Bavarian Gentians.' It is almost always the sign of *der romantischen Sehnsicht*, the soul-consuming pathos of the *Unendlichkeit*. One finds this tiny clue and emblem of the infinite struggling upward in some tangled brake of denser growth or in the rarefied air of a mountain summit or, as it happens, on a chip of baked clay glinting in a pile of debris.

Also, the romantic poets were in love with the fragmentary, with all that was cleft (like the devil's hoof), splintered (like diffracted light), parenthetical (like folk songs and fairy tales), and especially *unfinished* (like so many of their love affairs and longer poems). Even the views my wife prefers are sudden, fragmentary disclosures of sea and cliff, "cut-outs," as she says, bits of scape and scarp, momentary surprises, or as Hopkins chants, glimpses of "all things counter, original, spare, strange," flashes of "dappled things." As I watch her brooding over the rubble heaps in what she calls "the valley of the shards," a part of the terrain herself, and try and slip lexically into an imagination so different and remote from my own, "teutonic" becomes "tectonic." She is of the earth, an authochthonous being; at the same time she is a psychical mosaic of bits and pieces that are not intended to cohere, for coherence and integration are the death of the infinite. Who is this complex, paradoxical creature I am living with, rooted in peasant stock yet the bearer of a ghostly genealogy? There she is, stooping to dislodge another shard that will not fit any of the jigsaw fragments she collects, yet will reappear in her dreams as the crockery that graces the tables of heaven.

❖

I've been speculating again on the ubiquitous habit of spitting in this country and wondering if it is not also a means of taking or renewing possession of the earth. The peasant has made the land his by burying his dead in its stony, parsimonious soil generation after generation; by fertilizing it with animal dung and with his own feces; protecting it with mulch and enriching it with compost; quickening it daily with a cumulative avalanche of refuse and ordure. Whatever he has within him, he has given back to the land and thus established his proprietorship. The generous gobs of sputum which seep, ooze, filter and percolate through every inch of penurious subsoil ratify his contract with the chthonian depths and ensure another meagre harvest. By contrast we merely pay our water taxes and move on, and are decently repelled by these acts of fructification and kinship expressed through the medium of bodily excreta.

Third thoughts about our local paragon of retentiveness and greed, Myro Mourtis. The petrolgaz bottle he so magnanimously offered last week belonged, actually, to his son and daughter-in-law whose house nudges the out-skirts of Vassilatika. Myro and Marina live in their hobbit quarters above the restaurant in Lakka. It was his son, in fact, who would have found his family deprived of heat through his father's unforeseen liberality. (That is, had the bottle not been empty. Or was it?). It is, literally, no coat off Myro's back. So reluctant is he to undergo even the slightest expenditure on behalf of his own health and comfort or his wife's that the idea of heating his own premises never crosses his mind. He wears several layers of thick clothing and crawls into bed when the cold becomes unbearable. So I am back where I began with regard to Myro and his heraldic identity, and am convinced that not only will I never get to the bottom of Paxos (Karin neither, no matter how deep she digs), I will never get on top of it either.

I think it's time to leave Paxos for a while and visit friends in Italy, provided we can manage to get off the island, which seems unlikely at the moment. There have been only two crossings in the last couple of weeks and Captain Lakkis (a potential lift), who apparently sailed a few days back, seems to have vanished completely. One rumour is that he is weathering out the storms in Preveza; another locates him on a drunken binge in Mourtos; and a third affirms that he never left Paxos in the first place and that his caique is safely moored in Loggos harbour. Meanwhile our situation has become desperate. The three bottles of petrolgaz I borrowed from Christos were practically empty and we are now effectively without heat. The electric heater is unreliable. To compound the matter the propane supply in the kitchen sputtered out yesterday morning and we can no longer cook at home. We sit here in the cold and eat out of tins. A cup of tea is a luxury out of the Golden Age. There are only two restaurants open on the entire island and no hotels where I could lodge the family for a couple of days of warmth and modest comfort. The rain drums down incessantly and the wind hurls itself at the walls of the house; there are sudden updraughts which threaten to suck the roof right off its joists like a bubble in a straw. The situation is, in fact, absurd. We have to keep reminding ourselves that we are in Greece, a name which has only cartographical significance. For we are really on a mountaintop in a desolate place called Moungelatika, without heat, without cooking facilities, in the midst of a prolonged winter gale and zero temperatures, sheltering in a house that admits the rain and welcomes the wind, with a three-year-old child suffering from chronic bronchitis and no immediate way of alleviating our predicament, no place to go, no means of leaving the island. We are simply trapped. And this, I think, is not what anyone signifies by the term 'Greece,' by which is meant something entirely different, a kind of imaginary construct, an ideal or hypothetical condition supported by the appropriate props and buttresses: sun, sea and service. 'Greece' does not exist except in the imagination and on the map. It is a fiction backed by the transitory compliance of the elements and given a semblance of permanence by a complicated scaffolding of ritual ministrations and devout credulities. But I solemnly assert that 'Greece' does not exist, despite the attestation of postcards, sun-tans, brochures, brochettes, cassettes, history books, travelogues and embassies. 'Greece' is both a state of mind and a condition of the flesh, or alternately a lucrative stratagem and an immaculate delusion. But Moungelatika exists. It banishes the first twinge of Cartesian doubt with the first prickling of frostbite. (Descartes, one recalls, for all his radical scepticism, composed his opus warming his toes at a crackling Dutch stove.) And at this very moment as I write, as if to accentuate the irony of our dilemma and italicize my deposition, the power has failed. I complete this entry by candlelight at the parlour table with the members of my family shivering and coughing round the factitious warmth of its Lilliputian flame. We have shut off the rest of the house on which (as it feels to us) the dark of this starless night has clamped like an epoch out of Velikovsky. Greece is truly Moungelatika, the community of the dumb whose only voice is that of the storm that howls rhetorically around us like an army of klephtic irregulars bent on reprisal. The more fortunate down in Lakka and Gaios gather round their fireplaces, plentifully supplied with rich-burning olive wood: they are to some extent still in 'Greece.' Irony upon irony. We, who are foreigners, are among the last inhabitants of this island who can still be said to live on Paxos.

There is a good reason why the foreign visitor and the native Paxiot, despite the assumption of mutual intelligibility, face each other like incommunicable monads. Paxos remained deep in the neolithic age until very recently. Up to less than a generation ago, the people worked in the fields with primitive *tsapas*, a cross between a hoe and a spade whose shape had not undergone any change or development for countless generations, like terrestrial crustaceans. They hewed and chipped the great stone ashlars one sees everywhere with simple, aboriginal tools and raised them into the mosaic of quasi-mycenean walls which reticulate the entire length and breadth of the island. Traffic was pedestrian or by donkey and mule. Clothing consisted of wool and hides worked into the simplest of wardrobes, including the long shaggy caftan worn during the winter. Social attitudes pretty well corresponded to the physical conditions of life: the clan was predominant and is still reflected in village names; marriage proceeded according to a loose phratry system in which a man from Gaios would take a wife from Fontana; labour, at any rate since the Venetian occupation, revolved around the olive tree; the onerous picking followed by the crushing and grinding (one still sees the great wooden presses and cyclopean millstones abandoned in tumbling workhuts) kept the people in a state of vassalage to their Corfiot overlords and to the rigid constraints of a single cash-crop economy; education was minimal or non-existent. Almost overnight as it were, once the tourists discovered this small, green island with its three idyllic ports and its limpid waters, the influx of unexpected wealth changed life decisively and instantaneously. From one year to the next, so to speak, the people acquired the whole external armature of modern civilization — motor vehicles, television sets, electric ranges, antibiotic medicines, synthetic textiles — without at the same time naturalizing the structures of belief, perception and intuition appropriate to it. For hundreds, indeed thousands, of years the women cooked on tripods over wood-fire grates and pits. Then, abruptly, they were using microwave ovens. The jump from the wooden saddle of the donkey to the vinyl seat of the motorbike was instantaneous: in a twinkling something like three thousand years of insular transport was negated. The Paxiot neolithic persisted more or less intact until recently. Now it is all disco, subtitles, aqualungs, currency exchange, pocket calculators, telephones, and wives from England or France.

Because the transition from one age to another was not gradual and insensible, allowing the mind to adapt to the implications of modernity, but was in fact a qualitative leap accomplished in one quick, running stride, it should come as no surprise that the Paxiot mentality is in a state of shock, that there is something numb, inarticulate, inchoate, undefined and anarchic about it. The English tourist who sojourns for three weeks in a Corfu Villa or Paxos Holiday apartment believes he is speaking or dealing with a contemporary whose distinctiveness from himself is matter of language and culture. It never occurs to him that he is conversing with someone whose psyche, beneath the surface embellishments, bobs like a fishing cork in a temporal matrix inconceivably ancient and unapproachable: in effect, with *Homo Paxolithicus*. And I must confess that in my daily transactions with the local people I also tend to forget that the psychic chasm which divides us is unbridgeable, incommensurable, which explains why I am so often baffled, exasperated, provoked and infuriated. The majority of the people are still , imaginatively, dwellers in the neolithic era; the more 'advanced' are space-age medieval.

A concluding aside: it seems to me the preoccupation with 'filthy lucre' that is so glaringly evident, and even disruptive of the small, domestic reciprocities that sweeten everyday life, is not simply a function of rampant greed (it is that in part), but is also a form of translatability between incompatible modes of thought. The scale of currency operates as a kind of mediating language between two discrepant and irreconcilable grammars of existence. Prices are like handles, they enable one to get a grip on objects that would otherwise appear sinister, fugitive and inexplicable. (Yanni's Christmas visit.) Money is the recodification of ignorance and fear into substantial fluency, a sort of Pentecostal materiality. Land is transubstantiated into collateral, not only fiscal, but psychic collateral. Briefly, it is money that subsidizes a precarious mental and social equilibrium. In a sense very different from that intended by the cliche, *money talks* or it at least prevents the rapid declination into autistic silence and social psychosis that threatens to engulf these prehistorical Caspar Hauser regions which pucker and crease the Teilhardian 'noosphere' and which make true communication among the peoples of the world one more millenarian enchantment.

Captain Lakkis is back after two months of stalling and dithering, and we have heat once again. Bobby has replenished his stock of gasoline and I spent a morning lining up on the narrow road that leads from Makratika to Gaios.

The protracted storm that has pummelled the island since before Christmas gave us a one-day reprieve of hard, dry sunshine before tipping its inexhaustible buckets of rainwater over us again. But we are still unable to get off the island. The *Kamelia* is in drydock in Corfu and the *Anna Maria* cannot transport motor vehicles. The only way to return my Kadett to the Hertz agency in Corfu is to book a place on the *Keffalinia*, a large ferry that plies once a week between Paxos, Cephallonia (Keffalinia), Patras and Corfu, arriving in Paxos at 2:00 a.m. every Friday theoretically. It has not put in an appearance for many weeks, and though it is scheduled to dock tomorrow morning, the general consensus among the nautical drinkers at Spiro's cafeneion is that it will bypass the island once again. Port facilities in Paxos are inadequate to handle shipping in winds above five Beauforts, and it is blowing a steady six to eight today. I have had to keep the car much longer than I intended and it may be another two weeks before I can dump my exorbitant albatross and begin licking my financial wounds.

We have spent freely since coming to Paxos and the car has consumed a month's resources out of our shrinking budget. We will start feeling the pinch in the spring, unless I can perform a bit of fiscal thaumaturgy from afar to stave off encroaching destitution. Odd, but I haven't enjoyed a single carefree moment since the day I first set foot on this lovely and accursed island immemorial eons ago.

The old question of what constitutes a 'travel book', one of the inquiries I am pursuing in these pages, continues to peck away at my conscience. Being so near to Corfu, I am naturally spooked by the rotund and capacious presence of Lawrence Durrell. *Prospero's Cell* is, in its own fine, ingeminated way, one of those troubling books which distort, intimidate, challenge and beckon all at once. One resents its high polish yet tries to rub and buff one's own work with all the vigour of a manic shoeshine boy. The gloss one manages to attain will never equal the definitive Durrellian lustre. One distrusts its bombinating rhetoric and nevertheless attempts in imprudent moments to out-purple the master at his own Tyrian game. The result smacks of pastiche. One is constantly on the prowl for interesting people to match Durrell's polymathic friend Zarian (or for that matter the Katsimbalis of Miller, also mentioned by Fermor who tries his hand at the dubious trick of amplifying the famous rooster cry that concludes *The Colossus*) and has to settle with mixed gratitude and despair for a reduced fraternity of Haralamboses and Lucianos. Or is it possible that the Zarians and Katsimbalises who stride magisterially through the accounts of the masters, enlivening the *perivalon* with brilliant talk, eccentric speculations and lyric effusions are merely a species of literary efflorescence, iridescent bubbles in the rich genetic foam of their creators' imaginations? In life they are, let us say, ordinary geniuses, but in folio they are something quite different, beings kindled by exponential zeal to a seraphic radiance and splendour. I don't know, but I suspect this may be the case. (Though Katsimbalis may be a special case, a species of one.)

Nor does the sceptical and humorous, southpaw perspective help to deflate the myth of privileged status. Gerald Durrell in his *My Family and Other Animals* presents us with the comic and at times vaudeville side of the singular Durrellian menage: a pixilated mother perennially unflustered by disaster; a sister obsessed by an apocalyptic case of acne; and a literary brother, short and plump, given to bursts of melodramatic rodomontade and demonstrations of thoroughgoing incompetence but who, as everybody is well aware, is the future author of *The Alexandria Quartet*. The myth of Lawrence Durrell emerges from this douche of wry and affectionate disparagement corroborated and enhanced. For so towering a figure to be also so short, so assured a writer to be also maladroit and preposterous, argues an achievement of many-sided humanity equal to the sublimities of loftiest genius. And in addition to all this, the illustrious figure of Zarian, quaint, eloquent and doubly verified, puts to flight one's tenuous sense of common sufficiency. *He* exists; therefore one's circle of friends must, it appears, be impoverished.

Still, after the tremors of doubt have passed and one's house remains standing, the question recurs. Is the world which Durrell describes as authentic and unimpeachable as it seems, or is it nothing more, though manifestly nothing less, than a magnificent fiction, an allegory of what I have called 'significant life'? Is the reader not being presented with a heightened version of reality, a touched-up reproduction which by virtue of its consummate execution solicits his conviction and assent? Such augmentations of the world, while compelling and uplifting, may also be destructive in that they despoil one of a necessary confidence in the adequacy and scope of one's own experience unless, of course, that experience *is* paltry and exiguous.

My own feeling is that Lawrence Durrell may be a great writer but that the Corfu he depicts with such painterly excess has more in common with the melodious isle of Shakespeare's *Tempest* than with the Corfu one discovers reposing ambiguously behind its long literary seabord. Durrell is not writing travel literature. Durrell is Prospero. He does not portray Corfu, he evokes with the aid of an Ariel pen the enchanted region of his own fertile sensibility which is superposed, grounded, anchored on the social and physical substratum of the island itself. Genuine travel writing, on the other hand, seeks to dispel the opalescent mists and tragic exaltations, the larger magnitudes of being, the assumption of theatrical pre-eminence, the subtle tumours of anointment, and instead to render with ever-faltering scrupulousness what has generally acquired an auxiliary and subordinate position to the writer himself, namely, his subject. Orestes needs Pylades in order to be Orestes, but given half a chance, Pylades may prove to contain unsuspected depths. For most travel writers, as indeed for most writers considered as a privileged and gifted species, the world is a foil, an accessory, a silent Pylades. The great writer is the one who can bring off the swindle without his reader feeling cheated or abused. But to reproduce the world in its approximate shape, allowing for the inevitable warp of subjectivity, to disinter and re-present the world we have buried under our congenial and explanatory fictions, is also a plenary act of the imagination, which is to say, an act of motiveless love. One has to assume, at any rate, that the world is at least as interesting as oneself, and this is, perhaps, the supreme achievement of the imagination.

One book about modern Greece that strips the Arcadian finery off the subject is Nicholas Gage's *Eleni*. To begin with, it deals with a historical period that is religiously avoided by most travel writers, the civil war which decimated the country between 1945 and 1949. It is almost as if a tacit covenant exists which regards these four years as taboo and somehow indigestible. The reason for this literary boycott is not hard to find. A candid and extensive treatment of this period would explode the prevalent myth of Greece as the dancing floor of the gods, the land of archetypal clarity, the embodiment of the cardinal virtues of hospitality, rugged decency and spontaneous delight in life. The military exploits of modern Greece we tend to dwell on are the heroic War of Independence against the Turk, the incalculable suffering that followed in the wake of the Asia Minor disaster in the early twenties, the repulsion of the Italian invaders in the Albanian mountains, and the courage and ferocity of the resistance in Crete and elsewhere during the Nazi occupation. In these cases the western imagination is enabled to preserve its version of Greece intact. But a description of the partisan conflict after the Second War would give a very different picture of Greek reality and one that is strictly incompatible with those we like to hang in our communal Hellenic gallery.

There are exceptions. Kevin Andrews' *The Flight of Ikaros*, published in 1959 (one year after Fermor's *Mani*), deals largely with the civil war period, wheeling in the dramatic *eccyclemata* but shying clear of political commentary. Andrews recounts his wanderings and adventures in the *andarte*-infested mountains and describes his encounters with some of the *dramatis personae* of this debased, latter-day Greek tragedy. He does not appear demonstrably to take sides, though he seems rather more sympathetic to the Left, if only because he dwells on the sufferings and indignities of the captured *andartes* being shipped to the infamous prison camps on islands like Makronisi. His evaluation of the four-to-five year debacle is fairly represented, I think, by the following reflection: "Perhaps . . . the slaughter itself may not have been quite so important as the wholesale and nationwide distortion of values for which a civil war is directly responsible."

Another exception to the general rule is to be found, a little surprisingly, in Helen MacInnes' thriller, *Decision at Delphi*, published two years later, in 1961. Her knowledge of the period in question is laudably detailed and extensive: she is familiar with the currents of political intrigue that shifted and blurred the underwater shapes of Greek national life, she is aware of the methods and techniques by which the communists gradually dominated the various resistance groups in their loose alliance against the Nazis, and she knows about the egregious *paidomasoma*, the kidnapping of 50,000 Greek children to the East Bloc countries. That she should command this information in the late fifties when readers in the mid-eighties, Greek as well as foreign, should be astonished or incredulous at Gage's revelations, strikes me as one of those literary ironies that flourish in the no-man's land between fiction and history.

A Domestic Bulletin

From the sublime, or rather the infernal, to the ridiculous. Little Anthia is our current provocation. One morning she arrived at the door with her hair shorn to the scalp, a depilation explained neither by the shears of fashion nor apparent necessity. Like imbeciles we complimented her on her disfigurement and thought nothing more of it. Two days later when Hannah's ears and neck were caked with blood and her hair swarming with lice, we still did not understand. For at first we believed the cats to be responsible and exiled them ruthlessly from the house; only after a few more days did the truth gradually begin to dawn upon our invincible naivety. All that subsequently ensued, the trip to Dr. Alexandros at eleven at night, the repeated washing of Hannah's verminous hair with vinegar, pharmaceutical shampoos and military powders, and a week of boiling and fumigating every shred of linen in the house, might have been avoided had Anthia's mother Stamatella conquered her petit-bourgeois horror of appearing *déclassé* and alerted us in time to take precautions.

In fact, she was in the house to fetch Anthia after an evening of play when Karin discovered the sores on Hannah's neck and feigned utter astonishment. Next day Anglaia, who is Anthia's grandmother, knocked at the kitchen door with a gift of fresh eggs and *loukoumathes* ("for the child"), which we realized only later was feeble and belated restitution for the contretemps. (Now, whenever Stamatella appears with a head of cheese or stack of biscuits, Karin immediately subjects Hannah to a delousing shampoo.)

Several weeks have elapsed and we have succeeded in washing and combing the last clutch of white, dandruffy nits from Hannah's clipped locks. Today Anthia was over suffering from an explosive cold, her sleeves brittle with dry snot and her nose dripping like a tap, sneezing full in Hannah's face. So Hannah has, of course, come down with the mandatory sniffles. I have grown to hate Anthia. And it seems to me now that if Helen has forsaken Greece for the favourable climate of an imperishable mythology, she has been succeeded by a formidable claimant to emblematic supremacy. Helen may not yet be dead, but Anthia, thick, muscular, resilient, is richly and humidly alive past all heraldic designation. For Anthia, if I may permit myself a Parmenidean inflection, does not merely represent; Anthia *is*.

Returning after a month in Italy to Greece, it is very difficult to continue in good conscience with the observations and reflections I started a half year ago on Paxos. I feel a little like Henry III after his visit to Ruritanian Venice from which, according to legend, he never managed to recover. At any rate, I have become a biased witness, cranky, distempered, bellicose. Greece now seems to me an *underdeveloped* country in the spiritual and historical sense of the word. There is nothing like Florence to be found here with its magnificent Piazza, its monumental sculptures, Brunelleschi's double-shelled dome, the picture galleries of the Uffizi overlooking the Arno and the Ponte Vechhio; nothing like craggy Voltera with its Etruscan tombs or San Gimignano bristling with seigniorial towers or aristocratic Lucca or tempestuous, seething, yet marmoreal Rome.

Four weeks in Italy yielded a richer crop of interesting and memorable encounters than seventeen years of desultory ploughing in Greece. I think of Maria Luisa Spaziani, Italy's dowager poetess, witty, ebullient and charming despite her many years. Enso Biagi, grave and basilican at his table in *da Luigi*, courteous even in the midst of personal bereavement. Elio Chinol, the critic, arranging his English to diffract nuance and intimation. Alfredo Rizzardi of Bologna, Italy's leading authority on English and American poetry, with his immense erudition and kindly, diffident manner. Gilbert Reid, the Cultural Attaché, his lanceolate intelligence educated beyond the Canadian norm, speculating over a campanile of tapering fingers on the myth of personal identity. In all my years in

247

Greece I have never met anyone like Ferdinando Carrozza, a banker retired to a villa in Soiana in the Tuscan hills, who has devoted himself to his vines and olives and to the great passion of his life, the science of malacology. In that elegant and rambling villa with its terraces, gardens and views, he maintains an immaculate laboratory crammed with treatises, bagged samples of exotic sediments and thousands of species of shell life, one of which he has discovered himself and named after his wife, Diva. (*Raphitoma Divae*). The few hours I spent in his laboratory, finding my own hobby of shell collecting raised to a pitch of professional competence and expertise I could never hope to emulate, led to an agreement in which I will send him the trouvailles from my summer diving for inspection and analysis. More to the point, the supper that followed at the long refectory table garnished with local wines and good conversation has rendered me eternally unfit to dine at Myro Mourtis' blowsy, mucilaginous trough or to drink Haralambos' parching Villa Blotto wine of which he is so inordinately proud.

And yet I am aware as I write that I am setting up a pair of rigged alternatives, an unequal combat, introducing a brawny, heavyweight Italy in one corner and a scrawny, undernourished Greece in the other and, like a jaded referee, advising them to fight fair. No doubt if I had spent the greater part of my time in Athens rather than on the islands, I would have come to know a fascinating company of idiosyncratics and genuinely cultivated people. But abstracting from my current prejudice, I think there is a considerable amount of truth in these splenetic contentions of mine. In our frequent debates on the subject, Karin takes up a different position, seeing most of what I find objectionable as a function of class and citing the shrewd, polemical and rapacious Bavarian peasant as a case in point. I counter by opposing on the one hand the 'aristocrats' I have met here over the years, some of them world-famous scholars, for whom the broken promise is a way of life, the Greek kalends all over again; and on the other hand, the turbulent, predictable course of Greek political history from the time of the city-states to the present, right here on this representative island. "But Italian political history is equally turbulent," Karin says. "Yes," I retort, "but it has *flair*!" "You're just prejudiced," she replies, accurately.

And yet, and yet. Prescinding from my own enthusiasms and prejudices as scrupulously as I can, and accepting as far as it goes the argument from class stratification, I am left after so many years in this land with a stable and coherent set of impressions: the volatility of temperament that cuts across class distinctions, the political vehemence as a constant fact of *domestic* life, the inflammable friendships as easily extinguished as ignited, and the inveterate capriciousness and irresponsibility of ideological convictions (the upper-class Papandreou who received asylum in the West is presently in Moscow delivering himself of anti-American sentiments and seeking closer relations with the Eastern Bloc. In this he is being not so much expedient as Greek). For me the allegorical embodiment of the Greek temperament is not Achilles, though an element of his vain-gloriousness persists (as in the boast that Greece is not outnumbered by Turkey since one Greek is worth ten Turks), nor Odysseus who for all his cunning was in the habit of conversing with gods, but Proteus, the shape-changer, whom ordinary mortals will never succeed in pinning down, and from whom no disclosures will be compelled or extracted.

The first thing I did on disembarking at Corfu was drive to the Arkadion Hotel and order a coffee. The shock of that tepid, watery brew after a month of espressos and cappuccinos was enough to disenchant me with the place forever. On the *Anna Maria* steaming toward Paxos and loaded to the funnel with laryngeal women and heavy-set, self-important men, I wondered why I bothered to return. A family crowds toward the table beside ours and heaps innumerable plastic *tsantas* bulging with foodstuffs on the bench. Gradually they discover they have nowhere to sit and begin slipping their impedimenta to the floor to clear a space for themselves. One of the sacks plummets down the open hatchway. Stunned astonishment, followed by keening desperation as everyone scuffles helplessly about in several opposed directions in a flurry of feverish unproductiveness. Finally the *tsanta* is retrieved and the discommoded family once again begins its peristaltic weave around the freshly-cluttered table. Once I would have found this piece of vaudeville amusing and delightful; now I see merely the gracelessness and plain stupidity of it all.

I recall what Ferdinando said when I first met him and we discussed his several visits to Greece: "If you want to see classical Greece, you must go to Sicily." My prolonged love affair with Greece appears to be over. Paxos, the *real*

Paxos, bruised it beyond recognition; Italy buried it beyond redemption. I am still convinced that reality is to be preferred to illusion, that the world is superior in substance and depth and grandeur to Arcadia, but one is under no obligation to love it. Better a divorce predicated on fact than a marriage founded on desire. It now remains to discover what a more intimate and extensive acquaintance with Italy will beget (is Italy *my* Arcadia?), and whether it is possible for love and knowledge to live together happily, and if beauty and truth may indeed, in certain rare instances, despite the vexed conclusion of the renowned ode, be approximately equivalent.

There is a race of *Homo Arcadiensis* which may have scaled a ridge of wisdom not to be discounted. Since the world insists on its imperfection, it must be accepted on its own terms, but not without a certain preliminary screening and filtering. The traveller who is infected by ideal paradigms, who seeks like Shelley's Alastor for an unattainable purity of relationship, must inevitably be disappointed. He will come to Paxos and after the first euphoria has worn thin confront an island whose inhabitants fill the air with the bitter reek of cordite and fling garbage indiscriminately about like modern Cadmuses come down in the world. The only alternative for the perfectionist is the lifeless, glacial beauty of the North Pole. The wise Arcadian is instinctively aware of the romantic infirmity and counters the threat or the temptation by cultivating superficial relationships, confining his gaze to the perimeters of an astute and topiary modesty, and maintaining his independence by cleverly neglecting to learn the language of the people among whom he vacations or dwells. The *Ursprache* of money is sufficient. Thus he keeps out of trouble, preserves his illusions and remains more or less content.

But there is another race of traveller who is neither wise Arcadian nor Shelleyan idealist, who neither trains his watchdogs to hold the 'natives' at a respectable distance nor drowns in the Viareggio of romantic inappropriateness. For this peculiar soul the real is the ideal, the world is his poetic terminus, and a winter on Paxos underwrites the lyrical effusions of a hesperidean temperament. Travel is a way of avoiding Omaha, of discovering his true home, of learning how to acknowledge the whole hybrid creation, of accepting the plural and the demoniacal at their own outrageous valuation. Travel is the complex and labyrinthine grammar that eventuates in a simple, monosyllabic affirmation. Or, at least, such is the intention. What happens to this benighted and archaic representative of a specialized romanticism when the world proves intrinsically unlovable or, even worse, when it assumes the shape of its eternal adversary?

For I must still remain a considerable time on Paxos. It is still distressingly cold and moist. The cigarettes I left on the kitchen table are too wet to smoke and the cinders in the ashtray have turned to grey mud. The temperature in the house trembles around the zero mark: it is colder inside by several degrees than it is outside. The portable heater creates a small island of largely ineffectual warmth in a sea of frost and medullary damp. The clothes we left hanging in the corners have mildewed and the blankets feel like tracts of eutectic sludge. Spring will arrive one day, if rumour is to be credited, and the garden will be abloom with asters, anemones, lilies, forsythia and hyacinths, but the hunters will be stalking through the olive groves in a frenzied parody of Prokofiev. The birds will all be gone, dead or fled. (Norman Douglas, in his *Siren Land*, comments in a similar vein on the inhabitants of Capri: "No doubt an ornithologist would find much to interest him here during the spring and autumn migrations, for a number of rare birds alight at these seasons. But . . . every feathered thing is shot and eaten, irrespective of size or species.") The tourists will arrive by the arkload and the cafes will blossom with chairs and tables and the air will pullulate with disco vibes and artificial laughter and the night sky will rainbow forth its *son et lumière*. And now I have begun to understand that Arcadia is here to stay, that it has become a visceral and inalienable part of the real world, and that whatever we mean by *reality* must include its sworn antinomy, much as any classical city is partially defined by its core of resident traitors. The concept of reality has grown blurred past all attempts at clinical refocusing. The quotation marks will not be prized loose like rusty nails from the stigmata of the real world: Greece is also "Greece" and Paxos remains, among other things, "Paxos." Truth is undermined by its own definition and reality shows the character of dissimulation. Experience in the modern world has come to deny the very nature of experience and betrayal has grafted itself into the deepest fibres of our integrity.

❖

The phenomenon of mass tourism, deplored even by those who have derived the greatest advantage from it — the nostalgic 'local' as well as the discriminating expatriate — has nevertheless, for all the animadversion and contempt heaped upon it, been consistently underestimated as a factor in the molding of the contemporary sensibility. Together with its chief accessory, the refinement of the technological instrument (the relation is reversible), it has altered the configuration of the world in which we live. Entire populations respond to its demands in such a way that the emotional substrate of life built up over generations of felt and transmitted experience is radically transformed. People begin to travesty their own past, their own selfhood, their own humanity, on the one hand by turning themselves into the stereotypes decreed by the *Guide Michelin* and on the other by allowing themselves to become parasitical organisms at the cost of their dignity and historical identity. Greece with its chronic poverty and lack of natural resources is an illustration of this dynamic *in extremis*. What else can the Greeks do? Without the common market, without the emigration of more than a third of its population, without remittances from abroad, and especially without the millions of tourists who throng here each year, the country would inexorably sink into a condition of medieval stupor. But causes are not reasons and reasons are not justifications. Understanding need not force acceptance.

Something like thirty-five percent of the inhabitants of modern Tuscany hail from elsewhere. Yet Tuscany is still intact, much as Mary McCarthy described it in 1959 in her evocative *The Stones of Florence* which traced the persistence of its Renaissance character right into the present age. Its diversified and self-subsistent economy goes a long way to accounting for this degree of historical continuity, but there is also something in the psyche of the Tuscans which has survived the vicissitudes of time, the upheavals and sieges and revolutions and floods and miscegenations and uprootings, and retained an attitude to the world whose lineage is still discernible and relatively unmixed. The sense of ordered space in Florentine painting is still evident, McCarthy observes, in Tuscan agriculture with its perspectival allotments of field and garden, its ruled symmetries and graduated dispositions. And the Tuscan peasant, as I can myself attest, has achieved a personal cultivation and civility that bears the watermark of what might elsewhere pass for aristocratic discrimination. These are aspects of the Tuscan character which, however they may be explained, demonstrably exist. Whether they will continue to exist under the onslaught of modern tourism is another question.

But Paxos is largely dependent for its charm upon its ambrosial reserves of natural beauty which might satisfy the most ravenous of aesthetic appetites. Haralambos professes to be content with sunsets and seascapes. But Paxos is not only a green rock in a blue sea or a backdrop for atmospheric displays. It is also a living creature, a social entity, a small chunk of the human world. Paxos is as much its people as it is sea, sunset, and mountain pomanders of orange and lemon. (It is also at least as much its winter torrents and terrible cold as it is almond-scented spring and fig-ripening summer.) But in its social manifestation it is plainly compounded of greed, pettiness and deception but a deception of a peculiar sort, for the nature of deceit has changed and become more radical, intimate, pervasive, more interior than ever before. It is not simply the bankbook that is cheated but the diminishing fund of human expectations and, more critically, the exchequer of the mythopoeic imagination. We are paying with ever greater extravagance for fictions, stereotypes and hallucinations and increasingly coming to resemble the chimeras of self, the factitious identities, with which we barter for our livelihood. This is the singular curse of the modern world. And we must acknowledge that projections and ectoplasms are difficult to repel. When an entire world with only a few exceptions begins to believe in the congenial fables, iconologies and personae it manufactures industrially for its own consumption as well as for export, reality is contaminated at the source. As McCarthy remarked in *Venice Observed*: "There is no use pretending that the tourist Venice is not the real Venice, which is possible with other cities, Rome or Florence or Naples. The tourist Venice *is* Venice." This remark must now be amplified exponentially and should be applied not only to cities and countries but to concrete, specific individuals as well. People, even sedentary people, have become, in essence, tourists. One can no longer be saved even by dismemberment. We may recall in this connection the old war joke about the English P.O.W. who has his amputated limbs sent home one by one for interment with the approval of the sympathetic Kommandant until the latter puts a stop to these bizarre and macabre shipments. "I understand at last," he cries, "you are trying to escape."

Paxos is the most beautiful island I have known and lived on. It is also the most austere, rude and inhospitable. But it is, over and above all this, as Europe prepares its vernal invasion, its own caricature and negation. Thus, Paxos provides us with a modern definition of 'reality:' beauty, hardship and fraud. As for Italy, it will not doubt become for me, as it is politically for its citizens, a complicated way of avoiding the issue. Perhaps it will one day teach me to love Paxos better, a little more tolerantly, than I do now. Or perhaps it will lead to one more in a series of increasingly bitter refusals. Ultimately and ironically, it may culminate in the most painful recognition of all: *Et in Arcadia, Ego.*

Epilogue. Spring.

The hunting season is on us again, in fullest blast. The *trigonia* came wheeling in two weeks ago in their great seasonal migration from the littoral of North Africa to the grain fields of the Ukraine, the sky over Paxos all speckled and brindled with innumerable birds. It was a kind of advent, the enormous flocks performing their evolutions above us in complete silence, circling and careering in their mile-long looped trajectories like animate constellations, obeying cyclic, instinctual rhythms that must remain forever inscrutable to us.

The next day the activities of normal life on the island were suspended as the hunting mania triumphed over every other consideration. Lakka wore a sad, deserted air, shops closed or on skeleton staff, the incessant building of tourist facilities abruptly stopped, houses locked up. And from morning to night the island reverberates with the sound of gunfire. Up here in Moungelatika one has the impression of being in the middle of a battlefield. The windowpanes rattle, grapeshot plummets into our hair, strangers beat their way through Karin's garden looking for fallen turtle-doves, and the booming detonations from the double-barrelled shotguns at distances of ten to twenty-five meters have us involuntarily ducking our heads, spilling our coffee, jumping startled out of bed, glancing nervously over our shoulders. Suddenly a bird comes plunging through the olive branches like a stricken fighter-plane in an explosion of leaves and twigs, hits the earth near our feet with a deep thud, coughing blood, and then lies there dead with its talons neatly folded and a feather in its beak. We pick it up and give it to Arete, who cannot understand how we should part with so delicate a sweetmeat.

The men have donned their hunter's green, which resembles military fatigues. The theory is, of course, that of camouflage, but the reality is something very different, namely, transfiguration. An island of tourist entrepreneurs, prosperous merchants, and lazy and incompetent young men has undergone a radical metamorphosis. Everyone has become and instant hero. The landscape swarms with fierce *andartes* and dedicated royalists, with magnificent hunters bristling with rifles and adorned with cartridge belts slung bandoleer-fashion from the shoulder. You see them stalking with exaggerated and grotesque slow-motion steps under the olives and cypresses, their white running shoes glittering in the sun and subverting their elaborate attempts at invisibility. At night they gather in the cafes, lean their guns against the wall, and talk of nothing but *trigonia*: the one they shot but could not find, the wily one that escaped, the fat one caught in a deadly crossfire.

But it is a curious sort of hunting, a hunting without the slightest element of danger or risk except from other hunters, and requiring not an iota of *dexiotis*, of skill or ability. Their is hardly any need to aim. You merely raise your gun and fire, and the conic section of the pellet spray takes in half the sky. Whatever is up there is immediately riddled, including a large number of inedible finches, swallows and titmice. From time to time the *trigoni* obsession claims its human victim. Two years ago one of the hunters was reclining against a wall, the top of his head showing over the coping. This unfortunate extremity was very quickly mistaken for a perching bird and accordingly pitted by a blast of grapeshot. The man was flown to Germany for an operation. And Lambi, Anglaia's husband, opened his door one morning to be greeted by a double volley in the midsection which blew him, metaphorically speaking, clear to Corfu for a visit of several weeks in the hospital.

We have no choice but to wait out the fever and hope for the best. Little Anthia has been shipped off to Athens by her parents for the rest of the month. Hannah is the only child on the hilltop now, and we have trained her never to look up when she hears gunfire, the main hazard being an eyeful of scorching pellets. We have pleaded with our neighbours to shoot form a safer distance, but to no avail. I have complained vehemently to the police, but they are also powerless, being understaffed and too prudent to interfere with the consuming and insensate passion of the islanders. We have fought back in the only way we know how, by caring for a wounded *trigoni* we found one morning in the garden. With its wing shot through, it had made a small nest for itself among the lupine and calendula and prepared to die. We placed it in the chicken shed and Karin has been feeding and attending to it ever since, applying a balm of wood ash and olive oil to its wound. Yesterday morning it managed to escape and flew into an olive tree in the neighbouring yard, which was as far as its mending wing would carry it, and proceeded to sit there like a plump, stationary target in a shooting gallery. It took us a good part of the morning to dislodge it by climbing part way up the tree and tugging at the branch with a fifteen-foot pruning hook. It is now back in the shed and suffering from deep depression.

At this very moment as I write, someone has fired from just behind the garden wall. The pellets ripple through the lemon tree beside the table and Karin raises Huxley's book on Greek flora to protect her face. The air is a-twitter with bird panic, the chirr and flutter of myriad wings and arpeggios of syncopated trills in different registers. Evangelos, Arete's son, is patrolling his front garden just below our property, the long gleaming barrel of his gun performing its symbolic labour of priapic substitution. Another blast and the dead seed sizzles and cools on the ground between the snapdragons and the dogrose bush.

Easter has come and gone with its predictable glories and absurdities. The Friday night ceremony at church took place on two parallel levels of mutual and interpenetrating significance, like the double row of images on the local iconostasis. Papa Diamantis sang the liturgy with rapt devotion and solemnity, flanked by two ministrants who wept prolifically and kept sponging their tears with hand-kerchiefs the size of small flags. At the same time Aleko Apergis and Kyrios Aronis, off to the side of the altar, were busy counting the coins from the sale of candles and rolling them up into tidy, bankable little cylinders. The church was packed to the clerestory and everyone, from the youngest child of three to the veteran of eighty Easters, carried the obligatory lighted candle, so that I failed to understand the general consternation that ensued after Anthia's newly-grown hair caught fire. This appeared inev-itable to me, the only possible question pertaining to the identity of the sacrificial victim. The aureole was quickly doused and the service proceeded amid billows of sweet incense-and-honey smoke undercut by the faint, acrid stench of burnt hair. Then the candlelight procession round the village was spoiled by a nasty, secular wind that extinguished the prismatic twinkle of tiny flames in tardy restitution for the near disaster in the church. And the midnight service on the day of the *anastasis* was not free of its element of bathos either. Papa Diamantis, surrounded by his expectant congregation, approached the locked portals of the church and knocked the prescribed three times for symbolic admittance to the tomb in which the miracle had been enacted. After the echoes had faded, the door failed to open. It required a fourth, vigorous, determined pounding to alert the distracted sacristan who, I imagine, was probably attending to the rolls of candle money.

We keep mainly to ourselves, although the children have integrated splendidly into the community. Alki is rarely at home, having become a popular, sleek, tavli-playing Paxiot, and Hannah is making friends right and left and even dreams in Greek; in fact, she is no longer Hannah, but Annoula. All our fears of last September and October have dissipated with respect to the children, but we ourselves have come to feel increasingly confined and deprived. The other day it occurred to me that the narrow circumference of our garden has been one of the limits of my horizon for the better part of a year. I long for extended travel, for conversation, for the brisk exchange of ideas, for new books, different foods, other views and perspectives, for people who can help me replenish my dwindling stock of words, thoughts and exhilarations. I realize I am not ready for retirement or a meditative hermitage, and a steady diet of hunting talk, local gossip and pedestrian arithmetic (the people are perpetually counting: money, birds, rummy scores, votes) provides me with a little nourishment. Karin has taken *Candide*'s advice and tends her garden. She has coaxed a few sceptical artichoke bushes from the rocky and depleted soil, planted dill, parsley, tomatoes and peppers, is constantly pruning and watering. And the garden has responded: red poppy and mist-white nigella, clusters of wild garlic, jack-in-the-pulpit, the creamy upthrusting beakers of the arum flower, roses, geraniums, blossoming cherry, pear and almond. I see her walking among the Spanish broom and petticoats of lacy, white vetch, pausing under the pink mallow, struggling with the water can among the corn-yellow crown daisies and blue-petalled borage.

Which brings me back, as I see her tending to the borage, to the blue flower again, on the rim of a shard, or here in the garden beneath the orange trees, or in the elegiac poetry of those yearning, umbilical romantics. For this is Arcadia in its noblest, most vulnerable and necessary manifestation, the single aspect of the myth without which we would be truly impoverished. It is a curiously apt and heraldic scene, a *tableau vivant*, as if it had been invented for the occasion: my wife standing there in the garden, ankle-deep in borage flowers, beside the one sick almond tree whose leaves are turning brittle and red with what she calls *trigoni*-blood. And in the shed the crippled bird sits immobile and hieratic as part of the emblematic necessity I seem to recognize, the symbol of this flawed and beautiful island and of our own perennial desire for wholeness, consummation and flight, Arcadia being nothing else than the mythographic embodiment of that desire, as indispensable as it is deceptive.

The islanders talk about the quality of their stones the way other people do about the pedigree of their livestock or the different grades of the tea or tobacco they grow. Here, they are connoisseurs in the appreciation of subtle distinctions of density, shape, hue and friability. Pepitsa, showing us the old property in Manasatika that a feud between her husband and brother had allowed to fall into a state of utter dilapidation, commented proudly, "But these are good stones." And so they were: flat, trim, balanced, plate-like imbrications raised into walls that from a distance look as neat and clipped as English hedges. The best stones on the island come from Manasatika and Kastanida. The stones around Dendiatika are notable for their roseate hue, the stones in Boikatika for their massiveness, and those on the hill of Aghios Georgos for their detachable cores. Labour requires the avoirdupois scale; appreciation, that of Troy weight. Apart from olives, what other natural resource to the Paxiots have to be knowledgeable about?

It is interesting to note the degree to which the liturgy has influenced secular life, as if it were a structural paradigm for even the most common of profane activities. I was fascinated by Stavros reading a newspaper article aloud to his cronies in the cafeneion. The story had to do with a passion killing: husband, wife, lover, bullets, neighbours, all the predictables. Stavros read each sentence in plain-song, a perfect representation of liturgical chanting, raising pitch only to signify the full stop. He had become an officiating priest, the men assembled before him into an attentive congregation. At the end of each sentence, responding to the signal of inflection, they would emit a series of antiphonal phrases, commentary, judgement, elaboration. When the hubbub of voices subsided into the canonical and expectant silence, Stavros would begin his recitation anew and so it went for the better part of an hour, a classical rite and sermon. I realized that the cafene-ion had been converted into a church and that I, sipping my morning coffee and reading the mail, had been observ-ing a kind of mass.

It is in ways like this that the influence of the orthodox church can never be seriously challenged. However casual people are about their religion, however disestablishing the tendencies of government, the Sunday service is diffracted six mornings a week into the communal reci-tation of the newspaper in practically every cafeneion in rural Greece.

I am thinking of Karin's shard collecting again, and of the universal passion for collecting *per se*, and wondering if there does not exist a wider explanatory context for this preoccupation. The Kabbalah tells us that the Macro-prosopos created the vessel of the universe by emitting a beam of pure light from between His eyes. A second luminal emanation produced the stuff of life itself but was so powerful that it shattered the vessel it was intended to fill. Thus the cosmos was flawed at its very inception, and man was subsequently created to descend into the abyss in which the original fragments had fallen in order to find and reclaim the shards of the philoprogenitive vessel and return them, on ascension after death, to the Creator. As a result mankind works in a kind of synergism with the divine, one of the collaborators of God. (As in Manichean theology as well, which considers the hybrid world to consist of 'undelivered' light particles absorbed by the demonic element of darkness.)

We detect the same idea at work in nineteenth century German idealism, in which human life and thought is variously understood as a gambit on the part of Spirit or a strategy devised by Nature to assist in the great work of Self-consciousness. The human mind is regarded as a perfectible mirror in which the Creative Impetus is progressively enabled to recognize its own features. The notion of human collaboration in the prolonged act of divine redemption is once again paramount. It is taken up a little later by the French philosopher, Henri Bergson, who understands the *élan vital* as the effort generated by the Transcendent to liberate itself from its congealment in Matter through a laborious, upward process of spiritual evolution. Nikos Kazantzakis in *The Saviors of God*, *The Modern Odyssey*, and *Zorba the Greek* developed his thought along identical lines, inventing literary vehicles to carry this freight of metaphysical speculation. Man becomes God's accomplice and helper, as the divine flame is gradually freed from its fleshly wick and rises toward unencumbered spirituality. (It occurs to me that an analogous treatment of Creative emergence, or rather merger, is to be found in Spinoza as well.) And, of course, the Catholic theologian, Teilhard de Chardin with the wonderful pun encoded phonetically into his name elaborated the same perennial theme in his concept of the nous-sphere that is slowly enveloping the planet like a sort of atmosphere or Van Allen belt. It is tempting to consider each separate, individual consciousness as a mental shard being gradually fused and annealed into the translucent substance of the original Kabbalistic vessel.

Does this longing for wholeness, for the reconstruction of the primordial monad, this profound desire for lucidity, understanding and integration explain the human passion for *collecting*: coins, stamps, seashells, music boxes, prints, first editions, coloured stones, porcelains, African masks, anything at all, including, most appropriately, fragments and shards of something that was once whole and now lies scattered and dispersed, like the body of Osiris? Is this not, finally, what the blue flower symbolizes? In Manichean terminology, collecting would be the expression of the basic human need to deliver or redeem the particles of contaminated light obscured by the chaotic, mixed and dispersed condition of our existence. The venture is essentially a function of our desire to encompass totality, to reassemble the elements of some pre-existent category or *series* that has been sundered and cast adrift. It is the same obsessive urge we discover behind the need to solve jig-saws and crosswords, or to reconstitute the component parts of any original set or aggregate at all. And Karin's quest for the original blue-flowered plate that lies splin-tered and pulverized in a million irretrievable shards on all the rubbish mounds of Paxos is an aspect of that primal human compulsion to achieve wholeness, to recover a pristine auroral identity. It is the Kabbalistic quest, in miniature or parable.

The climax of the day occurs for us, not at the canonical moment of sunset, but at quarter to nine or so in the morning when the sun floats over the tops of the olive trees and floods the garden with its alluvial light of orange and saffron. At that precise instant the cicadas strike up their resonating overture, the sound swelling rapturously, hugely, symphonically, until every cicada in this part of Moungelatika is fiddling the sun higher and higher in its laborious journey through the heavens. And then it seems as if the sun is actually buoyed up on this massive wave of orchestral sound and that should the cicadas cease for even a moment it would immediately plummet into the abyss and vanish from our sight. The cicadas, like the Pueblo Indians, seem to feel this too. The work of accompanying and sponsoring the sun goes on all day, and is taken up again during the night as if they felt responsible for the moon as well. The quiet descends in the small hours of the morning as the cicadas pack up their tiny stradivarii and take their rest, with the intuitive awareness, no doubt, of having played the world safely through another day.

Spiro Minimarket, who is among the most fanatic of the *trigoni*-hunters, is also distinguished for the depth and fervour of his political loyalties. With the elections looming people have begun taking sides with an inner conviction and certitude eclipsed only by the insane blare of the perambulating, vehicle-borne loudspeakers. "I am green, green," Spiro declares, referring to the PASOK colours but reminding me bizarrely of Lorca's poem. Each day I solicit his membership in some new political party of my own invention, like the *Trigoni Exoteriko*, but he refuses to respond to the joke, vowing that he is "socialist to the last breath." I wonder what it means to be "socialist" in Paxos. Spiro's family, for example, runs the most flourishing market in Lakka, operates the lucrative Tourist Agency on the port, and owns considerable property not only in the town itself but in the hills above Monodendri as well. Spiro drives about in a vw minibus, and his brother Panayotis, when he is not on the phone to Italy or strolling about with a walkie-talkie pressed to his ear in earnest confabulation with his subalterns, is to be seen behind the wheel of his Fiat Pony or the handlebars of his Honda motorbike. In the offseason they enjoy the benefits of continental travel and Panayotis recently visited Saudi Arabia, returning with a portfolio of new contacts if not contracts. Spiro cut short his own travels in order to return in time for the *trigoni* hunt.

Spiro's socialism is approached though perhaps not matched by that of my landlord, Costas, who is constantly rushing to and fro with PASOK pamphlets, posters and flags, one of which he has planted on the back of his tractor. As ardent and vehement a socialist as he may be, he continues to enjoy the unearned increment of his wife's dowry, namely, the house I am renting, the use of the family villa in Vassilatika, the indulgence of his restaurateur father, a winter of uninterrupted card playing and a spring filled with the delights of the hunt. I keep asking what it means to be a socialist in this island and the only answer I can come up with is that the definition is purely nominal and negative: to be a PASOK socialist has nothing at all to do with Socialism, as one glance at the oligarchic lifestyle of George Papandreou should make abundantly clear, and everything to do with not being a KKE radical or a Nea Demokratia centre-rightist. Greek politics, whatever their intellectual origins, are entirely self-referential. Loyalties are defined by delimiting animosities, assent by corresponding repudiations, a political plus by a double, multiplied minus (+PASOK = -KKE x -N.D.). I can conceive of Spiro and Costas turning their colours only under two, albeit unlikely conditions: if the Socialist party should prohibit *trigoni* shooting; or if, in a sudden and implausible access of conscience, it should adopt a socialist platform.

❖

Eleni, standing black and massive at the door of her dry goods shop, surrounded by a party of English tourists. She is holding a service, chanting the endless liturgy of her complaints that makes entering her shop such a risky, time-consuming venture. It is the usual gravamen: her prolonged widowhood, the burden of supporting her son in medical school in Romania, inflation and devaluation, and the fact that she has never taken a vacation in her life. "I ganna do vacation every year," she mumbles, and the English tourists misinterpret the first three words slurred thickly together with the gamma pronounced as gh sounding partly like a shallow, frontal 'r' as Grenada. "Oh," pipes one of the ladies in that high, chirpy, half-surprised intonation they all have, "you go to Grenada for your vacation every year. How nice for you." And she is utterly serious in her delight.

Eleni is dumbfounded. "No, No," she sputters, "no Grenada."

The sympathetic lady does not know what to make of this contradiction. It seems perfectly logical to her that Eleni, proprietress of a tumbledown shop with the paint peeling off the window-frames, should jet to Grenada every year for a little frolic and relaxation. Eleni I know well and the Greeks I understand in part, but the English with their invincible politeness and cheery, brisk, ritualistic fellow-feeling that renders them so insensitive to the things and people around them, have always escaped me.

❖

Marigo sits in her cigarette-cum-grocery shop, her hair mottled brown and grey, wearing her dusty, brown potato-sack of a dress. She is watching television, an American rock video with Greek subtitles. A tall black is cakewalking behind a half-naked, punk-shorn nymphette, miming intercourse to the heavy metal beat. Marigo looks up and says, "They are all barbarians over there." "Maybe," I reply, "but there are barbarians everywhere." "Ah," she reflects and smiles, "but surely there are no barbarians in Greece." "In Greece especially," I say.

Marigo is taken aback. "Impossible" she draws the word out to indicate disbelief. "In America there are barbarians. And in Turkey. But not here. Where do you find barbarians in Greece?"

Marigo, who has spent all her life on Paxos and enjoyed little schooling, does not know her history nor can be expected to. But she does know her cigarette shop which, being on the point of collapse, was demolished this winter in order to be reconstructed in the spring by her son, who is a professional builder. But the *trigoni* season intervened and for the last month he has been stalking through ilex and arbutus blasting everything out of the sky while Marigo sits behind a makeshift slat-and-billet counter surrounded by a free-standing cement blocks in lieu of a wall, covered in dust and *asvesti* which turns to mud when it rains through the perforated ceiling. When she is not at the counter, she is hauling bricks back and forth in a hod or small wheelbarrow. Marigo is over sixty. I remind her somewhat theatrically that my four year old daughter is in considerable danger from the cartridges her son is busy

272

peppering our house with — his moustache is frequently to be seen decorating the geranium bushes in the adjoining garden. All this, I tell her, strikes me as a mild form of barbarism, at any rate. Marigo nods and smiles ruefully. "Maybe you are right," she concedes, and as I stumble out over the chicken-crate steps, I hear her musing aloud, "In Greece, too!"

Evangelos the butcher (our neighbour Yanni's son) is once again in disfavour with Karin, who is raging at least five or six Beaufort of housewifely fury. I can't say that I blame her. The Mastoras family has been a veritable thornbush in our sides since that ill-fated Christmas eve visit. It seems that every week or two I have to cross the yard with another complaint. During the hunting season Evangelos is one of the chief offenders. At one point I had to tie a white towel to a pole to ensure safe passage for Karin and Hannah along the Moungelatika road which winds past our adjacent houses. During the remaining nine months of the year, Rocky, who is a rather indifferent retriever, is chained day and night to his jerrybuilt kennel and hurls all his ninety pounds into a feverish cachinnation of howling and moaning. He generally ceases around one o'clock in the morning and resumes at seven, a disruption of normal life I have only recently come to terms with by mobilizing the rest of the community which consists of Anglaia's and Stamatella's households further up the road. From time to time Rocky is taken down to Lakka to give us a breather.

We are largely dependent on the Matoras butcher shop for our meat supply, a fact which has played havoc with our diet and driven us into occasional adventures with vegetarianism. Neither Evangelos nor his father have any experience of their trade, having purchased the shop from a relative two years ago. They can distinguish beef from pork and can slam a heavy cleaver through bone and gristle: this is the extent of their combined virtuosity. Several months ago Yanni sliced through his finger with a rusty blade while flensing a hunk of semi-frozen meat, but neglected to attend properly to his wound which eventually festered and led to two operations for blood poisoning. After his recovery, he underwent a fresh spate of difficulties with a defective grinder, which had to be sent to Athens for repairs. The machine returned as rebellious as ever, and Yanni immediately proceeded to get his arm stuck to the elbow in the metal funnel, managing to switch off the contrivance just as it was about to mince a goodly portion of his hand into the ground meat. (It was Alki who released him with a borrowed screwdriver). A kilo of this ambiguous substance which I brought up to the house turned out, when unwrapped, to be shot through with flecks and striations of vermicular whiteness. This posed a considerable enigma until Karin figured out that the meat had been mixed with the stringy vestiges of Yanni's bandage.

Yanni displays an unimaginative and authoritarian disposition which renders him rather unappetizing, but Evangelos, who has inherited both of these patristic traits, has added several of his own, including laziness, indifference, sullenness, and a degree of avarice more rampant than the norm. Never have I seen him exert himself. Except during the *trigoni* season, he never walks, driving to the shop down the steep Lakka path on his little red Honda motorbike or taking the long way round through Apergatika in his Nissan pick-up. I have rarely seen him contribute to the work on the new bachelor's house his parents are having built for him; on the few occasions when he is present I have to step across and ask him to turn down the tape deck which is bellowing disco at full volume. He is also forgetful: the half-lamb we ordered for the long Easter weekend was never delivered and we were three days without food, except for a few packages of paleontological spaghetti, a quandary from which Anglaia rescued us with a timely invitation. Today we discovered that the two chickens he sold us had rotted in the fridge and had to be thrown out to the cats. Karin is livid. "Tell him he shouldn't sell his chickens, he should bury them," she rants. But we know that short of complaining to the *koinotita*, the only satisfaction we will get is to see Evangelos shrug his shoulders and smile with that peculiar mix of inanity and ineffability we have become so accustomed to. Afterwards he will hoist his overweight belly into the cab of his Nissan and drive off to the Aloni discotheque. Then Rocky will curdle the night with his Baskerville howl and Yanni and Areti will bolt the shutters, lock the door, and let the television loose. Last night, rather, early this morning during one of Rocky's infrequent remissions, we were awakened by the unexpected grate of American speech from the film they were watching. "Are you crazy?" a Bogartian voice rasped.

275

✥

Visa problems again. It took us nearly two months of driving back and forth between Lakka and Gaios last autumn to procure our original visas. First we needed to produce a set of official photos, but since the only recognized photographer on Paxos is the mute shopkeeper in Gaios whose whereabouts are often as obscure and mysterious as those of the Graia in classical mythology, it was some time before we could pin him down. Furthermore, since he has no studio, all his work is done alfresco. On the day of the session, there was a gale-force wind blowing off the sea, which forced us to spend much of the morning trying to find a suitable wall against which to have our pictures taken. Several days later we picked up the photos: we resembled a party of the condemned, hair blown straight up, an expression of terror frozen on our faces, and a blank wall in the background. Having delivered these to the police station, the next requirement was to purchase the necessary stamps: another wasted morning trying to locate the appropriate office. Afterwards we set about filling the requisite forms in quadruplicate, twenty sheets of paper all told. Next the forms had to be processed. Finally, after several more weeks, the visas were ready and we had received permission to stay in Greece for the year.

But we had not reckoned with the local genius for complication. When we left for Italy in February, the visas were confiscated by the customs authorities in Corfu, who assured us that they would be forwarded to the police station in Gaios where they would be waiting for us on our return. That was nearly half a year ago and the visas have not yet surfaced. I made a trip to Corfu last month to track down the missing permits. The customs officials had sent them to the Corfu Tourist Police, who had in turn dispatched them to Gaios, where they must presently lie moldering beneath one of the pyramidic stacks of files that teeter against the yellowing walls, but three visits to that chaotic hutch have proven equally fruitless. I go again today on the 11:30 bus, but expect to return empty-handed. It is too late to apply for new visas, which means that I will have to pay a fine at the International airport on the day of our departure. I am beginning to suspect a lucrative method in all this systematic madness.

I ask Haralambos how it is that Yanni and Areti, to whom he is distantly related, do not seem to mind the noise that spews nonstop from their property. He smiles pityingly. "Ees you not understand? Ees being stupid? Bang. Bang. All the life." Finally I get it. Like so many Paxiots, they are partially deaf from a lifetime of gunfire.

Drive back from Loggos (pronounced Longos, but the double gamma does not discourage *reading* it as 'Logos,' the 'word,' the other pole of Moungelatika) with Michelakis in the tiny, cramped, red Austin Mini that has

277

replaced his now defunct taxi. We played the popular game of guessing one another's age to while away a little more of it. For the Greek taxi driver a silent passenger is the curse of his profession and a sign of the incomprehensible depravity of the foreign temperament. Michelakis shrewdly assessed the white prickles in my stubble and the copious grey over my ears, toted up the lines and wrinkles, and produced his estimate with a slight note of triumph. "You are fifty-five," he said. "You are wrong," I replied. "Surely it is not more?" "Less." He reflected a few moments, squinting as if I were a passing *trigoni* in his cross-sights. "Forty-nine?" "No." "Forty-five?" "No." He gave it up, growing visibly embarrassed at the possibility of having committed an outrage against my *amour propre*. "Forty-three," I said, trying to smile reassuringly. He whistled through his teeth and exclaimed, "But you are just a child." "I have many problems," I said, to take him off the hook. It was my turn now to compute his sum of physical deterioration and degradation of spirit, but I was determined not to make the same mistake and deliberately underestimated. "Forty?" "No." "Forty-five?" "No." I threw up my hands and confessed myself stymied. "Fifty," he said, his earlier mortification now tempered with pride and relief. For Michelakis looks every crease and pucker of his age and probably feels ten years older. He is one of the few Paxiots who has not demonstrably prospered with the tourist rush. He goes about constantly unshaven, his tall, angular figure stooped and racked with a perpetual cough, and he is often drunk. His father owned the first motor vehicle on Paxos and he himself possesses a chauffeur's licence; in fact Michelakis taught many of the auroral motorists here the rudiments of driving. Now they swerve and careen around the island like the infatuated Toad, amassing money, vehicles, houses, land, while he remains in Lakka with a broken-down taxi, a superannuated dog, and a narrow, crooked little house. And he is often bitter and aggrieved, complaining that the Paxiots, learn-proof to a man, are unforgivably ignorant of the fine art of driving and that it is one of God's miracles they have not utterly destroyed themselves yet.

As for myself, I take a bit of consolation in the fact reported by De Quincey that Wordsworth was once riding in a coach in which the age-guessing game was taking place. Though he was still in his thirties, the passengers assumed that he was a sexagenarian who would never see his grandchildren grow to maturity.

As the day of wrath and tears, or is it laughter and rejoicing, approaches, I am gradually taking inventory of our year in Paxos. My thoughts dwell mostly on the people I have met and gotten to know in that time. They are on the whole an eidetic group, but remind me of that description in Paul Theroux's *The Consul's File*: "And he had failed at being a person, so he tried to succeed at being a character." The majority of the people I have grown acquainted with here strike me as essentially anecdotal, Theophrastian, curiously heraldic. They are not an altogether agreeable lot.

There are exceptions, those whom I acknowledge and respect as redemptive figures. Spiro Petrou is one of the quiet heroes of my attestation, a man whose avuncular presence smoothed over many difficult moments. Whenever I needed a taxi to meet the boat in Gaios after one of our trips to Corfu, it was Spiro who made the arrangements. Spiro who lent me money when the bank's coffers were depleted, who saw us through a particularly bad week in the middle of the winter with a drum of petrolgaz, and who tutored Alki in his career as part-time garçon. It was directly owing to this quarter-year stint as a waiter that Alki managed to pick up a working knowledge of Greek and to integrate so effortlessly into the community. Without Spiro's comforting presence down the hill in Lakka, we would have had a lonelier and more dismal time of it than was often the case.

And of course the redoubtable Anglaia, perhaps the most vital and energetic woman I have ever met. She is crowding sixty, plump, muscular, bustling and gyroscopic. So ceaselessly vigorous is she that she has consumed the very marrow and life-force out of her immediate family: her husband Lambi dodders by, laconic and self-encapsulated (As Karin puts it, "And wherever Anglaia went, her Lambi was sure to go"), her daughter Stamatella is a moody type, suffers from chronic lumbar pains and recently contracted chicken-pox (Anglaia claims she has never been sick in her life), and her son Pericles, who is presently visiting from Preveza, moons about in a pleasant, vapid, inoffensive way, leaving no wake when he departs. (In contrast Anglaia is a human bevetron). When

Anglaia is not feeding her chickens and goats, she is weaving at her loom; when she is not at the loom, she is busy crocheting, or perhaps she is pressing olive oil; otherwise she is cooking up stews, baking *pitta* and *kourabiethes*, preserving jams, brewing various herbal teas, and casefying thick bulbs of *mezithra*, among the best I have sampled. In her off-moments, she is to be found carding and spinning. She is up at six and turns out the light at midnight. And yet amid the perennial hum of all this activity, she has found the time to be a sympathetic and congenial neighbour, pampering us with the specialties of her kitchen and instructing Karin in the garden.

These two, Spiro and Anglaia, have rescued me from an onslaught of terminal misanthropy, and if I am not more cynical than I feel at present, after Maria's lunge for extra rent, after Fat George trying to dun me twice for the pedal boat I rented for the children, after Evangelos' poisonous meat and decrepit chickens and the Mastoras circus-barrage of unneighbourly noise, after months of pleading with the tribe of frenetic hunters to shoot *away* from the house, after a winter of nigh-indescribable cold and a year of nigh-perpetual insomnia, I have Spiro and Anglaia to thank for whatever residue of human warmth remains in my jaundiced and dyspeptic system. And yet, paradoxically, I regret not a single moment of it.

And then there is Barba Grigory.
Barba Grigori moves in that ambiguous region between

characterhood and seership. There is no doubt that he is a 'character,' but there is enormous humour and imagination and wisdom in him too. Our first meeting in the *plateia* in Lakka last October was a disaster: tempers flared, harsh words were exchanged, and we avoided one another religiously for the next month. The issue, as was so often the case in the early days here, was Hannah, wholly unprepared as we were for the lavish and physically intimate attention that young children and especially little girls tend to receive. Sometimes little girls are treated — dressed and addressed — as dolls, and the epithet *kukla*, heaped so abundantly on all creatures of the human species and female gender under the age of five, is more than a merely metaphorical expression. It is on occasion frighteningly close to the truth. Sometimes the need for the somatic expression of emotion can scarcely be distinguished from a physical assault. The clutching, grabbing and squeezing can resemble an unprovoked attack on the physical integrity of the diminutive victim, and at one time Hannah sported such a collection of bruises and lacerations that she looked as if she had been tattooed. And sometimes, though rarely, the assault is disturbingly pedophilic. This was one of the reasons we chose not to settle in Ozias in the southern part of the island, where the proprietor of the cafe-grocery store swooped down on a terrified Hannah and devoted himself with rapt devotion to pinching and squeezing her nether regions. There followed a bizarre tug of war in which I had literally to tear my daughter out of his arms and fend off a number of repeated 'passes,' plucking motions, at her unripened delicacies while a grotesque chorus of black-garbed crones chortled and wheezed, enjoying the scene hugely.

It was shortly after this perverse encounter that I met Barba Grigory. I was still smoldering and Hannah tended to cringe whenever anyone approached her, when Grigory seized her by the shoulders and lifted her in the air, nuzzling his grizzled chin in her neck with gruff affection. He was, of course, only being sociable, and the twin bruises that he left as evidence of his friendliness were simply the result of his old man's lack of dexterity. But I was in no mood to make allowances, retrieved Hannah from his vigorous grasp, and held him at arm's length.

"Leave her alone," I shouted, "Can't you see she is afraid?"

He grew angry in turn. "Why?," he growled, "She has nothing to be afraid of."

"She is afraid," I repeated, "She is not used to your customs."

And for the next month I kept Hannah away from practically everyone, developing a local reputation for unneighbourliness and eccentricity.

Eventually relations improved and I explained to Grigory, who was after all a kindly soul and Anthia's grandfather and an Olympian part of the Moungelatika *ratsa*, the reasons that underlay my inexplicable reaction to his attempts at welcome. He merely grunted and laughed. "*Tha synethisi*," he said, "she will get used to it." But after a moment's reflection, added, "But you are also right."

I saw Barba Grigori at his best and most theatrically entertaining during the Easter meal that Anglaia prepared for the entire clan. Grigori sat at the head of the table and dominated the assembly with his rhetorical effusiveness, tossing back great beakers of Antipaxos wine and swallowing Lestrygonian mouthfuls of *pitta*, *keftedes*, and *arni*. He was developing a theme on which he had obviously brooded for many years: the degeneracy of women in the modern world as compared with the strength, dignity and uncomplaining fortitude of their mothers and grandmothers.

"Today, you can watch them tripping down to Lakka, dressed up in their finery, three times a day. What do they want?"

"They want to go shopping," said Lambi, amusement tempered with disapproval, his fear of the scandalous.

"Shopping! Sheepshit! They want to show off their fine clothes and new hairdos to one another. They want everyone to say how pretty they are. They are good for nothing!" He slammed his fist on the table and then performed a kind of paralyzed minuet with his torso in a mimetic caricature of femininity.

"And how were they in the old days," asked his son Stavros, Stamatella's husband, enjoying the spectacle to the hilt.

"Ah, yes," said the old misogynist, looking down into the well of the past situated somewhere between his knees, then pounding on the table with so much force that all the crockery hopped to attention, and raising his voice in tragic exaltation: "I'll tell you how it was in the old days. The wife woke up at three in the morning. Then she walked a kilometre to the well to fetch the water. She washed the clothes. She fed the animals. She raked up the manure for fertilizer. She swept the olive leaves from the garden."

"And the husband?" enquired his plump, elder son Vassilis.

"He slept. By God, he slept."

"And then?" Stavros pursued.

"And then, the wife wakes up the husband and prepares his breakfast." He had switched tenses, reliving in the actual moment the dubious splendours of the past. "For everything depends on the husband. He must work in the olive groves. He must go out to sea in a small boat to catch fish and who knows if the storm will permit him to return? He must cross the water to trade with the people on the Mainland." He swivelled in his chair and gestured out the kitchen window at the Epirot coast fifteen miles away. "I remember when those mountains were full of *andartes*. A few times I almost didn't make it back."

"And that life was better than we have today?" asked the sceptical Lambi.

"A thousand times better! Men were men and women were . . . ."

"And women were mules," Vassilis completed the sentence.

"And women were mules," Grigori agreed. "But what is wrong with a mule? It works and it does not complain. It does not revolt, it does not join a political party, it does not dress up in expensive clothes and wiggle its behind in the village square . . . ."

"Muliebrity," I whispered to Karin, and evoked a conjugal groan.

285

Grigory was in full career. "Yes, they are mules, God knows, that is what He intended them to be. What does a woman understand? To work, to bear children . . . ."

"How can they bear the children if they are mules?" asked Stavros, laughing uproariously as Grigori choked and sputtered, trying to find a way out of the conundrum.

"Never mind my father," Vassilis said to me in English, "he liked the women plenty in the old days," and then repeated this libellous revelation in Greek. Grigori's wife, Dina, sitting across the table form her husband, and who spoke not a word during the meal, smiled ruefully.

"Oh yes," Stavros fairly whooped with glee at his father's evident discomfiture, "He liked the girls very much during his prime. Hey, *Patera*," glaring in a severe and judicial manner at Grigori, "How many half brothers and sisters do I have in the Epiros?"

"*Asta*," rumbled Grigori, "let it be."

"How many? Ten? Twenty? As many as the beads of your *koumbaloi*?"

Grigori could restrain himself no further and began to chuckle, and Anglaia, positively gelatinous with laughter, chimed in, "He is not a Paxos artichoke, our Grigori, his seed multiplies, multiplies . . . ."

"Six legitimate children," Stavros began counting on his fingers, "and how many others? Lend me your fingers everybody. Let us count the harvest of the old days."

"In the old days," interrupted Mimi, the youngest of Grigori's sons and the shortest, "in the old days before Homer, men were giants. But they had small brains."

"I am not speaking of the days before Homer," thundered Grigori, "I am speaking . . . ."

". . . of the days before *us*," said Stavros.

". . . when men were strong *and* intelligent," Grigori continued, "and women were strong and devoted. But now, we are in the ass-end of time," and he slapped his rump emphatically.

"The ass is still good for something, is it not," Stavros leered.

"Certainly," the old man retorted, "it can still be spanked," and raised his hand menacingly in Stavros' direction.

"And you certainly had an eye for a shapely behind," said Vassilis with mock severity, modelling a callipygian sculpture with two hands in the air.

"I had a good eye," said Grigori, glancing lasciviously at Stamatella, "and so does Stavros. But you, you have an eye . . . a nose . . . for nothing but your mother's cooking. And a belly to match."

"Ah well," sighed Vassilis, looking down at the hummock beneath his belt and confessing to me in English, "Greeks love eating. That's the trouble."

Queried by his father, he repeated the remark in Greek and Grigori responded, "Me, I had no time for eating. That's today's generation. Eat. Eat. Eat up the earth and turn it into ordure. What is the mouth for?"

"For promising the world," replied Stavros, "as you should know."

"In the days before Homer," said Mimi, who was evidently in the heroic mood, "it was for biting into the flesh of your enemy and for shouting battle cries!"

"*Asta* with your days before Homer," said Grigori, scanning the table portentously. "I will throw light on the mystery for you. The lips are for kissing but not the whole mouth. The teeth are for clenching against the sea wind. The tongue is for framing wonderful lies. The throat is for swallowing wine. But on Easter afternoon, then the mouth is for eating." And to demonstrate his point he tore off a chunk of lamb haunch in his almost toothless gums and began to masticate with noisy, histrionic relish.

And in this way the Easter meal continued all through the afternoon until we subsided into a pervasive alcoholic stupor, slumping in our chairs, yawning, rubbing our eyes. Suddenly, as I leaned back to stretch, I saw in unbidden revery the young thug who had hurtled us in his taxi through the streets of Athens. I could still see the muscles of his jaw casually working at a wad of chewing gum and those cold, glabrous eyes occasionally flicking toward the meter. Then his face gradually faded into the smoky light of the kitchen. Grigori began to snore gently and I thought, "I love this man." And in fact we all loved him, including the silent Dina who had endured his soaring and tempestuous vehemence for over fifty years, borne him six children, and never complained once. And in that love, so manifest, so *palpable*, it was as if we had for a brief moment, strangers that we were, become one with this joyful, ancestral family, shards annealed into a precious if ephemeral unity.

N O T E S

1. See Sannazaro's paradigmatic *Arcadia* (1502). Virgil suggested Arcadia as a *locus amoenis*, based on the Idylls of Theocritus; Sannazaro established it. The *real* Arcadia, of course, was poor, bare, and rocky.

In the Fifth Eclogue, Virgil had raised a tomb in his ideal, pastoral landscape. Sannazaro erected three in his Arcadia, of which the third in Eclogue 12 probably gave Poussin the idea for his *Et in Arcadia ego*.

2. In the late 1960s, after Anthony Quinn's rendition of the Kazantzakian hero, Europe and America set out on its Zorba hunt. This became the principle quest of the cruising Grecophile. I remember swearing blood-brotherhood with a Peloponnesian fisherman, who subsequently raped my girlfriend and vanished in his boat.

3. And even modern 'Greece' was assembled only gradually and piece-meal. After the war of Independence, Greece consisted mainly of the Peloponnese and Thessaly. Crete was incorporated only in 1912; Macedonia after the Treaty of Bucharest in 1913, at the end of the Balkan Wars; Thrace as part of the peace settlement after the First War, and the Dodecannese only after the Second War.

4. There is another reading of the legend which strikes me as somewhat idle. Rabelais interprets the death of Pan, in the fourth book of Pantagruel's adventures, as signifying the death of Christ, since Pan in Greek signifies the All and Christ, a 'shepherd' as well, represents all the world to the devout Christian.

5. In Mauritius? According to V.S. Naipaul, "the travel writers . . . have set to work . . . the island is a 'lost paradise' which is 'being developed into an idyllic spot' and which the visitor leaves with 'a feeling of peace.' " Naipaul continues: "To the Mauritian who cannot leave it is a prison," and proceeds to anatomize the economic deprivation, political confusion,

topographical monotony and social hopelessness of which life in paradise consists. See *The Overcrowded Barracoon* (Penguin 1981).

6. "The better classes had long abandoned their national costumes as everyday dress and dressed in the manner of the European culture which surrounded them. The women in particular were said to deprive themselves of necessities and neglect their houses in order to make a smart appearance on the Esplanade." In today's unisexual youth culture, the same observation would apply to the men as well. One thinks of Giambattista Vico's cutting remark: "There are too many whose carriages are drawn by their own guts."

7. To give Miller his due: in his prodigious, unstanchable flow of rhetoric he writes like a man under threat of execution: no time to consult the world. It is done breathlessly, *con amore*. In a key passage, Miller makes an oblique allusion to his own nature and practice, using his hero Katsimbalis as a kind of stalking horse. "Certainly in those endless and seemingly fabulous stories which Katsimbalis was in the habit of recounting there must have been a good element of fancy distortion, yet even if truth was occasionally sacrificed to reality the man behind the story only succeeded, thereby, in revealing more faithfully and thoroughly his human image." Miller is evidently referring to himself, and this is the *modus operandi* of his book. *He* is the colossus. He is also, essentially, a miller, grinding the truth down into flour to be later kneaded, leavened, and baked into the bread that satisfies the imagination's hunger. My objection, or perhaps it is merely a cavil, is that the world is a pretty good bakery in its own right, and that this is sometimes forgotten by writers who, in obsessively sacrificing truth to 'reality,' often conclude in worshipping the image and simulacrum at the expense of the thing itself. To round off the metaphor, instead of good country pumpernickel, we are served a thin, white, urban loaf, in the belief that what was has been subjected to refinement and enlivened with additives is invariably superior to the coarser and primitive substance. Miller knows this too, as he makes clear in his essay on the staff of life.

OTHER TITLES OF INTEREST FROM VÉHICULE PRESS

Prose

White Desert Stories by Jean Ethier-Blais, translated from the French
    by Jane Brierley
Birds of a Feather Stories by Catholyn K. Jansen
A Private Performance Stories by Kenneth Radu
Deathly Delights Stories by Anne Dandurand, translated from the
    French by Luise von Flotow

Stone Voices: Wartime Writings of Japanese Canadian Issei edited by
    Keibo Oiwa, foreword by Joy Kogawa
Mapping Literature: The Art and Politics of Translation edited by
    David Homel and Sherry Simon
An Everyday Miracle: Yiddish Culture in Montreal edited by Ira Robinson,
    Pierre Anctil and Mervin Butovsky

Poetry

Evenings at Loose Ends by Gérald Godin, translated from the French
    by Judith Cowan
The Proving Grounds by Rhea Tregebov
Modern Marriage by David Solway
Fortress of Chairs by Elisabeth Harvor
New and Selected Poems by Michael Harris
WSW (West South West) by Erin Mouré
Continuation II by Louis Dudek